5-50

4-8-63

(63 - 11/52)

THE NEW EUROPE

Today—And Tomorrow

The New Europe

TODAY—AND TOMORROW

George Lichtheim

FREDERICK A. PRAEGER

Publisher • New York

BOOKS THAT MATTER

Published in the United States of America in 1963
by Frederick A. Praeger, Inc., Publisher
64 University Place, New York 3, N.Y.

Printed in the United States of America

PREFACE

This book has been written as an attempt to acquaint the non-specialist reader with some of the arguments underlying the current debate over Western Europe's future role within the emerging Atlantic Community. It does not pretend to do more than generalize from the growing literature on this theme. Much of this is devoted to technical questions, notably in regard to the economics of European integration. The aim has been to summarize the discussion surrounding this subject, and here it has inevitably been necessary to draw upon a good deal of specialist writing, including some recent studies of the European Common Market and of the rather problematic future of Britain as a member both of the Commonwealth and the new Western European grouping. In dealing with such a complex subject there is always the danger of causing the treatment to become at once too dry for the general reader—to whom this book is primarily addressed—and not sufficiently detailed for the expert. The author can only hope that he has somehow managed to steer his boat between these familiar cliffs.

THE NEW EUROPE: TODAY—AND TOMORROW is a rather ambitious title. It really covers more ground than can be adequately surveyed in what is after all intended to be an introduction to genuinely specialist literature. The framework of this study is, moreover, frankly political, though much of it is devoted to an analysis of facts and figures relating to economics. A certain underlying commitment to the solidarity of the Atlantic world is taken for granted, and the question is then asked how Western Europe can be expected to fit into this world now that the era of European hegemony is finally closed. This approach is one of several that could in principle have been chosen. The assumptions it implies—that Western Europe and North America form a whole and that this community of interests also represents a community of shared values—are indeed common to many writers in the Western world today, but precisely for this reason they exclude other possible approaches to the subject. Both the East-West conflict and what is sometimes called the "North-South" tension between industrialized and emergent countries can be viewed through a variety of more or less idiosyncratic lenses, depending on the political sympathies and intellectual preconceptions of the writer. If in what follows a mid-Atlantic standpoint has been chosen, the immediate reason is quite simply that it was thought desirable to discuss the subject in a manner that might be of some use to readers on both sides of the oceanic divide. But there is also a further reason: The author happens to believe that a certain kind of West European parochialism is best avoided by trying to adopt an Atlantic viewpoint.

In this particular context, Britain's geographical location offers what is at present still the most convenient vantage point. One may be critical of the British performance since 1945 and yet feel that one is fortunate in being domiciled at the principal point of intersection of the European and American orbits. For the benefit of American readers it may be added that there is also a built-in advantage in the traditional employment of political terms—conservatism, liberalism, socialism, etc.—of Continental European origin, which in Britain still retain their original meanings. Thus, in what follows, to take one example, "liberalism" does mean liberalism, not populism, democratic radicalism, or socialism, as it frequently does in the United States. British political terminology retains the sense that conservatives are either old-fashioned agrarians or—in more recent times—defenders of corporate management, liberals are concerned with individualism and competition, and socialists advocate public ownership and planning. These distinctions are important in practice, and for this reason it is desirable that they should also be retained in theory.

It remains to be added that the "Europe" in the title of this study is Western Europe. A comparable survey could no doubt be devoted to the present problems of Eastern Europe, but that would be a different subject altogether and one which the author is not competent to undertake.

G. L.

London
November, 1962

ACKNOWLEDGMENT

Part of Chapter I has appeared in *Commentary* magazine (New York). The author is obliged to the Editors for permission to make use of this material.

CONTENTS

INTRODUCTION

In 1945, when the dust of battle cleared, Europe's former eminence in world affairs was found to be among the casualties of the Second World War. Instead of the familiar "concert of powers," there were two rival poles of attraction—the Soviet Union and the United States—and a congeries of medium-sized Continental states, plus the deeply shaken British Empire, which rapidly transformed itself into a Commonwealth of autonomous members. Since then, the emergence of China and India as rival, though unequal, colossi in Asia, and the emancipation of Africa, have confirmed a trend already obvious to thoughtful observers in 1945. The novelty, during the past decade, has been the countermovement to bring about an integrated Europe in the place of the old system of mutually hostile entities. Since in what follows it will be argued that this recent development is both necessary and to be welcomed, there is no harm in asking to what extent it is compatible with what has customarily been thought to be the peculiar character of European civilization. After all, even if it should turn out that a considerable price has to be paid for the final burial of Europe's now senseless rivalries, there need be no lament over the transaction. Whatever it may be that the Europeans—including it seems the British—are being asked to give up, it is clearly not worth a major war every generation. What then is it that is going to distinguish the future integrated Europe from its predecessors?

Although there are various ways of approaching this question if one thinks of the world scene and Europe's diminished importance thereon, there is, it would seem, only one sensible answer in terms of the Continent's own recent past: The new Europe is not going to be an assemblage of sovereign nation-states. Sovereignty after all finds its ultimate expression in a war-making capacity, and if the prospective members of a Western European Union are to renounce the right to make war on each other, they are to that extent abrogating their sovereignty. The near-certainty that this is going to happen between now and 1970 is what chiefly distinguishes the European consciousness of today from that of the past generation, which still took the sovereign nation-state completely for granted. That generation of course also took it for granted that Europe formed a whole and that the countries now under Soviet rule were part of it. When states-men and their advisers considered the possibility of future trou-ble, they thought in terms that today sound archaic, although some of the familiar landmarks are still visible. Dangers were seen to arise from the weakness of the Versailles settlement in 1919, and in particular from the well-known ambitions and resentments of Germany. Thus when, in 1925, the chief historical adviser to the British Foreign Office, Sir James Headlam-Morley, in what has been described as "a remarkable and prophetic memorandum," warned the Foreign Secretary, Sir Austen Cham-berlain, of coming conflicts between Germany and her neighbors, he observed that "the danger-point in Europe" was not on the Rhine but on the Vistula, and he went on to ask:

> Has anyone attempted to realise what would happen if there were to be a new partition of Poland, or if the Czechoslovak State were to be so curtailed and dismembered that in fact it disappeared from the map of Europe? The whole of Europe would at once be in chaos. There would no longer be any principle, meaning or sense in the territorial arrangements of the Continent.[1]

The reason why this kind of language seems to belong to the past—though a rather recent past—is that one can no longer

[1] James Headlam-Morley, *Studies in Diplomatic History* (London, 1929), pp. 182, 184; quoted in Hajo Holborn, *The Political Collapse of Europe* (New York, 1951), pp. 128–29.

think of the European political system as being autonomous. That
system today is plainly controlled by the reactions of the two
superpowers. What this realization has meant to Europeans is
not easily grasped by outsiders. It strikes at the roots of the old
concept of Europe as a stage on which sovereign national entities
enact their historic rivalries. Now it may be all to the good that
this phase is closed, and it certainly need not be lamented that
Germany is no longer able to play off East against West (as she
still did, with devastating consequences, during the interwar
period of 1919–39). But the transformation has certainly gone
much farther than most people even in 1945 thought likely.
After all, in those days the British Empire still ranked as one
of the Big Three, and it seemed probable that Germany, though
defeated, would emerge once more as the dominant power on
the Continent. That the old historic Central Europe would
vanish for good, and that Britain might decide to enter a
Western European confederation (for the time being decorously
disguised as a mere customs union) was not foreseen by the states-
men who met at Potsdam to settle Germany's fate.

Now if Europe's traditional way of life has been built upon
the coexistence of a multiplicity of sovereign entities, what is to
be its future in a world in which only the thermonuclear superpowers retain what used to be called sovereignty? This question
cannot be dismissed as academic. It is eminently practical. It also
accounts for the fact that many prominent Europeans are still
unenthusiastic about the whole idea of integration or federalism.

The nation-state has in the past mattered to Europeans because
it seemed to them to have recaptured some of the virtues of the
classical polis. This feeling was particularly strong in the late
nineteenth century, when liberalism had altered the relationship
between the state and the citizen. It then appeared possible that
the nation would outgrow its rather haphazard origins in absolutist and dynastic power politics and become a genuine community. We all know what became of these dreams, but it is
important to realize that in the liberal age they supplied the
rationale of a sentiment that was not simply self-adulation or

xenophobia. Even today such patriotism as exists in England, France, West Germany, Italy, and the smaller European countries is fed by remnants of this attachment to one's country as one's spiritual homeland: the place where the deepest values are genuinely shared; where men and women can meet and talk the same language (in every sense); where public affairs can be discussed in a spirit of mutual comprehension; where it is not wholly senseless to quote Pericles' speech to the Athenians. The Germans never quite joined in these sentiments, mainly because German liberalism had failed to win power; and most East Europeans to this day hardly know what it is to live in a country where the government is not a strange and hostile power beyond the control of the citizens. But in Western Europe—leaving Spain and Portugal aside—a sense of community did exist and made it possible for people to think of the State not as a monster but as the emanation of their own collective thoughts and aspirations. In the smaller countries of Western Europe which were overrun by the Germans in 1940, and thereafter struggled to get free, this feeling has perhaps grown even stronger, because democracy and patriotism were successfully tested at the same time. It is therefore a hopeful sign that the stablest of these countries, Holland, is also in the van of European federalism, for this would seem to show that the old national loyalty is not incompatible with the new European spirit.

For all that it has to be recognized that it is going to cost the Europeans a considerable effort to let go of their past. Public spirit and self-respect have hitherto been bound up with an almost exclusively national patriotism. To describe such sentiments as "irrational" is a trifle absurd. After all, it is not in the nature of primary loyalties to be entirely rational; nor is it altogether reasonable to dismiss them as irrelevant obstacles to the goal of European integration, for the opponents of federalism could well retort that a unified European structure will have to be built upon the sacrifice of all that has given meaning to European life in the past. The familiar parallel with the Italian city-states is valid at this point. No one would wish to go back on

Italian unification, but it cannot be denied that Venice, Florence, and Naples have long sunk into provinciality. Are London, Paris, and Rome to suffer the same fate? And if they do, will their citizens still feel that they are leading a meaningful existence?

In what follows an attempt will be made to answer some of these questions. For the most part, however, we shall be concerned with more baldly factual matters, principal among them the economic organization of the new Europe that is now arising before our eyes. Yet there cannot be a rigid distinction between the material framework within which political decisions have to be made and these decisions themselves, for what is done by those in authority is crucially important in shaping the environment in which people will have to live and trade. To a large extent, the history of the European Union movement since 1945 is a story of opportunities seized or missed by the national leaders —including the intellectual spokesmen—of the various European countries which on the morrow of World War II found themselves exposed to the twofold menace of the East-West split and the nuclear age. There was no overwhelming material drive— whether military or economic—that could have been said to determine the respective behavior of the British, French, West German, and Italian governments and publics. Rather, there were conflicting pressures, which in turn gave rise to different and sometimes conflicting reactions. If in the end one particular solution—the European—has prevailed, this must not lead us to suppose that the outcome was fated, or to underrate the strength of the opposing forces. In particular, it must not obscure the truth that the British have been extremely reluctant converts to Europeanism, and that but for constant American urging they might have succeeded in slowing down the movement towards integration until its original drive had spent itself. In a factual study, no blame is attached to anyone, least of all when it is a question of measuring the spiritual cost of renouncing past glories. We shall simply register these reactions among the other elements of the European synthesis and for the rest attempt to sketch the outline of a new supranational grouping that is taking the place of the Europe of sovereign nation-states.

THE NEW EUROPE

Today—And Tomorrow

I

HISTORICAL BACKGROUND

CONTINENT OR CIVILIZATION?

Europe can be thought of in several ways. The simplest way perhaps is to think of it in geographical terms, as a peninsula of Asia, in which case of course the historical dividing line between Eastern and Western Europe appears irrelevant. This was the viewpoint adopted by a French geographer—writing as it happens for Americans—who some years ago outlined the frontiers of the Continent so as to include within them the great central land area of what is commonly called European Russia:

> Between the heavy land masses of Asia and Africa, there is a sort of puzzle of mingling lands and seas called Europe. Between the Arctic Ocean, the North Atlantic, the Mediterranean, and the widening forests and shrublands of Soviet Asia, the European lands consist of peninsular and isthmian areas, plus a scattering of islands all around. It scarcely deserves to be called a continent. However, it is and always has been an exceedingly important part of the globe.[1]

In terms of this definition, Russia to the west of the Ural mountain chain is part of Europe, a circumstance duly emphasized by this writer:

> The eastern limit follows traditionally the "line of the Urals"—that is, the crest of the Ural mountain range from the Arctic shores southward, then the course of the Ural River, which empties into the

---

[1] Jean Gottmann, *A Geography of Europe* (rev. ed.; New York, 1954), p. 1.

3

Caspian Sea; the limit crosses the Caspian southward and swings back to the Black Sea westward along the crest of the Caucasus range.[2]

What can be said in favor of this conventional definition is that it is indeed "traditional"; moreover, it takes account of the fact that European Russia is primarily inhabited by Slav peoples whose long-standing connection with other European nations is unquestionable. Population and culture, however, introduce a different criterion, or rather two. If all the Slav peoples can be said in some sense to form a historic whole, then we arrive at a cultural and language frontier that runs between Eastern and Western Europe, more or less along the line of the present political East-West cleavage. This division may appear arbitrary, but it reflects a circumstance that goes back a long way and is not dependent on politics: the distinction between the great East European plain and the coastal lands bordering upon the Atlantic and the Mediterranean. Seen in this perspective, the important difference is between the continental and the maritime halves of Europe, the frontier between them running right through the middle of Germany: a division corresponding to a definite cleavage between two distinct types of civilization. When it is borne in mind that the great discoveries and sea voyages of the fifteenth and sixteenth centuries, which led to the rise of the New World and the spread of European influence to Africa and Asia, were chiefly associated with the countries of the Atlantic seaboard, it no longer seems arbitrary to run the historic frontier through the area usually called Central Europe: with Hamburg and Trieste very much on the western side, and the lands further east joining European Russia to form a distinctive whole. The historian may qualify this picture by stressing now the unity of the entire European land mass, now the creative tension between Eastern and

---

[2] *Ibid.*, p. 8. See also Margaret Reid Shackleton, *Europe: A Regional Geography* (4th ed.; London–New York–Toronto, 1950); p. 4: "Europe is almost equally divided into two great physical regions, an eastern and a western. Even from a small-scale atlas-map it is possible to perceive the contrast between the great monotonous plain of eastern Europe and the varied relief of the rest of the continent. . ."

Western Europe. But although the question whether "Russia" does or does not belong to "Europe" must in some sense depend on how the Russians themselves see the matter, it can at least be said that, however defined, "Europe" is made up of two distinctive halves. The dialogue between Eastern and Western Europe is at least as old as the civilization traditionally called European, and if in what follows we shall mainly be concerned with the maritime half of the Continent, it is well to bear in mind that the great eastern plain is inhabited by peoples whose history has since the early Middle Ages been inextricably intertwined with that of the West European nations.

To the geographer such memories are irrelevant. Economic geography has its own criteria, among which population density is not the least important. Europe as defined above—i.e., including European Russia—is the most densely inhabited of the continents, as well as being the smallest: less than half the size of North America, and one-quarter the size of Asia. Although it accounts for only 8 per cent of the world's land area, it is inhabited by about 550 million people, or more than a fifth of the globe's population, which gives a density of some 140 inhabitants per square mile: twice the figure for Asia, three times that for the United States, and ten times that for Africa. Here the inclusion of European Russia tends to confuse the picture. Subtracting the U.S.S.R. and its East European satellites, and adding Turkey on the other side, we arrive at some 300 million people whose political representatives take part in common Western institutions, principally the various parliamentary assemblies in almost continuous session at Strasbourg since 1949.[3]

It is evident, then, that in the context of our discussion the geographer must yield place to the historian. For practical purposes we are concerned with the western half of the Continent, that is to say, with the historic Western Europe; plus, on the one hand, those parts of Central Europe which after 1945 did not fall under Soviet control (chiefly Western Germany) and, on

---

[3] Max Beloff (ed.), *Europe and the Europeans: A Report prepared at the request of the Council of Europe* (London and New York, 1957), p. 3.

the other, Mediterranean lands such as Spain, Portugal, Greece, and Turkey.[4] Yugoslavia is a borderline case; so, for different reasons, is Finland. It is impossible to state exactly where either of them belong, for the concept of "Western Europe" is only in part determined by geography. To take the most obvious example: were Britain in the end to refuse to join a *political* union of Western Europe, the British Isles would nonetheless continue to form part of the West European civilization to which they have traditionally belonged. Conversely, one may say that, whatever the political pattern, there are limits to the extension of "Western Europe" beyond the cultural frontiers set by history.

These difficulties were touched upon at a European Round Table Conference held in Rome in October, 1953, when some eminent statesmen and thinkers were asked to give their opinions on the subject. Professor Arnold Toynbee—perhaps not the most eminent, but certainly the best known among them—had this to say:

> The Europe with which we are concerned is not the geographers' conventional continent. . . . When we speak of "Europeans" we really mean, I believe, those inhabitants of the north-western peninsula of the Old World, and of the adjacent islands, who are ecclesiastical subjects or ex-subjects of the Patriarchate of Rome: in other words, we mean those Catholic and Protestant Christians who live in this north-western corner of the Old World.[5]

In the ensuing discussion, Professor Toynbee felt obliged to make room for "among others, Serbs, Greeks, Bulgars, Rumans [*sic*] and Turks," thus raising doubts concerning the usefulness of his formula. To exclude the Russians while including the Turks is in any case a dubious procedure for a historian who places so

---

[4] And at a further remove Cyprus, Lebanon, and Israel, although not Egypt and (probably) not the territories formerly constituting French North Africa, unless they should decide to seek permanent links with Western Europe. Even in that case, however, they could scarcely qualify as prospective members of a West European political confederation. It can, of course, be held that Turkey does not qualify either.

[5] Beloff, *op. cit.*, p. 7.

much emphasis upon religious affiliation.[6] In the end all historical thinking is to some extent arbitrary and depends upon self-definition. But so far as antecedents can be allowed to count, the peoples of Eastern and Western Europe have a common starting point in the classical, or Mediterranean, civilization. If today the line of division separates the Slav lands from the West, it does not follow that this particular cleavage can be traced back to antiquity. Even so important a cause as European union does not entitle the historian to read his current preoccupations back into the past.[7] Thus the current division of Europe into two halves identified with conflicting sociopolitical systems takes on different aspects depending on the standpoint of the viewer. One may grant the essential unity of European civilization and still hold that the political rift runs along an ancient cultural frontier.

Independent of this issue there is the question whether the entire "European age" may not have come to a close during the past half century. Here writers of both schools can afford for once to agree that it has, and that since 1914 we have been witnessing the end of European pre-eminence in the world and the emergence of a new global system controlled by two powers that are non-European. Western historians—whether European or American—are disposed to speak of an "Atlantic" age; to the Russians it doubtless looks different, and probably would look different even if Soviet political orthodoxies were to change. But here we may provisionally ignore the Russian (and still more the rather parochial Chinese) viewpoint, and inquire in what sense it can be said that—in the Western world anyhow—a European

[6] This was pointed out by Professor Beloff (see *Europe and the Europeans*, p. 11), who observed that Russia "is a principal member of the European family of nations, and through its Byzantine inheritance might well be regarded as no less close to the Mediterranean world of Greece and Rome than the countries of north-western Europe."

[7] See Oscar Halecki, *The Limits and Divisions of European History* (London, 1950; New York, 1952) for an illuminating discussion of European origins. Professor Halecki, as a Polish historian, is perhaps in a better position than Professor Toynbee to appreciate the contributions of the peoples of Eastern Europe in fashioning the peculiar European civilization out of the confusion of the early Middle Ages. In his terminology, the pre-European epoch is defined as the Mediterranean, rather than the classical, age.

era has been succeeded by an Atlantic one. If such statements are examined in terms of what they imply about a civilization and a whole way of life, it will be found that they do not refer simply to power relationships: What is meant is that a particular form of political organization, based upon the nation-state, is no longer the determining pattern in world affairs. For European history since at least the close of the Middle Ages has been the history of conflicting and competing nation-states, as Mediterranean history was the record of rival city-states. To say that the European age has closed is to imply that the nation-state is no longer the dominant political form.[8]

Before reverting to this point it is worth considering what is signified by the familiar statement that the traditional European balance of power has ceased to function. This is a different matter from Europe's loss of global pre-eminence, although the two are connected. To start with the internal European balance: This can be thought of as a mechanism that came into being when the modern states began to form, and indeed it has generally been so regarded by historians. Ever since Leopold von Ranke formulated the concept in the introduction to his *History of the Latin and Teutonic Nations* (1824), Continental historiography at any rate—but the British soon followed suit—has operated with the notion of a Western European "unity in diversity" founded on the mutual relations of the "six great nations of the Romano-Germanic world": French, Spanish, Italian, German, English, Scandinavian. The Slavs were outside this construction, but Russia was brought in by way of the balance of power. Ranke himself described in his later writings how in the eighteenth century the Russia of Peter the Great was gradually introduced into the "European concert"—partly as a means of balancing the suprem-

[8] For this and the following, see in particular Geoffrey Barraclough, *History in a Changing World* (London and New York, 1955), pp. 135 ff.; Max Beloff, *The Great Powers* (London and New York, 1959), pp. 24 ff.; Ludwig Dehio, *Germany and World Politics in the Twentieth Century* (New York, 1959), *passim;* Alfred Weber, *Farewell to European History* (London, 1947), *passim;* H. Stuart Hughes, *Contemporary Europe* (Cambridge, Mass., 1961), *passim;* George L. Mosse, *The Culture of Western Europe* (Chicago, 1961), *passim.*

acy of France in the West. Russia therefore was only semi-European—unlike Poland, which French historians (if not the Prussian Ranke) treated as an important member of the European family. This traditional viewpoint is still substantially that of Marx, as the reader of his polemics against Czarist diplomacy in the 1850's can verify.

Now to a nineteenth-century European familiar with this picture, the question presented itself whether the non-European powers would be permanently drawn into the vortex of European affairs and adopt its peculiar rules of behavior. Ranke himself dated the crystallization of the modern European "balance of power" (as distinct from the medieval rivalries) from the years 1494–1514, when France and Spain began their long struggle for hegemony in Italy. As the other powers were slowly drawn into this complex play of ambitions, the circle gradually widened to take in newcomers like Russia and Sweden, while at the same time the discovery and settlement of the Americas transferred the Franco-Spanish and Anglo-French rivalries to the New World. By the eighteenth century the original balance of power had become Atlantic; in the nineteenth century it became world-wide and merged with the industrialization of Asia and Africa to form a world system, of which Europe, however, was still the center. Until 1914 it could be argued that all that had happened in the intervening four centuries was simply a gradual widening of the original circle, and that Russia, North America, Latin America, Japan, and China were so many newcomers to the game who had eventually learned its peculiar rules—chiefly the rule that no single power should be allowed to dominate, and that wars should be conducted for profit and broken off when they threatened to get out of hand. It took the 1914–18 war to shake these assumptions, and the 1939–45 war to shatter them completely. Since then, people have gradually become used to the notion that the "European era" is finished, to be succeeded by an Atlantic—and possibly a Pacific—one, just as Europe itself at one time replaced the old Mediterranean civilization. Indeed, it is beginning to be felt that even this is too parochial a perspective, and that we may have to learn to think in global terms *tout court*.

From the European viewpoint the implications of this change are revolutionary. If one adopts the traditional perspective one can say that the European era of world politics lasted from 1494 to 1914. Two years before its start, Columbus had accidentally discovered America and thus provided a suitable counterpoint. The emergence of Russia cannot be dated with the same precision, but sixteenth-century Muscovy had got rid of the Tartar domination and begun to spread out, while at the same time the Turkish threat to Christendom receded, thus making it easier for the European powers to shed their medieval preoccupation with the defense of the faith against the unbelievers. The subsequent story has already been briefly summarized. If now the whole of this familiar chapter of history lies behind us, to what is this due? Apparently to the fact that in the end the play of rivalries became self-defeating and led to a state of affairs where America and Russia emancipated themselves from European leading strings. This is the prosaic circumstance underlying the familiar phrase about Europe having "committed suicide" in two world wars. Europe did not in fact commit suicide. What happened was that its internal conflicts could no longer be settled by its own efforts. The flanking powers—America and Russia—had to be called in, and their superior weight decided the issue, both in 1918 and in 1945, though on the former occasion the Germans just managed to defeat Russia before they were themselves overwhelmed and so retained the illusion that the old familiar balance of power had not in fact disappeared. It took another war to enlighten them.

There is one further aspect that needs mention: the manner in which the European balance was controlled by British statesmanship so as to prevent the hegemony of any one Continental power. But the British did not simply control the European system; they also acted as the link between that system and the outside world. There were two circles, European and global, and England belonged to both. The circles intersected, and because England was at the intersection, British statesmanship could mediate between the Old World and the New. This opportunity arose in the eighteenth century, came to a peak in the nineteenth, and was lost in the twentieth, though the manner in which it was lost did not fulfill the anticipations of those European governments who had hoped to "balance" America against Britain. During World War I, the Germans made such an attempt, and failed. After 1917, the Soviet Government and the Communist International spent twenty years waiting for what they regarded as the inevitable clash between America and Britain. It never materialized. The fact was that the European "balance" did not really operate outside Europe. The rules of the game had been worked out by absolutist regimes in the sixteenth and seventeenth centuries, and their peculiar rationality did not cover the behavior of the new Atlantic powers. Thus, even before the European "system" of perpetual rivalry and balance had collapsed, it had shown itself unable to draw America into its operation. The Americans—unlike the Russians— preferred to stay outside until they could become Europe's heirs. By now, of course, American "isolation" is as dead as Russia's old position on the outskirts of the European system, and the two "flanking powers" have taken over the control of the central mechanism.

If this is one moral to be drawn from the course of events during the era of European hegemony, another conclusion has to do with the contrast between integration outside Europe and disintegration—or at any rate territorial fragmentation—within. It has rightly been remarked that "every European war has resulted in greater division, every colonial war in greater cohesion." The operation of the European system kept the several nation-states in equilibrium by keeping them all relatively limited in size; meanwhile, the non-European powers spread across ever larger land masses until they had acquired the extent necessary to overshadow their erstwhile European mentors. The "liberties of Europe" were paid for by fragmentation. Because no single power was allowed to dominate, the Continent in the end pre-

sented the picture of a congeries of sovereign entities too weak
to carry weight on a world scale. This fate had already overtaken
Holland in the eighteenth century; it overtook France, Germany,
and Britain in the twentieth. Since then, it has dawned on
thinking people in Europe that the pursuit of the "balance of
power" has become self-defeating. Federalism is a reaction to this
discovery. Is it the only one? Europeans are better aware than
outsiders of what their traditional anarchy has cost them; they
are also aware that their civilization has grown up with the
nation-state and quite possibly may not survive it. This is a
disturbing notion, and to non-Europeans an unfamiliar one. It
may be unduly pessimistic, but it cannot be dismissed out of
hand, and we shall have to revert to it. For the moment, however,
what concerns us are not the growing pains of Continental Europeanism but the manner in which the British have adapted themselves to their new role on the edge of the European system.

EMPIRE IN TRANSITION

In 1914, the British Government controlled the destinies of a
quarter of the human race and could afford to be on distant
terms with most of the remainder. The British Empire had no
equal among the powers, as the Royal Navy had no serious rival
among the world's maritime forces; its nearest competitor, the
German fleet, had barely half its strength. Britain was aloof from
Continental Europe, and in competition with Russia in Asia.
She employed France as a counterweight against Germany, and
Japan as a constant threat to Russia, but for the rest paid little
attention to the views of either friendly or hostile powers. With
the United States her relations were friendly but distant. The two
Anglo-Saxon powers—to employ a cant phrase of the time—
steered along parallel courses, though serious danger might draw
them together. Of the two, the British Empire was unquestionably
the greater as well as the older. Indeed, until 1917 it was not
certain whether the United States cared to play the part of a
world power at all.

It has taken less than half a century to bring this structure to the ground, but the seeds of change were already at work before World War I. Britain's territorial basis was too narrow, sea power was about to be eclipsed by air power, free trade was on the wane, and the colonial Empire was beginning to stir. At home, democracy—long kept within the decorous bounds of a parliamentary system controlled by the Conservative and Liberal parties—made growing inroads upon oligarchy. All these factors working together, plus two world wars and the rise of nationalism in the original white-settler dominions—Canada, Australia, New Zealand, South Africa—gradually transformed the Empire into a commonwealth of sovereign nations no longer held together from the former imperial center. Sea-power, empire, oligarchy, the unchallengeable pound sterling—these assets have gone with the wind. Their place has been taken by island conscious-ness, democracy, the welfare state, and faith in international organizations. The recent decision to apply for membership in a European confederation of more or less sovereign states—for the time being disguised as a customs union—places the seal on a development which farsighted observers had already begun to envisage in the early years of the century. For all the apparent solidity of the surviving Commonwealth, and the enduring ties of language and tradition, the record of the past half century pre-sents itself as a prolonged retreat along the road back from world empire to island state.[9]

So rapid and complete a transformation—decline is perhaps the wrong word—would have seemed unlikely even as late as 1945, when Great Britain counted as one of the Big Three, its leaders still meeting their American and Soviet counterparts on an equal footing at the Potsdam Conference. Yet it is clear in retrospect

[9] The imperialist school in Wilhelminian Germany had been banking upon this happening from about 1900 onward, but of course they expected Germany to be the chief beneficiary; see Dehio, *op. cit., passim*. Theodore Roosevelt, on the other hand, though he felt some uncertainty over England's continued ability to rule countries like Egypt (where nationalism was beginning to stir even before 1914), had nothing but admiration for what he termed the civiliz-ing role of the British Empire, and took care to express these sentiments publicly in the course of a visit to England in May–June, 1910; see Beloff, *The Great Powers*, pp. 215 ff.

that they owed this role very largely to the dominant personality of Winston Churchill and his personal relationship with President Roosevelt. Anglo-American solidarity was emphasized throughout the war by the British rather than by the American partner, who was already beginning to think in terms that implied a shrinking role for postwar Britain. Where their interests diverged, it was generally the British who yielded on essentials, with the Foreign Office putting up a rear-guard action against the Prime Minister's determination to let nothing disturb the personal tie he had established with the President. This fleeting relationship masked a real if silent transfer of power and prevented the British public from realizing how precarious their country's global position had become by 1945, and how much it depended on American goodwill.[10] In matters of crucial importance (e.g., Roosevelt's readiness to strike a bargain with Stalin at the price of the permanent partition of Central Europe) British resistance was of no avail. The story was continued with the Truman Administration's abrupt ending of Lend-Lease in August, 1945—a measure which effectively prevented the newly elected Labour Government from making an orderly transition to peacetime conditions. Much of the rapid weakening of British influence was due to Whitehall's lack of imagination and its obstinate adherence to outworn policies, but Washington's coolness to a Britain that had elected a quasi-Socialist government played its part.[11] Still, the basic disproportion between financial means and political burdens was one for which the Americans bore no responsibility. Like France in 1918, Britain in 1945 had

[10] For particulars, see Llewellyn Woodward, *British Foreign Policy in the Second World War* (London, 1962); also the review of this work in the *Times Literary Supplement*, March 16, 1962.

[11] See in particular R. F. Harrod, *The Life of John Maynard Keynes* (London, 1952), pp. 586 ff. The story of how the Labour Government, almost in its first week of office, had the rug pulled from under it by the Truman Administration has been told in the third volume of Hugh Dalton's memoirs, *High Tide and After* (London, 1962). Dalton was Chancellor of the Exchequer in 1945–47 and had to cope with the catastrophic consequences of American policy in this period (and, it is true, with the British Treasury's ready acquiescence in such weird experiments as the establishment of full currency convertibility in 1947).

won an empty military triumph, which masked the reality of a decline from Great Power status. It was a symbolic matter that the first explosion of a nuclear bomb in August, 1945, should have occurred a few days after the conclusion of the Big Three conference at Potsdam.

In recent years, the gradual release of memoirs and biographies has disclosed how difficult it was for the postwar British Governments—notably the Churchill-Eden Government of 1951–55, and the ill-fated Eden Government of 1955–57—to adapt themselves to a changed world. Again and again one finds the Cabinet—whether under Attlee, Churchill, or Eden, though less so under Macmillan—unwilling to cut its politico-military coat according to its economic cloth. Leaving aside such mental aberrations as the Suez expedition of 1956, there is the Labour Government's pathetic decision in 1951, under the impact of the Korean War, to embark upon an arms program of crippling proportions in order to impress American opinion. This misuse of scarce resources added little to the West's military strength, but it had the effect of breaking the Attlee Government's back and precipitating a financial crisis which swept it from office in October, 1951, in circumstances not very different from those attending the collapse of the MacDonald administration twenty years earlier. Yet ever since the negotiations over the U.S. loan to Britain in 1945–46 it should have been obvious that the United States was not disposed to prop the British economy beyond the minimum extent necessary to prevent a wholesale disaster and the effective transformation of Britain into a disarmed and pacifist neutral. This obstinate clinging to Great Power chimeras, for which the economic foundation was lacking, makes up one half of the postwar record. The other half is constituted by the remarkable story of the British Government's relations with Continental Europe.

Since Anglo-American partnership on approximately equal terms was an illusion (as was the fiction of Big Three harmony), it might have been thought that one or the other of the two main political parties would espouse the idea of European union, so as to give Britain a leading part in a European system that could hold its own in a world of supranational giants. In the event, neither the Conservatives nor Labour did so in time, though each managed to sound "European" while in opposition. The result was to leave the Continent with the firm impression that the British—except for a relatively small body of Liberals— were either indifferent or positively hostile to European integration. On the face of it, such insularity seems odd, at any rate in the case of Socialists who had never quite shared the Tory faith in the Empire. It cannot be accounted for in terms of Commonwealth loyalty, for this need not by itself have prevented people from grasping that Britain was inescapably part of Western Europe. The French, too, were the inheritors of an imperial past, yet it has rightly been remarked that they did not regard themselves as being closer to West Africans than to the Dutch. The truth is that between 1945 and 1960, most British people of all parties still tended to believe in the possibility of an exclusive Anglo-American partnership that would become the core of an Atlantic system. The gradual abandonment of this dream—first by the Liberals and then by elements within the two major parties —made it possible for the British Government in 1962 to sound rather more convincing on the subject of European unification; but down to the first half of that year, the prevailing standard of political behavior was set by the ritual affirmation that as between Europe and the Commonwealth, the latter must take precedence. This may be regarded as a triumph of faith over mere fact, or alternatively as an escape door towards the hypothetical Atlantic Union of the 1970's.

The record of informal parliamentary meetings at Strasbourg is a good test of British feelings and intentions during this period, for unlike the subsequent Common Market treaty, they were brought into being with the official, though unenthusiastic, participation of the British Government.[12] The Statute creating

12 In the third volume of his memoirs, Dalton describes the traumatic effect produced upon the Continentals by the British delegation's appearance at the Council of Europe session in Strasbourg in 1949. Churchill was then in opposition and busy embarrassing the Labour Government by being pro-European. It therefore fell to the Labour Ministers at the head of the British

the Council of Europe at Strasbourg was signed in London on May 5, 1949, on behalf of the governments of Belgium, Denmark, France, Ireland, Italy, Luxembourg, the Netherlands, Norway, Sweden, and the United Kingdom, and entered into force on August 3 of that year.[13] It was preceded by an unofficial campaign sponsored by influential public men of all parties and given more or less official backing by all the West European governments concerned. It could look back upon some striking wartime utterances by Winston Churchill, then at the height of his power,[14] and forward to the time when West Germany would be able to join the circle. In the immediate postwar period there was some uncertainty over the role Britain might want to play, but Churchill—then out of office—accepted the chairmanship of the United Europe Movement in Britain, and on September 19, 1946, in a public address at Zurich, once more affirmed, "We must build a kind of United States of Europe."[15] He was echoed by the Foreign Secretary, Mr. Ernest Bevin, who told the House of Commons on January 22, 1948, "I believe the time is ripe for a consolidation of Western Europe," and cautiously supported by the then Prime Minister, Mr. Attlee (who in 1939 had declared

---

delegation to pour cold water. In this they were greatly helped by the fact that the veteran William Whiteley, Labour's venerable Chief Whip in Parliament, had never before crossed the Channel and was known to be deeply distrustful of all foreigners, as well as ignorant of their languages: his colleagues promptly put him forward as candidate for President of the European Assembly. See Christopher Layton, "Labour and Europe," *The Political Quarterly* (London), January–March, 1962.

[13] See A. H. Robertson, *The Council of Europe: Its Structure, Functions and Achievements* (2d ed.; London and New York, 1961), p. 1.

[14] E.g., the following communication to the War Cabinet in October, 1942: "It would be a measureless disaster if Russian barbarism overlaid the culture and independence of the ancient States of Europe. Hard as it is to say now, I trust that the European family may act unitedly as one under a Council of Europe. I look forward to a United States of Europe. . . . I hope to see a Council of perhaps ten units, including the former Great Powers . . ." (See *The Council of Europe*, p. 1.). By "the former Great Powers" Churchill clearly meant France and Germany: not, however, Britain, which he regarded as a present Great Power.

[15] See Andrew and Francis Boyd, *Western Union, UNA's Guide to Western Recovery* (London and Washington, D.C., 1949), Appendix B.

that "Europe must federate or perish").[16] M. Spaak, then Prime Minister of Belgium, and the French and Italian Foreign Ministers, M. Bidault and Count Sforza, lent their weight, and at a "Congress of Europe" convened by the International Committee of Movements for European Unity and held at The Hague from May 8 to 10, 1948, the 713 delegates from 16 countries present could feel that they were borne along by a victorious tide.[17] They could afford to be hopeful, for on March 17, 1948, the governments of Britain, Belgium, France, Holland, and Luxembourg had signed the Brussels Treaty providing for "economic, social, and cultural collaboration, and collective self-defense," and for the creation of a Consultative Council of Foreign Ministers; while on April 16, 1948, there was signed in Paris the Convention for European Economic Cooperation binding together the sixteen countries which had responded to the American initiative resulting in the Marshall Plan. Yet in July, when the French Foreign Minister, M. Bidault, made the first official proposal for the creation of a European parliament, the British promptly responded with a counterproposal for a purely governmental organ of consultation, thus giving the Continental Europeans their first inkling of London's reluctance to accept binding commitments. The difficulty was eventually overcome when the British, realizing the strength of feeling on the Continent, agreed to take part in a European Assembly. It is worth noting that the subsequent agreement to establish a Committee of Ministers and a Consultative Assembly, together forming the Council of Europe, almost coincided with the signing of the North Atlantic Treaty on April 4, 1949. The British evidently gave way because the Americans (in the words of a State Department declaration issued

16 Robertson, *op. cit.*, pp. 2–3.

17 Mr. Churchill was President of Honor on this occasion, and the three principal committee chairman were M. Ramadier, the French Socialist leader; the veteran Belgian statesman M. Van Zeeland; and Professor Salvador de Madariaga, on behalf of the exiled Spanish Liberals. The subsequent "European Movement" international committee set up on October 25, 1948, was headed by Mr. Churchill, M. Léon Blum, M. Paul-Henri Spaak, and Signor Alcide de Gasperi (then, and until his death in 1954, Italian Prime Minister), as Presidents of Honor.

in July, 1948) "strongly favored" the "progressively closer integration of the free nations of Western Europe."[18] But they continued to regard themselves as the link between "Europe" and the United States, an attitude made clear by British delegates of all parties in the subsequent meetings of the European Assembly at Strasbourg. Since the Assembly, unlike the Council of Ministers, was a parliamentary body consisting of members of the various national legislatures acting in their individual capacities, these expressions of feeling had the additional significance of being quite spontaneous and, so to speak, unpremeditated.[19]

This is not the place to go into the complex story of the European Union negotiations and the plethora of official and semi-official bodies that emerged from these protracted labors; a brief account of the matter will be given in the following chapter. What concerns us here is the attitude adopted by the British Government and the dominant political parties and personalities throughout the period when the Continental Europeans were making their first great effort to overcome the historic divisions of the past.

The fifteen years following the close of World War II were for Britain a period of adaptation to an age in which the British Empire (like the French, but unlike the Russian, which expanded in all directions under its new name and under cover of a new ideology) gradually disintegrated. Whether one attributes this to the triumph of democracy and the Liberal-Labour legacy in British politics or to "the indifference of the British people and the self-hatred and political death-wish of a social elite exhausted by two European civil wars"[20] matters less than the realization that the British public could not immediately foresee how far the process would go. There were intermediate stations on the

[18] Robertson, *op. cit.*, pp. 5–6.

[19] When the Assembly got around to passing the first European Statute—a Declaration of Human Rights—the British Labour delegation distinguished itself by abstaining, and even managed to muster a solitary "No" (see Layton, *op. cit.*, p. 41). It is only fair to add that some individual Labour delegates eventually took their own line in these matters, and one or two of them indeed became outstanding proponents of European unity.

[20] Hugh Seton-Watson, *The New Statesman* (London), March 16, 1962.

way, even after India had gained autonomy in 1947, when it
seemed that the Middle East might be preserved as a British-
controlled region. When Arab nationalism, in its new Pan-Arab
and aggressive form, proved unmanageable, these hopes were in
part transferred to Africa, until there, too, the rise of black
nationalism and white-settler resistance compelled the British
Government to make an awkward choice, the symbol of which
was South Africa's self-exclusion from the Commonwealth in
March, 1961. At every point the old imperial sentiment rallied
within and behind the Conservative Party, while the Labour and
Liberal opposition wavered between crypto-Europeanism and the
hope that, given sufficient concessions to Indian, Arab, and
African nationalism, the Commonwealth might take on a permanent identity of its own. Indeed "the Commonwealth" came
to signify for many Liberals and Socialists precisely this vision
of a new supranational and multiracial brotherhood. Conservatives naturally hoped to escape with minor concessions to nationalism and democracy (mostly of a symbolic kind), while preserving
the substance of the old imperial position and the status of a
world power able to look America and Russia in the face. In this
atmosphere, a genuine commitment to European integration,
which would have signified the tacit acceptance of a totally new
position in the world, was not possible. It was the less likely to
appeal to the electorate since to the ordinary person "the Commonwealth" signified countries such as Australia, New Zealand,
Canada, and—rather more doubtfully—South Africa and Rho-
desia, where millions of British people had made their homes.
To argue that Britain had less in common with these "members
of the family" than with European countries like Germany,
France, and Italy seemed to most people not only outrageous but
positively absurd; indeed it is fair to say that on this point public
sentiment has not really changed, and may not change for
another generation, whatever official arrangements are made to
facilitate the gradual transition to Europeanism.

If these were illusions, they were sustained by ingrained attitudes, a record of statesmanlike behavior in the postwar period,

some ingenious legal camouflage, and a certain amount of self-deception.[21] They were also sustained by a factor that is seldom mentioned, but to which considerable importance must be allotted: the dream of an Atlantic partnership in which Britain would share control with America. Atlantic Union means different things to different people. To the United States it has recently come to mean a partnership with a unified and federated Western Europe. British opinion may yet come to accept this goal, but there is no disguising the fact that British policy has hitherto aimed at something else.

ATLANTIC CROSSCURRENTS

Since 1945, the movement towards European Union has had its counterpart in a sustained attempt to popularize the concept of Atlantic Union. Lately indeed it has become fashionable to treat the two as complementary, but this was not always the case. In the early postwar period, and almost throughout the 1950's, the military alliance which had been brought together in the North Atlantic Treaty Organization (NATO) was viewed as a global system embracing three major groupings of states: North America, the British Commonwealth (with or without Canada, depending on how the latter's role was viewed), and the countries of Continental Europe. A good instance of this attitude was furnished by a report issued in 1952 by an extremely high-powered and influential group of people in London, in which the formation of NATO was attributed to the fact that "Western Europe and Britain alone could not organize sufficient strength to prevent attempts at aggression against free Europe. Its essential novelty in 1949 lay in the fact that it brought the North

[21] To quote Seton-Watson (*loc. cit.*): "The manner of the ending of the British Empire was more elegant than that of [the Ottoman, Habsburg, or French], though we might be well advised not to exaggerate. Mau-Mau, Cyprus and Malaya were small affairs compared to Vietnam or Algeria, but they were not much pleasanter for those concerned, and there may be Congos still to come. Whether the total number of Balkan people killed in the 19th-century rebellions and wars against the Turks was larger than the number of Moslems and Hindus killed in India in 1947, would make an interesting subject for research."

American continent—the United States and Canada—into close association with Britain and Western Europe not only for defence but for all activities involved in planning deterrents against total war."[22] To the authors of this document, who included some eminent representatives of the military and diplomatic "Establishment," the distinction between "Britain" and "Western Europe" seems to have been self-evident enough to require no further explanation. The report indeed goes on to explain that Britain, although a member of the Western European grouping set up under the Brussels Treaty of 1948, "is a world Power with vital interests outside Europe which preclude a complete merger with European neighbours and restrict what it can do for Western Europe."[23] In regard to Western Europe indeed, "Britain's responsibilities should be no greater than—or very little greater than—those accepted by the United States."[24]

If today one marvels how such notions could have been held by influential people a bare ten years ago, part of the answer is to be found in the observation that "Britain, as in other great crises, has been the main link between the two hemispheres, and to keep a balance between its interests in Europe and its interests outside has been one of the major problems of British policy. Without the existence of NATO the maintenance of the balance would have been even more difficult."[25] NATO was then viewed as a convenience enabling the British Government to continue its traditional role of intermediary between Europe and America— as though the British Isles were not themselves part of Western Europe, and as though in the thermonuclear age Britain's fate were not inexorably tied up with that of the Continent! This peculiar notion, however, was only one aspect of a semi-official creed which laid it down that in the post-1945 age, Britain had come to occupy the "intersection of three circles": Europe; the Commonwealth plus the newly emancipated lands of Asia and

22 Royal Institute of International Affairs, *Atlantic Alliance. A Report by a Chatham House Study Group* (London and New York, 1952), p. 1.
23 *Ibid.*, p. 2.
24 *Ibid.*
25 *Ibid.*, p. 3.

Africa; and North America; with the implied corollary that British statesmanship was called upon to mediate between all three. That this conviction was firmly held at least by the Foreign Office became evident when the principal architect of British foreign policy in that period, Sir Anthony Eden, became Prime Minister in 1955. Readers of his reminiscences have since been offered an opportunity to perceive how a fatal misjudgment of what was called "the Anglo-American alliance" betrayed Eden into a course of action that eventually climaxed in the Suez disaster of 1956.[26]

It might seem that since 1957 there has been no need to elaborate upon the theme that the Anglo-American partnership so conceived was an illusion. Yet the strange attraction of this mirage continued to deflect British policy even after the Suez debacle had shown up its insubstantial nature. These were the years when on the Continent a union of states was beginning to take shape under the aegis of the Common Market and the Rome Treaty of 1957. In the words of a recent study on the subject:

> Time and again Britain was offered the chance of leading a united Western Europe and helping to mould it, but each time she refused the role so nearly thrust upon her. It is no wonder if the continent then turned suspicious of her wooing; and today efforts to reach a commercial and political settlement with the Six are doomed to fail unless they take full account of the historical and ideological context in which these nations have begun to build their new community, and of the spirit which inspires the politicians and civil servants who lead it.[27]

When one inquires into the attitudes underlying this curious reluctance to perceive the obvious, one comes upon a complex interplay of feelings that cannot be reduced to simple terms like insularity or traditionalism. "European" and "Atlantic" argu-

[26] *Full Circle. The Memoirs of the Rt. Hon. Sir Anthony Eden* (London and Boston, 1960); for an instructive comment on this work see the review in the *Times Literary Supplement* of March 4, 1960: itself revelatory of a state of mind sufficiently close to that of the author.

[27] U. W. Kitzinger, *The Challenge of the Common Market* (Oxford, 1961), p. 1.

ments intermingle in one and the same publication, sometimes in
one and the same passage. An author who has no doubt about
the essential unity of Europe, including the British Isles, nonetheless feels constrained to emphasize that Britain lies at the
intersection of two different worlds. As late as 1957, an influential
historian felt able to assert that "the idea of an Atlantic community . . . to many people appears to be more in accordance
with the facts of international life than a community based upon
'Europe.' "[28] A few pages earlier the same writer draws attention
to the persistence of specifically European cultural patterns that
make nonsense of national claims to uniqueness. "Thus in Ireland the sandshoes used for hunting wild duck are similar to
those used in Scandinavia. Norwegian nationalists have been
shocked to learn that their 'local' costumes originated from
France and that the national symbol, the red cap, is really the
bonnet phrygien of the French Revolution."[29] One may wonder
why after this the reader is told that "if Britain or Norway are
asked to choose between the Atlantic Community and Europe,
they will choose the Atlantic Community."[30] Why should anyone
confront them with such an unreal choice? And what of France
or Holland, both bordering on the Atlantic? It seems at times as
though even liberal-minded historians have difficulty recognizing
that to a transatlantic observer all these West European countries
look remarkably alike.

What then is meant by the frequently heard assertion that the
true solution for Britain—and for the United States, too—lies in
the promotion of an Atlantic Community embracing North
America, Western Europe, and the British Commonwealth? This
question must be considered before we take the plunge into
European affairs proper, for on the answer to it depends the
perspective in which one views the European Unity movement.
If an "Atlantic" orientation signifies something more than the
commonplace that most of the countries concerned are grouped

[28] Beloff, *Europe and the Europeans,* p. 25.
[29] *Ibid.,* pp. 17–18.
[30] *Ibid.,* p. 25.

around the Atlantic trade routes,[31] it must have a bearing upon the "three circles." Otherwise why should the proponents of "Atlanticism," both in the United States and in Britain, be so frequently found among the same people who until lately promoted the idea of an exclusive Anglo-American partnership?

A brief excursion into the recent past may help to set matters in perspective. World War II was fought—at any rate so far as Britain was concerned—under the banner of Anglo-American resistance to Continental tyranny. The maritime powers were once more exercising their historic role, and would continue it in the postwar period if the German menace should be succeeded by the Russian peril. The classic formulation of this faith is to be found in the six volumes of Sir Winston Churchill's account of his wartime stewardship, but *The Second World War* is only the most impressive document of a vast literature—mostly originating from Britain—in which the accent falls on Anglo-American partnership and unity-in-adversity against all comers. Since the flood of postwar publications set in from the American side, it has gradually become evident that the matter was viewed somewhat differently in Washington, where the President and his circle were more concerned to establish tolerable postwar relations with Russia, and to maintain the American hold on China, than to gratify British longings for an enduring Anglo-American comradeship.[32] When British proponents of "Atlantic Union" today denounce the idea of Britain entering a "narrow" European framework at the expense of the "wider" Atlantic one, they are in a respectable tradition; the only question is whether

[31] This of course is not true of such British Commonwealth countries as Australia and New Zealand, not to mention India. But here the tacit assumption appears to be that their links with the Anglo-American or English-speaking world confer honorary Atlantic status upon them.

[32] See Woodward, *op. cit., passim.* The literature is endless, but it can perhaps be said by way of summarizing it that on balance it shows Anglo-American partnership to have been a British concept which the Americans accepted with some reluctance and not a few mental reservations. This state of affairs really goes back half a century to the period around 1900, when the British Government first made the conscious decision to bank on a close relationship between the two countries.

they are not deluding themselves in imagining that it is possible for Britain to be half in and half out of Europe, while at the same time heading a Commonwealth group within an "organic union" of the entire Western world, so called.[33]

What can be said about these proposals is that while they may offer the United States a means of coordinating the policies of the alliance, they scarcely enable Britain to elude the choice between a European and an Anglo-American orientation. When one is told that the Western alliance "can be thought of as a 'tripod' —including Western Europe, the Commonwealth, and the United States,"[34] it is clear that this ingenious formula evades the question whether Britain is to count as a member of the West European group. From the viewpoint of those who continue to cherish Churchillian notions of Anglo-American partnership in policing the world—or at any rate the "free" world—this of course is precisely the virtue of the scheme. Whether it has much attraction for Americans is another question, and one that writers sympathetic to the general idea of an Atlantic Community have latterly come to view with skepticism.[35]

The economics of Atlantic Union will be considered in a later chapter, together with the analysis of the European Common Market. Here it remains to be said that the ideology sustaining it has had the unfortunate consequence of blinding British spokesmen to the quite evident determination of three successive

[33] For an exposition of this viewpoint, see Professor George E. Catlin's article "Putting Atlantic Union First," in The Daily Telegraph (London), January 24, 1962, where reference is made to statements by such American spokesmen as Senator Fulbright, Walter Lippmann, and the late Wendell Willkie, all favoring such a union. This, of course, was before President Kennedy had entered the arena.

[34] Catin, loc. cit. One wonders how Latin America, India, and Japan fit into this tripod. They are likely to find it an uncomfortable resting place, notwithstanding the author's assurance that their subsequent application for membership will be considered in a tolerant and nonracial spirit. Recent official U.S. declarations on the subject of Atlantic Union notwithstanding, the "Atlantic world" and the "free world" represent different concepts; to say nothing of the moral-political problems offered, e.g., by South Africa.

[35] Cf. Professor Beloff's article "The Prospects for Atlantic Union," in The Times (London), February 2, 1962.

U.S. Administrations to make European Union a success. Until 1961, it was believed in Whitehall that Britain could afford to stay out of the Common Market because Washington in the last resort would hesitate to promote an economically powerful bloc of all West European countries which might discriminate against the United States. Wishful thinking must have had a considerable share in perpetuating such illusions, just as it presumably had a share in the persistent attempts to denigrate the leading Continental countries in the eyes of the American public.[36]

These attitudes had their counterpart on the other side of the Channel. Nothing is to be explained in personal terms alone, but the condescending treatment Western Europe, and above all France, received from the victorious Anglo-Americans in 1944–45 cannot be discounted in an analysis of the subsequent story. In the second volume of his war memoirs, General de Gaulle has related the extraordinary scene he had with Churchill in June, 1944, when the Prime Minister urged him to visit Washington and, so to speak, obtain Roosevelt's authorization to act as the representative of France. It was in the course of this stormy session that Churchill, in the presence of Eden and Bevin, cried out: "Here is something you should know: whenever we have to choose between Europe and the open sea, we shall always choose the open sea. Whenever I have to choose between you and Roosevelt, I shall always choose Roosevelt."[37] Since Roosevelt for his part intended to exclude France from the postwar settlement, this impassioned declaration amounted to a fairly clear announcement that Churchill preferred a secondary status within an Anglo-American partnership to the role of defender of

---

[36] An influential British commentator has remarked: "It was breathtaking to hear Mr. Macmillan announce in the spring of 1961 . . . that he had discovered that the U.S. Administration did not after all object to the idea of enlarging the European Common Market by bringing Britain into it." (Andrew Shonfield, "Atlantic Dialogues," *Encounter* [London], March, 1962.)

[37] Charles de Gaulle, *War Memoirs,* vol. II (London and New York, 1959), p. 227. The style of this translation has been slightly altered.

Europe's interests.[38] Subsequently, de Gaulle had the American standpoint explained to him in Washington by Roosevelt himself.[39] What it amounted to was that the postwar world would be ruled by a quadrumvirate composed of the United States, the Soviet Union, Great Britain, and China, with a parliament of smaller countries—the future United Nations—acting as a chorus and giving a democratic look to the directorate of the "big four." Among the latter Washington then counted on having China on its side, so that the U.S.S.R. would be isolated and outmatched. For the rest, there would be American bases throughout the world, some of them on French soil. The coming peace would be an American peace, and the world would enter the American Century—all in the name of democracy, of course. It is scarcely surprising that after hearing these views, de Gaulle betook himself to Moscow in order to sign a brief wartime alliance which supplied him with a counterweight to Roosevelt's stifling embrace. His real orientation had been fixed somewhat earlier during a visit to Rome, where the subject of a postwar union of the West European countries—Germany, France, Italy, Belgium, Spain, and Portugal—came up, not surprisingly, during conversations at the Vatican.[40]

It is useful to bear this background in mind when considering the complex story of Europe's postwar efforts at political integration. The personal factor enters into every arrangement, but it does so effectively only where it can give direction to impersonal forces waiting for a lead. In Western Europe after 1945, these

[38] In this he was not altogether supported by all his Cabinet colleagues, nor indeed by the Foreign Office, but during the crucial period his influence prevailed. Hence his postwar support for European-union movements could not fail to evoke some skepticism on the Continent, where his wartime role was remembered.

[39] See *War Memoirs*, vol. II, pp. 239–44. It must be said that de Gaulle is rather generous about the pettiness and malice Roosevelt displayed in his relations with him.

[40] De Gaulle, *op. cit.*, p. 238. Eighteen years later, and four years after his return to power in 1958, President de Gaulle still thought of European union in terms of a loose confederation of states, though Spain and Portugal had disappeared from the list, to be replaced by Holland and (perhaps, if she proved sufficiently "European" in spirit) England; see his remarks at a press conference in Paris on May 15, 1962, when incidentally he disclaimed the authorship of the phrase *Europe des patries*.

forces grouped themselves around the axis of the wartime Resistance movements, which had been democratic and patriotic, although the Communists tried to influence them and here and there succeeded in taking over some branches. When the Communist grip was shaken off after the 1948 Prague *coup* and the Christian Democratic victory in the Italian elections that spring, it soon appeared that European Union appealed to a broad spectrum of political forces running from the Socialists to the moderate Catholic parties, and excluding both the extreme Right and Moscow's followers. The subsequent history of the governmental moves towards economic, and ultimately political, integration has its roots in this tangle of political and personal loyalties, not least in the fact that many of the leading proponents of European Union had made each other's acquaintance in wartime prisons and concentration camps. Among them were Germans, as well as Frenchmen and others from German-occupied countries. Thus the movement got off to a start quite different from the usual circumstances attending political or economic mergers. It is not too much to say that what has kept it going is this original impetus, which perhaps can be summed up in the formula that to avoid a final catastrophe Europe—or at any rate Western Europe —must federate. If this involved the end of national sovereignty in its historic form, the leading "Europeans"—though not traditionalists like de Gaulle, for all his belief in some form of European unification—were ready to draw the conclusion. What was lacking was an equal readiness on the British side to dispense with Atlantic and Commonwealth mystiques that no longer had much relation to current political realities. There was no disposition in London to renounce the exclusive link with Washington and—more important even in terms of public sentiment— the stance of a victorious great power with world-wide commitments. The other European nations were viewed as unhappy victims of a catastrophe that Britain had fortunately been spared.[41]

[41] See the discussion between Raymond Aron and Andrew Shonfield reproduced in *The Listener* (London), February 8, 1962; e.g., Shonfield's observation "It is true that Britain had, to put it brutally, written off the Continent of Europe by 1945." To put it even more brutally, the United States and the Soviet Union had simultaneously written off Britain's pretensions to great-

The share taken in the subsequent conversion to a more
realistic viewpoint by the increasing disproportion between financial means and military-political ends is disputable, but in Britain
at least it has been noteworthy that with every year—and every
annual budget—there has been a growth in the number and the
influence of people who felt that the smaller countries should
drop out of the nuclear arms race: not primarily on moral or
even on political grounds, but quite simply because their finances
could not stand it, and in Britain's case because the "independent
nuclear deterrent" was making only a trifling contribution to the
West's strength. In this respect there has been a notable change
of attitude since the early 1950's, when "Anglo-American" strategy was still discussed in traditional terms, as though it were a
question of sea-power versus land-power. By 1960, even opponents of British entry into a European confederation were
ready to advocate reliance on the U.S. thermonuclear "umbrella"
rather than the build-up of independent nuclear forces, whether
national or through NATO. It was beginning to be felt that as
long as the balance between America and Russia continued to
operate, the European countries, including Britain, could well
afford to dispense with efforts to establish their own striking
forces. Such an appraisal clearly facilitated a new approach to the
problem of European unity, though not all those who urged realism in military policy were willing to carry matters to the point
of advocating "entry into Europe." They could of course point to
the fact that some prominent European figures—with General de
Gaulle well in the lead—seemed determined to combine greater
economic integration with the build-up of nationally controlled
atomic forces.[42]

---

power status, and the former had just dropped the first atomic bomb to ram
the point home. But this was something the British public took time to
recognize.

[42] See Denis Healey, *The Race Against the H-Bomb* ("Fabian Research
Series," No. 322 [London, March, 1960]), especially p. 6: "Fear that the American nuclear deterrent may soon lose its validity for the alliance is the main
rational ground why European countries, led by Britain and France, are
beginning to produce strategic atomic weapons for themselves—though the
prestige argument is no less important."

The seeds of this uncertainty lay in the pledges of the 1949 North Atlantic Treaty, which paralleled the establishment of the Council of Europe and the first halting steps towards greater Continental unity. In Article 5 the signatories had agreed "that an armed attack against one or more of them in Europe or North America shall be considered an attack against them all." Since retaliation would have to be immediate, they further agreed to place some of their national forces under a joint command, to that extent limiting or abrogating their national authority to a central command which in practice could only be an American one. This arrangement was acceptable to most Europeans in the immediate postwar period as long as they felt reasonably safe under the protection of the American nuclear "umbrella." It became less satisfactory with the growing uncertainty over whether the United States would or could employ its nuclear power in support of a European ally after the U.S.S.R. had built up its own striking capacity to a point roughly equal to the American one. Without attempting to go into the complex subject of "nuclear credibility" it can be said that as time passed, the European partners in NATO discovered reasons for producing their own deterrents. They were strengthened in this resolve when the then U.S. Secretary of State, Mr. Christian A. Herter, told the Senate Foreign Relations Committee on April 21, 1959: "I cannot conceive of any President engaging in all-out nuclear war unless we were in danger of all-out devastation ourselves."

Though none of the various European states could seriously hope to build up a strategic force which by itself would be powerful enough to deter the U.S.S.R., they might conceivably get nearer this aim by pooling their forces. On the other hand, it could be argued that by doing so they might hasten the day when the United States would judge that the time had come to concentrate on issues nearer home. To quote a writer of some authority in these matters who has already been cited: "If America then had an invulnerable second-strike countercity capacity of her own, she might well prefer to write off all her strategic commitments in Europe rather than to put herself at the mercy of trigger-happy allies."[43] It is perhaps unnecessary to assume that the allies would in fact be trigger-happy. They could equally well be pacifist or even neutralist. After all, possession of a modest nuclear capacity (together with an enormously productive and fragile industrial civilization) would give them both a bargaining point and a sound reason for "contracting out" of global entanglements.

This is not the place to go into the complexities of the arms race, nor is the present writer competent to do so. The issue that concerns us here is at once narrower and less strictly a matter for military experts. It might be summed up in the question, Can Europe be defended? But there is an equivocation about the meaning of the term "Europe." Does one think of it as an assemblage of sovereign nation-states, each pursuing its own line and the whole loosely held together by an over-all commitment to the Western alliance? Or is Europe on the way to developing a political and military cohesion of its own? This question really leads back to the theme of our introductory section. If Western Europe is about to shed its ancient historical skin and become a unified supranational area with a central political authority, will its leaders aim to make it an equal partner of the United States within the Atlantic alliance or a neutral "third force"? It would be lacking in candor to deny that Europeans are divided on this question. So perhaps are some influential Americans. Among spokesmen of the U.S. Administration, Mr. McGeorge Bundy was thought to be expressing President Kennedy's opinion when on December 6, 1961, he told the Economic Club of Chicago: "My own belief is that the most productive way of conceiving the political future of the Atlantic Community is to think in terms

43 Healey, *op. cit.*, p. 8. *The Times,* in an editorial of January 5, 1962, preferred to stress the other side of the coin: "Fears of American reluctance to incinerate themselves in the cause of European freedom are not new—it is for this reason, not for the mythical influence in the making of policy which it is often claimed to confer, that Great Britain clings to its 'independent' V-bomber force and that General de Gaulle goes ahead with his nuclear striking force." This judgment was confirmed by the French President in his public statement of May 15, 1962, when he clearly envisaged an autonomous Western Europe, with its own nuclear-defense potential.

of a partnership between the United States on the one hand and a great European power on the other." Commenting adversely on this statement, Mr. Denis Healey—by then in charge of the British Labour Party's Commonwealth policy and a noted critic of the "European" viewpoint—remarked:

> It is inconceivable that if Europe, including Britain, became a Great Power, as Bundy predicted, it would not make itself wholly independent of the United States in the field of atomic striking power. Once it did so, NATO would have lost its *raison d'être* and the Atlantic Community would cease to develop, if not to exist. This may be what many Americans secretly desire. But I cannot believe that it would be in the long-run interest of the United States or Europe, or the world as a whole.[44]

This clearly is a decisive issue. It will later be argued that in the postwar movement towards European integration, which celebrated its first great triumph with the 1957 Rome Treaty, there was a built-in cleavage between the adherents of greater Atlantic solidarity and those who thought of a United Europe as a potential "third force" midway between the global blocs headed by the U.S.A. and the U.S.S.R. The concept of European unity was itself neutral as between these rival interpretations. But this cleavage will persist even if a federated Europe does not come into existence and does not become a great military power. It is inherent in Europe's geographical location and in the fact that North America is the only part of the North Atlantic Treaty area that could conceivably survive the consequences of a full-scale thermonuclear war. All Europeans know in their bones that if a

[44] See *The New Leader*, January 22, 1962. It is perhaps not wholly accidental that the same writer also dwelt on the possibility of civil war in France or a fascist dictatorship "with appalling consequences for the Atlantic Community as a whole," and for good measure suggested that "Europeanism is already on the wane in West Germany, as Bonn's rigidity on the Common Market's agricultural policy has shown." Bonn in fact displayed no rigidity, but on the contrary showed itself very accommodating; and the fascist *coup* in France obstinately refused to materialize, despite all the urgent solicitations of the British Left over a period of years. But writers in need of an argument to bolster their instinctive preferences can always find evidence to support their views.

military conflict in Europe begins to "escalate" beyond a certain point, their common civilization is done for. The point must be stressed because some Americans are willfully blind to it, or else confuse such arguments with "neutralism." In fact, the present situation arises from the collapse of the Pax Britannica and the simultaneous development of air-power far beyond the point reached during World War II (except at the very close). The fact is that nuclear power has put a stop to the kind of "classical" warfare that could still be sustained by the European nation-states in 1939–45. To quote a British authority on the subject, and one quite untainted by neutralist sentiments:

> It was one thing to endure ordeal by high explosive which, however much damage and suffering it might cause, still left the basic structure of society intact. It was, and is, another to look forward to the total destruction of one's civilization . . . beyond hope, so far as one can see, of repair; with the consolation only that the adversary is being annihilated as well.[45]

The question then for Western Europeans is whether the Pax Americana does in fact insure peace, or whether the present nuclear stalemate is to be regarded as an overture to a war that might rapidly escalate beyond the limit compatible with the inherited framework of European civilization. The word "European" must be underlined in this context. It is no use trying to conceal the fact that Europeans (like other people) are primarily concerned with their own safety; or that their society is more vulnerable to nuclear war than are the backward regions of the globe. It may be that the inhabitants of Europe have no moral claim to being placed in a relatively privileged position, but such considerations are not going to deter either the peoples or their leaders if it comes to choosing between alternative positions,

---

[45] Michael Howard, "Bombing and the Bomb," *Encounter*, April, 1962; see also in the same issue "Reversing NATO Strategy," by John Strachey (Secretary of State for War in the Labour Government of 1950–51), for a detailed exposition of the argument that Europe can and must be defended by "conventional" means, and by the Europeans themselves. On the British Government's reasons for retaining a national deterrent, see G. F. Hudson, "The Folly of 'Our Bomb,'" *Encounter*, July, 1962.

among which "armed neutrality" is certainly one. If U.S. strategy remains geared to the notion of the "deterrent," and to plans for countering a possible Soviet offensive with an "escalation" of "strategic" nuclear weapons, no prophetic gifts are needed to foresee that the political basis of NATO is going to melt away. Conversely, if the West European nations—with France and Germany in the lead—manage to build up sufficiently strong "conventional" land forces, plus an adequate assortment of tactical nuclear weapons under their own (separate or joint) control, and possibly a modest "strategic deterrent," they may in due course feel able to dispense not only with American bases on their soil—a wasting asset in any case—but with the American "umbrella." The Atlantic Community would then in fact consist of two independent halves, though one may suppose that the underlying unity would prove strong enough to outlast the change in military and technological relationship.

Whether one sees Britain as part of the European half, or as an independent power serving as linchpin of the whole structure, must in part depend on one's personal preferences. On the whole, European opinion has tended to favor the first view, and the movement of thought in Britain has recently been in the same direction, though powerful obstacles remain. Clearly they are not just economic, though in subsequent parts of this study we shall be mainly concerned with this aspect of the matter. The real issue has all along been one of national sovereignty—both as a matter of principle and in the context of a world strategy that treated Anglo-American solidarity as the cement of the entire Western edifice. For leading Americans to think of Western Europe (including Britain) as a unity *and* as an equal partner of the United States is something of a novelty, and not altogether welcome to British spokesmen of either the Right or the Left. The doctrine of Atlantic "interdependence" enunciated by President Kennedy in his important statement of July 4, 1962, has its dangers from the viewpoint of those who value Britain's "special position." That Britain is a West European country; that Anglo-American partnership is a fading myth; and that successive British governments since 1945 have been embarrassing three different administrations in Washington by pursuing this fata morgana—these are thoughts that have not yet sunk into the consciousness of the electorate and would be disputed even today by important sections of the opinion-forming minority.

To be fair, more is at stake than national pride. There are arguments against British membership in the European Economic Community—and *a fortiori* in the still undefined European political community of the future—which do not depend for their validity on the acceptance of the imperial myth or on the quaint vision of "socialism in one island." Setting aside both the nostalgic dreams of the Old Right and the tedious imbecilities of the New Left, there is a serious case against turning the United Kingdom into a member state of a political community of Europe. Basically, it rests upon the perception that Europe's interests are not easily reconciled with those of the Commonwealth. As regards foodstuffs and other economic issues this is a truism; but it applies also to Europe's future political orientation: not—as the more frenetic opponents of European integration are fond of asserting—because a European Union dominated by France, Germany, and Italy is bound to be "reactionary" and "militarist," as well as "protectionist" and "inward-looking," but because a federated Europe is much too great a force to be contained within the present Anglo-American framework. It is not necessary to go so far as to assert that "the European idea has an anti-American flavour,"[46] though it clearly does have such connotations for some influential people in Europe; it is quite enough to realize that its unspoken premises include the belief that Europe has been unduly overshadowed in the system built up after 1945 under Anglo-U.S. auspices. This notion has its advocates even in Britain among the sophisticated pro-Europeans on the left wing of the Conservative Party who have behind them the more alert members of the rising generation in industry and technology. It is a notion oddly at variance with Washington's reputed hope that Britain will act as America's most reliable ally in Europe. Con-

[46] Cf. Leonard Beaton, "The case against joining Europe," *The Guardian* (Manchester), July 26, 1962.

ceivably, there are people in Whitehall and in the State Department who still believe that, once inside Europe, the British will "manage" it—in the joint interest of the Anglo-Saxon powers. This is wishful thinking; the Europeans are in no mood to have their affairs run by people whom they regard as outsiders. If the British count on playing a leading role in the new Europe, they will have to demonstrate to their skeptical partners that in any serious conflict of interest between the two halves of the Atlantic world they can be counted on to come down on the European side. Clearly this must cast some strain both on the Commonwealth and on the Anglo-American partnership, which has been the sheet anchor of British foreign policy for so many years; and it is not impossible to foresee circumstances where a split might occur that would wreck what is left of the Commonwealth's political cohesion. This is an extremely touchy issue, for the Commonwealth is essentially a family affair, not easily understood by outsiders and capable of generating irrational sentiments perhaps as strong as the "European idea" itself. Indeed it might be said that if the British on balance feel more deeply attached to this far-flung group of like-minded countries than to their European neighbors, they would do better to stay outside the political community of Europe. Certainly they can do no good either to themselves or to the Continental Europeans by becoming halfhearted and disgruntled members of a partnership to which they do not really wish to belong.

What makes the decision crucial is that the community will clearly aim at autonomy, if not independence, in the field of politico-military strategy. This after all has been the issue between the United States and France since the advent of the Gaullist regime—and it takes a good deal of naïveté to suppose that it will disappear once General de Gaulle has left the scene. Gaullism may originally have been rooted in traditional French nationalism; it has now merged into something broader and more up to date that is not quite European neutralism but may become identified with a conception of "armed neutrality" between the blocs bound to attract support from almost all points of the political compass—not excluding the far Left. What lies behind the semitechnical dispute over the use of national or European "deterrents" is really the question whether Western Europe can become autonomous within NATO. To this question, as is well known, Washington and Paris return radically different answers.[47] The American view is that Europe neither needs, nor is able to afford, nuclear forces of its own, though the British "deterrent" is tacitly accepted as long as it remains *de facto* under American control. In setting up a center of resistance to this hitherto dominant viewpoint, Gaullist policy has set the stage for a Franco-American dispute that bids fair to become a European-American one. The London *Times* put the matter with commendable clarity when it wrote:

> It is clear that the Common Market, with or without Great Britain, is about to enter the next stage of its progress towards some sort of political federation. Out of this has grown a crisis of power and leadership in the western alliance and a revolt by the European powers against the American monopoly of strategic nuclear power. The natural tendency of power politics being towards bipolarity, the issue has developed into what is virtually a Franco-American debate. . . . By 1963 France will have a nuclear force which by the standards of the sophisticated "game-theories" of nuclear war is crude and unconvincing. It will consist, at any rate until 1965, of supersonic aircraft equipped with free falling nuclear bombs, and students of the intricacies of the nuclear balance of power insist that this presents no sort of credible deterrent.

There has been a tendency in the United States, and to some extent in Britain, to condemn General de Gaulle's attitude as *folie de grandeur*. Considerations of national prestige obviously come into his

[47] The U.S. position was clearly outlined by Secretary of Defense, Robert S. McNamara, in his Michigan speech of June 16, 1962. British policy is currently somewhat fluid, but appears in recent months to have come a little closer to the French position. This was one among several consequences of the British Cabinet reshuffle of July, 1962, which marked an advance for the "Europeans" who also form the left wing of the Cabinet and the Conservative Party. French opinion remains divided between convinced "Europeans," i.e., federalists, and Gaullist adherents of a national striking force; but neither side to this controversy favors complete reliance upon the United States.

calculations, but it would be wrong, and incidentally unprofitable, to dismiss the argument simply as one of stubborn pride against cold reason. It is a question, as Walter Lippmann has said, of "power politics played by the masters of the game." Between them sits Britain, equipped with the "independent" nuclear force which has done much by its example to influence French nuclear policy, enjoying the special relations with the United States which General de Gaulle finds it hard to forgive, and at the same time seeking admission to the European Community. Those who will shape Britain's defence policy for the next few years have this as their first and least tractable problem.[48]

Having reached this point, we do well to terminate our preliminary sketch of the framework within which the European unity movement of the postwar period must be placed. In what follows we embark upon our central theme, which is the integration of Continental Europe since 1945, and in particular the establishment of the European Economic Community, popularly known as the Common Market. The resurgence of "Europe"—here understood to signify the Continent, though it will be taken for granted that Britain in fact forms part of the larger whole—must be seen against the background which it has been the intention of this introductory chapter to set forth. But when it comes to understanding how and why the Continental movement towards integration got under way after 1945, the "Atlantic" frame of reference is not really very helpful. The drive came from the very heart of the old Continent before it spread outward. We are therefore obliged at this point to adopt a different and somewhat narrower perspective, before returning once more to that "open sea" which links Europe with America. Noth-

[48] *The Times,* July 26, 1962 (article by its Defense Correspondent). This happened to coincide with the French National Assembly's debate on the Government's policy of creating a nuclear striking force. It was noteworthy that on this occasion some of de Gaulle's most strident journalistic critics on the Left tied themselves into knots in their embarrassment at having to oppose (or accept) a venture that promised to make France militarily independent of the United States. Their opposite numbers in Britain, with their customary parochial fixation upon home affairs, saw in the whole issue nothing but another instance of Gaullist megalomania. They thus missed the whole point of the debate over Europe's future role.

ing that can usefully be said about the probable future shape of the Atlantic Community has much support in factual arguments unless we first manage to establish what the new Europe of the supranational age is actually like, and wherein lie the roots of its enduring importance. These roots are historical in a sense to which some precise significance can be given. It has to do with that unique phenomenon the nation-state—its growth, its catastrophic climax in two world wars, and the transformation it is currently undergoing. European integration would be a comparatively trivial matter if it were confined to economics and did not involve the issue of political sovereignty as hitherto understood in the birthplace of nationalism. Among Europeans it was taken for granted from 1815 to 1945 that politics was "about" the interplay of conflicting national claims and ambitions. Since 1945, this tacit assumption has given way to a new one—that in our age Europe must somehow evolve supranational institutions. The tension between the old and the new loyalties underlies the surface play of events, and imparts to it the pathos that raises the political drama above the level of mere interest-conflict.

II

TOWARDS EUROPEAN
INTEGRATION: 1945–60

FROM MARSHALL TO MESSINA

The movement towards greater political and economic integration in Western Europe has occurred against a background that has been briefly sketched in the preceding chapter. It also possesses a history proper, which must be summarized before we can move on to the theme of Europe's present resources and future prospects.

Setting aside the wartime plans of European exile governments in London, and the establishment of the United Nations (which falls outside our subject), the story may be said to begin with the formation of the Council of Europe at Strasbourg, to which reference has already been made. This was paralleled on the economic side by movements towards economic integration which sprang from the war-shattered Continent itself, though their success was made possible by the massive weight placed behind them by the United States. General Marshall's well-known initiative on June 5, 1947, and the British Government's unusually prompt response, set the ball rolling towards the goal of making Western Europe self-supporting and consequently independent of further U.S. aid. The sixteen countries whose governments on April 16, 1948, signed the Convention for European Economic Cooperation (popularly known as the Marshall Plan) were all represented either in NATO or at Strasbourg, where attendance also left room for neutrals like Austria or Switzerland who were barred by treaty or by national law from taking part in military alliances. The resulting picture looks complex, especially when account is taken of the subsequent division between the European "Six" and the "Seven," but the relevant point is that in one way or another every West European country—including Spain, which was diplomatically boycotted by some of the others—was eventually brought in. This can be shown in the form of a table listing the members of the six principal overlapping organizations: from NATO—which of course included the U.S.A. and Canada—via the OEEC (Marshall Plan aid) and the Council of Europe, to the rival economic communities of the Six and Seven (EEC and EFTA) which came into being with the signing of the European Coal and Steel Community Treaty, in 1952, and the Rome Treaty, in 1957. We thus anticipate our brief account of these integration moves in order to provide a pictorial representation of the resulting politico-economic checkerboard. It is worth remembering that the April, 1948, Convention for European Economic Cooperation (OEEC) had preceded the Hague Congress of the European Movement by only one month, and that NATO came into being at about the same time, whereas the European economic communities emerged in the 1950's. The tabulation naturally takes no account of these time differences.

It will be clear from the above that in practice these overlapping "tables of organization" were designed to take in all the European countries not controlled by the U.S.S.R.: including doubtful cases like Turkey (only half in Europe, though represented at Strasbourg), Yugoslavia (European but Communist), and Spain (Fascist and thus boycotted by the Strasbourg Parliamentary Assembly). Eventually they were all brought in somehow or other, and for good measure the U.S.A. and Canada lent their weight to NATO and to the OEEC's successor. These organizational tables, however, reveal little about the life that presumably animates such structures. After all, it was conceivable that the whole postwar movement would resolve itself into a complicated rigmarole of rival bureaucracies. In NATO this happened to some extent, thus giving rise to the joke that if the Russians ever started moving, they would have to fight their way through a

(x *signifies membership*)

	NATO	OEEC[a]	Council of Europe[b]	European Economic Communities	EFTA	Population (in millions)
Austria		x	x		x	7.0
Belgium	x	x	x	x		9.1
Denmark	x	x	x		x	4.6
Finland					Associate	4.0
France	x	x	x	x		45.4
Germany	x	x	x	x		52.1
Greece	x	x	x	c		8.8
Iceland	x	x	x			0.2
Ireland	x	x	x			2.8
Italy	x	x	x	x		49.2
Luxembourg	x	x	x	x		0.3
The Netherlands	x	x	x	x		11.4
Norway	x	x	x		x	3.6
Portugal	x	x			x	9.1
Spain		x				30.0
Sweden		x	x		x	7.5
Switzerland		x	x		x	5.3
Turkey	x	x	x			27.3
United Kingdom	x	x	x		x	52.3

SOURCE: Kitzinger, *op. cit.,* p. 8.

[a] In 1961, the OEEC was transformed into the Organization for Economic Cooperation and Development (OECD), with the U.S.A. and Canada becoming full members. Yugoslavia has an observer in the Organization.

[b] Cyprus joined the Council of Europe in 1961.

[c] A draft treaty for the association of Greece with the European Economic Community was signed in 1961.

forest of committees, and probably exhaust themselves in the process. There was perhaps a more serious danger that the movement to create a united Europe would get drowned in a bureaucratic "alphabet soup." It is a tribute to its sponsors that this did not happen, notwithstanding some severe disappointments on the way. The worst of these was the failure of the projected European Defense Community (EDC), which was rejected by the French Parliament in August, 1954, two years after a treaty providing for a German contribution to European defense had been signed by the governments concerned. Paradoxically, it was after this setback that Germany's partners agreed to let her have a national army and become a member of NATO—the very things the EDC had contrived to avoid in order to spare French feelings![1]

But before matters came to a head in the military field, resulting in a temporary defeat for the aim of Franco-German reconciliation, the two governments chiefly concerned had shown their determination in another sphere. On May 9, 1950, the French Foreign Minister, M. Robert Schuman, proposed the integration of the French and German coal and steel industries and invited other European nations to join. Four accepted the invitation—Italy, Holland, Belgium, and Luxembourg—and on July 25, 1952, the treaty establishing a European Coal and Steel Community (ECSC) came into force. Britain, invited to join the negotiations, refused, and Mr. Harold Macmillan, then still in opposition, voiced a sentiment shared by the Labour Government and its supporters when he said in the debate: "One thing is certain, and we may as well face it. Our people will not hand over to any supranational Authority the right to close down our pits or our steelworks."[2] Thus the economic community of the Six came into being, if not against British resistance, at any rate under circumstances that emphasized Britain's aloofness from the Continent. Its core was Franco-German, and was to remain so.[3]

The Schuman Plan (actually the brainchild of M. Jean Monnet, then head of the planning commission set up in 1946 to coordinate the reconstruction of the French economy) did two things: It bridged the historic Franco-German cleavage, and it set the ball rolling towards the wider European Economic Com-

1 Kitzinger, *op. cit.*, p. 13. For the proposed relationship between the EDC and the Council of Europe, see Robertson, *op. cit.*, pp. 94 ff. Britain was not a member of the EDC but became a signatory to the subsequent treaties which set up a Western European Union to associate the United Kingdom with the Six (including West Germany) for military purposes.

2 Kitzinger, *op. cit.*, p. 10.

3 Shirley Williams, *The Common Market and its forerunners* ("Fabian Research Series," No. 201 [October, 1958]), pp. 8 ff. John Pinder, *Britain and the Common Market* (London, 1961), *passim*.

munity of the late 1950's. Its principal authors were the effective
controllers of foreign policy in Germany, France, and Italy:
Adenauer, Schuman, and de Gasperi—all, as it happened, also
the leaders of their respective Christian-Democratic parties. The
"fourth man" was M. Paul-Henri Spaak of Belgium, who swung
the Socialists into line with the aim of making supranational
control of industry the means of overcoming the traditional, and
now senseless, European national antagonisms. Thus the drive
from the outset had strong Socialist support, though the German
Social-Democrats took some time to emancipate themselves from
British advice and the narrow nationalism of their own leader,
Kurt Schumacher. It would be foolish to pretend, however, that
even this powerful Catholic-Socialist combination could have
overcome the entrenched obstacles to integration if national interests had not been adequately met and if the United States
had not lent its benevolent support. The Schuman Plan in fact
squared the circle by enabling Western Germany to come into a
Little European community within which France provided the
political leadership. By pooling coal and steel on terms fairly
advantageous to the French, and by placing both under a common High Authority, the Plan subjected Germany's industrial
and political resurgence to a freely negotiated restraint; this was
acceptable to both sides and did away with the controls of the
occupation regime. It was therefore an essential step to that
German-French reconciliation upon which the whole subsequent
history of the European union movement has pivoted. The British, by excluding themselves, involuntarily lent the final touch:
Face to face at last, the Germans and the French decided to make
the best of it and become Europeans.

The Preamble to the ECSC convention signed by the Six in
1951 already looked forward to a full European Economic Community: "Conscious of the fact that Europe can be built only by
concrete actions which create a real solidarity and by the establishment of common bases for economic development. . ." This
was more than a rhetorical flourish: It actually translated into
words what the signatories had in mind. So far, however, it merely
stated an aim. The immediate gain was embodied in those clauses

that proposed the abolition of restrictions on movements of coal and steel between the six member nations. Steps were also taken to remove trade discriminations and to establish a unified transport system. The treaty further laid it down that after a five-year transitional period, ending in February, 1958, a common external tariff on coal and steel imports would be imposed. This provision and the time limit already pointed forward to the Rome Treaty of 1957, which established the full European Economic Community. On the executive side, the High Authority of nine members (eight of them appointed by the six governments) was given powers that led to its being described as a "supranational" body. These included the right to control prices, to channel investments, to raise loans and credits, to allocate steel and coal during periods of shortage, and to fix production if there was a surplus. Since the Authority financed its own administration by a levy on every ton of coal and steel produced in the Community, it was independent of the governments and thus virtually sovereign. At the same time, it was obliged to cooperate with a Council of Ministers made up of representatives of the member governments, decisions in the Council being taken by majority vote, as against the OEEC procedure, which was based on unanimity and thus gave every participant the right of veto. This abandonment of the unanimity rule was one of the reasons why the British at this stage felt unable to take part in the Community: It smacked of supranationalism and thus of abandonment of national sovereignty.[4]

The movement towards European integration was thus launched on a front considerably broader than was implied by the formal title European Coal and Steel Community. The Community was in fact, if not in form, the nucleus of a future supranational

[4] In addition there was a parliamentary Assembly which naturally conflicted with the Strasbourg Assembly set up under the 1949 Treaty, the more so since its duties were more specific. In appointing delegates to this Common Assembly from their midst, the national Parliaments disregarded party lines; thus not a single Communist deputy was appointed, notwithstanding the size of the Communist parties in France and Italy. Since the Communists were on principle opposed to European integration, they could hardly complain at being left out.

political authority, politics and economics being inseparable in matters affecting Europe's basic industries. This was already apparent from the provisions of the treaty setting up a virtually autonomous High Authority and a Common Assembly, which by a two-thirds vote of censure could force the Authority to resign, plus a Council of Ministers and a Court of Justice. The basic institutional pattern was that of the Strasbourg Council of Europe, with the difference that Strasbourg clearly had not become a genuine political authority, but had remained a mere consultative body. Equally clearly, this was due to the fact that at Strasbourg the foreign ministers of fourteen countries (plus 200 deputies from 15 parliaments) confessedly could not take political decisions in the absence of any understanding over the future of Europe. The Six meanwhile had made up their minds about integration and were going ahead within their narrower but more effective sphere. Significantly, the ECSC Assembly soon developed into a genuine parliament, with regular party affiliations and with a tendency to lay down guiding lines for policy:

The Assembly took to the supra-national aspects of the Coal and Steel Community like a duck to water. Again and again, Assembly members pressed for more vigorous use of the High Authority's powers against cartels, in investment policy, and in ruling out discriminatory actions. Criticism has been far more often that the Authority has bowed to some national interest than that it has overriden it.

This has had an effect on the behaviour of the members themselves. In the first year or two, most members talked like Germans or Frenchmen or Dutchmen. But in the last year or so, party loyalties began to cut across national loyalties. Political factions were formed— Christian Democrat (the largest), Socialist and Liberal.[5]

The trend, in short, was towards Continental groupings, and this tendency found expression in an unspoken alliance between the deputies and the supranational High Authority against vested national interests. So far from acting as a roadblock to integration, the parliamentarians wanted the High Authority to pro-

[5] Williams, *op. cit.*, p. 12.

ceed more rapidly against national obstacles. Thus the European
drive acquired a democratic character, making it easier for Socialists and trade unionists to participate in what had at first
looked to some suspiciously like a supercartel. In fact, the removal of internal barriers to trade in coal and steel was practically complete in 1958, when the wider European Economic
Community was formed. During the same five-year period, trade
in steel products within the Community rose by 157 per cent, and
steel output by almost 65 per cent, while the stagnating coal industry was helped to modernize itself. This success, which was
doubtless facilitated by the world boom, made it possible to envisage the next step, which was the formation of an Economic
Community embracing the entire field. The step-by-step advance
in itself made nonsense of the argument that the European federalists were wedded to a doctrinaire concept that had to be imposed in the teeth of economic reality. In fact it was the (mainly
British and Scandinavian) "functionalists" who during this period
were being doctrinaire in denouncing every move that threatened
to interfere with absolute national sovereignty. When the Foreign
Ministers of the Six met at Messina in June, 1955, they specifically
refrained from setting themselves political aims for which—as
the recent collapse of the Defense Community had shown—public
opinion was not ripe. "The next phase in the building of a
United Europe," their communique said, "must lie in the economic field." They thus returned to the approach exemplified in
the successful treaty that had set up the Coal and Steel Authority.

THE TREATY OF ROME

Messina proved to be merely a station on the way that led to
the Rome Treaty of March 25, 1957, inaugurating the European
Economic Community (EEC), popularly known as the Common
Market. The intervening governmental moves, with the inevitable jockeying for position, can be ignored here, but two points
are worth noting. First, the Messina conference had set up a
committee under M. Spaak, then Belgian Foreign Minister,

which met at Brussels for nine months to study, among other matters, the pooling of Europe's nuclear energy resources; and it was the outcome of these labors (formalized in the inevitable *Report* issued in the following April) that furnished the basis of the Rome negotiations. Secondly, the Rome Treaty,[6] in the words of a British writer, was "drafted in some haste to exploit the political constellation of 1955–57, when M. Mollet was French Prime Minister, before Dr. Adenauer had to face his electorate in the autumn of 1957, and while the economies of Europe were experiencing a boom."[7] This maneuvering underlines a circumstance already mentioned: the reliance of the European "federalists" upon the political strength of the ruling Christian-Democratic and Socialist parties. In fact, the political upheaval in France during the following year, ending in a partial collapse of parliamentary rule and the return to power of General de Gaulle, showed the wisdom of these precautions. For a few months it seemed uncertain whether the Treaty, which had gone into effect early in 1958, would be fully honored by one of its most important signatories. The crucial date in this respect was the first of January, 1959, when the preliminary round of tariff reductions became operative. In the event, the new French Government lived up to the legal undertakings it had inherited and made no difficulties about tariff cuts, though it showed a marked lack of enthusiasm about federalism. The first big hurdle was taken without mishap, and what is now generally known as the Common Market went into operation on the date foreseen by the signatories.

This decision on the part of the Gaullist regime to step into the inheritance of its predecessor doubtless owed something to

[6] Strictly speaking there were two treaties, dealing respectively with the Common Market and with nuclear energy. Both the agreement establishing the Economic Community and the one setting up a European Atomic Community were signed on March 25, 1957, on the Capitoline Hill overlooking Rome, thus providing the Italians with a tactfully contrived substitute for the short-lived Roman Empire promised them under the Fascist regime.

[7] Kitzinger, *op. cit.*, p. 17. For a brief history of the Common Market negotiations and Britain's refusal to join at an early stage, see Pinder, *op. cit.*, pp. 15 ff.

the fact that the Rome Treaty embodied some escape clauses compared with the Spaak Report, which was a more uncompromisingly federalist document. Unlike the agreement setting up the Coal and Steel Authority, the Rome Treaty was a "statement of intent" depending upon the willingness of the signatories to carry out its provisions. In the event, they not only did so, but in some respects even went ahead of the original schedule; this is the more remarkable since the Treaty in effect integrated economic policies in a manner incompatible with unrestricted national sovereignty. In principle at least it looked forward to ultimate economic *and political* union, and all the rearguard actions fought since then by individual governments have merely had the effect of slowing the process down somewhat. As formalized by the Treaty, the Common Market—or to give it its proper name, the European Economic Community—committed its signatories (France, West Germany, Italy, Belgium, the Netherlands, and Luxembourg) to a degree of integration that fell short of complete economic union but went beyond a customs union. Some of the implications will be discussed later, but the general principle is worth stressing because it had an obvious significance for believers in economic planning. It was in fact this emphasis upon integration—as distinct from mere removal of trade barriers—which made it possible for socialists and other supporters of planning to play so prominent a part in the negotiations, and for the bulk of the European labor movement to lend its support.

There is a seeming paradox here, for the Treaty called for the removal of national tariffs and other obstacles to free trade, as well as for the gradual abolition of governmental subsidies. But these decisions were themselves political and depended upon the central authorities being given sufficient power to override sectional interests. The State, in other words, was invoked to remodel the clogged and artificially restricted national economies, though the long-range purpose of the operation was to reduce bureaucratic controls. Immediately, the free-trade aspect of the Treaty responded to a very simple economic urgency. In the six years between the establishment of the Marshall Plan OEEC in 1949, and the coming together of the Foreign Ministers at Messina in 1955, intra-European trade had more than doubled in volume and was coming up against monetary and tariff barriers. In particular, France was falling behind in her trade-liberalization commitments, while the Benelux union (Holland, Belgium, Luxembourg) was pressing for more rapid removal of customs barriers. In fact, the whole liberalization movement was grinding to a halt. As long as every move depended on agreement among the eighteen member countries of OEEC, no significant advance was possible. The chosen solution—tariff cutting on a regional basis—had the twofold advantage of suiting the prospective members of "Little Europe" and of being compatible with the General Agreement on Tariffs and Trade (GATT) to which all the OEEC members were signatories.[8] What happened at Messina and Rome therefore was that the political drive towards integration merged with the economic pressure to remove barriers to Europe's growing internal trade. For the rest the Six chose this particular solution because it offered a means of getting the integration movement back upon the rails without giving it an overtly political character. The Common Market was both a means and an end, depending on how it was viewed. The British at this stage regarded it as a pipe dream and refused to take part in the negotiations. Instead, after some uncertainty, they put forward the idea of a European Free Trade Area surrounding the projected customs union of the Six.

THE SIX AND THE SEVEN

In view of what was to follow it is worth remembering at this stage that the first postwar attempts to provide the whole of Western Europe with a common legal framework had encountered British resistance, or at most very lukewarm support. The Strasbourg organization never became popular in Britain, and indeed the British Government had taken care, in associating it-

---

[8] Under Article XXIV of GATT, tariffs could be lowered on a regional basis, provided they were reduced to zero over a reasonable period of time. This was a way around the difficulty created by GATT's prohibition on tariff-cutting that discriminated against third parties.

self with the Council of Europe, to render it "as little embarrassing as possible."[9] The military "Western European Union" hastily set up in 1954 likewise continued to linger, and in 1957 Whitehall withdrew one of the promised four divisions which Sir Anthony Eden had undertaken to station on the Rhine until the year 2000! In the economic field, Britain had refused to join the Coal and Steel Community and to attend the Messina talks. It was thus with some surprise that the Europeans in December, 1956 (i.e., shortly after the Suez fiasco), heard Mr. Selwyn Lloyd, then British Foreign Secretary, propose a "Grand Design" for a single European Assembly, in which the Strasbourg institutions, plus various advisory and somewhat functionless international parliamentary bodies, would be merged with the Common Assembly of the Coal and Steel Community. Since the latter was now clearly on the way to becoming the nucleus of a European Parliament, this move looked to the federalists suspiciously like an attempt to "drown Europe in the Atlantic."[10] The Grand Design—a ludicrous title for an abortive scheme hastily produced to stop the European integration movement—had no effect other than to warn the Six that the British Government was hostile to their plans.

Proof of this was promptly furnished when London countered the success of the Rome negotiations with a Free Trade Area plan which had clearly been improvised to take account of the threat to British exports implied in the Rome Treaty. Since the low-tariff members of the Common Market—Germany and Benelux—were Britain's best customers on the Continent, it was understandable that Whitehall should not relish the idea of a common external European tariff which on average would be somewhat higher than the duties charged on British goods by four out of the Six, while at the same time internal barriers between the Six were to be removed. But the British proposals looked like de-

9 Lord Strang, *Home and Abroad* (London, 1956), p. 290, quoted by A. H. Robertson, *European Institutions* (London and New York, 1959), p. 13; Lord Strang, at that time Permanent Under-Secretary at the Foreign Office, clearly expressed the sentiments of his nominal chief, Mr. Ernest Bevin.

10 Kitzinger, *op. cit.*, pp. 86 ff.

liberate sabotage. They amounted to the creation of an all-European free-trade area embracing both the Common Market countries and those who did not wish to join the Six in promoting a genuine economic union. This area would have no common external tariff but would permit all its members to pursue separate tariff policies in relation to nonmembers. In other words, it would enable Britain to retain her special arrangements with the Commonwealth countries. For good measure, mutual customs reductions within the area would not apply to farm products. Since duty-free import of overseas foodstuffs was the cornerstone of Britain's trade with the Commonwealth—notably in the case of Canada, Australia, and New Zealand—it required no great astuteness to realize that the British Government was trying to obtain all the advantages of lowered tariffs on the Continent while continuing to grant preferences to the Commonwealth at the expense of European farmers. Maintenance of the mutual preferences extended to Britain and her Commonwealth partners ever since the Ottawa agreements of 1932 in fact ruled out British membership in a European customs union. At this stage, however, the British Government did not regard this as a reason for abandoning or modifying the Ottawa agreements. The argument was rather that if the Continentals wanted Britain to be associated with their projected Little Europe, they would have to pay the price of allowing the United Kingdom to have the best of both worlds. What this proposal amounted to was that Britain would continue to keep manufacturing costs artificially low through the import of cheap Commonwealth raw materials and foodstuffs, while enjoying free access to Continental markets. For all that, there was some support for the scheme on the part of the Dutch and the Germans, though the former disliked the exclusion of agriculture and the latter were split between the business community's pro-British orientation and Bonn's desire to conciliate the French. In the end, Dr. Adenauer and the Bonn Foreign Office opted for France, much to the chagrin of Dr. Erhard, upon whom the British had rather unwisely placed excessive hopes. What turned the scales was the intervention of the convinced federalists on the Common Market Commission, which had meanwhile come into being.

With this degree of German backing assured, the new French Government, which was anyhow more resolute than its predecessor (although not particularly favorable to federalism), in December, 1958, quite suddenly terminated the Free Trade Area negotiations, and thus compelled its partners in the EEC to do likewise. The British were left in the cold, and the Common Market went into operation on the ruins of the Free Trade Area scheme. The British response was to set up, at the end of 1959, the European Free Trade Association (EFTA) of Britain, Sweden, Denmark, Norway, Austria, Switzerland, and Portugal, to which Finland adhered as an associate member in 1961. Compared with the Common Market's 170 million people, EFTA's 90 million still looked quite substantial, but from the British standpoint it added only 38 million people to the United Kingdom market—mostly good customers anyhow, for Scandinavian tariffs were low and their abolition was unlikely to make much difference to British exports (which, in fact, rose no faster than they did in the Six). Britain's partners thus got considerably more out of EFTA than did the British. The whole scheme had been hastily concocted in the hope that it would teach the Continental Europeans—especially the Germans and the French—a lesson and thus induce a change of heart. What it did was to annoy the French while failing to impress the Germans.[11] EFTA provided for mutual tariff reductions leading to complete abolition by 1970, but for the rest did not call for economic unification. If it was thought that the Six might eventually accept the Seven as a single negotiating partner, the hope was disappointed. Meanwhile, the British Government itself was beginning to develop second thoughts. In January, 1960, Mr. Selwyn Lloyd admitted that it was a mistake not to have joined in the talks that led to the Coal and Steel Community; by June that year, Whitehall was belatedly trying to get in; in August, Mr. Macmillan traveled

[11] The French Government showed its resentment by refusing to let EFTA open its headquarters in Paris, President de Gaulle characteristically observing: *"Paris n'est pas un hôtel."*

to Bonn to meet Dr. Adenauer, and rumors began to spread that
he had asked the Germans to use their good offices in Paris. For
all that it took another year, and a really serious economic crisis,
before the British Government in August, 1961, publicly announced its readiness to start negotiations for joining the Common Market.

The difficulties involved in any attempt to integrate Britain
with Continental Western Europe necessarily form a recurrent
topic of this study. Here it is only proposed to set out some of the
problems that arose as a result of the antecedent splitting-up of
Western Europe into the rival Six and Seven. The original
British reaction to the Rome Treaty was to propose an industrial
Free Trade Area that would enable the United Kingdom to retain
the system of Commonwealth preferences instituted in 1932.
When this failed—chiefly because the French balked at the
thought of admitting British goods duty free as long as they were
indirectly subsidized by cheap food imports—it was no longer
possible to aim at an arrangement under which the tariff reductions of the Common Market and the Free Trade Area should
start jointly in 1959, and thereafter proceed concurrently. Instead, EEC and EFTA began to look like two rival and competing
blocs within the general NATO area, with the important difference that the EEC was a genuine customs union with central
organs strong enough to impose a common policy, while EFTA
had a looser structure and no common external tariff. As such,
it was a triumph for the "practical" and "functionalist" school,
which has always had strong support in Britain, where Continental logomachy and constitution-mongering encountered the
deepest suspicion on the political Left as well as on the Right.[12]

EFTA, however, failed to do the trick; that is to say, it failed
to impress either the Continentals or the Americans. The former

---

[12] For an eloquent, if somewhat strident and not altogether balanced, expression of this attitude, see William Pickles, *Not With Europe: the political
case for staying out* ("Fabian International Bureau pamphlet" [London, April,
1962]). This influential pamphlet by a well-known NATO supporter and ad-
herent of the Labour Party's dominant right wing has the merit of briefly
summarizing all the noneconomic arguments employed by Socialist—as well
as Liberal and Conservative—opponents of European integration.

regarded it as a mere holding operation; the latter preferred the EEC precisely because it promised to speed the political integration of Western Europe. Washington, moreover, had no interest in trade arrangements that would give Britain's overseas partners a preferred market in Europe at the expense of the American farmer and manufacturer. It therefore did not encourage the notion that the Six might extend preferential treatment to the British Commonwealth, thus practically shutting the European market to U.S. exports. If the British Government was angling for a form of discrimination favoring the Commonwealth, it was certain to arouse American resentment. All this became very clear during the period of a little over a year between July, 1960 (when EFTA began its tariff-cutting) and the following summer, when Mr. Macmillan suddenly announced Britain's readiness to negotiate for entry into the EEC.[13] The actual turning point had come a little earlier, in January, 1960, when an Atlantic Economic Conference of the NATO powers decided to replace the OEEC by a new grouping, the OECD, which latter included the U.S.A. and Canada. The significance of this move was that it enabled the European Commission in Brussels—now dominated by the federalists under Professor Hallstein and his very able French colleagues—to link hands with North America, thus bypassing the whole Free Trade Area scheme and reducing Britain to the status of just another European country. It was of course precisely this perspective that angered the British opponents of European federalism; they were doubly resentful when Whitehall—having at last seen the danger sign—reluctantly changed course.[14]

The history of the subsequent British negotiations with the Six falls outside this study. It is useful, however, to take a straight look at what has always been the fundamental British motivation

[13] *Hansard*, House of Commons, August 2, 1961. See also the statement made by Mr. Edward Heath, Lord Privy Seal and chief negotiator with the Common Market countries, in Brussels on October 10, 1961 (Cmd. 1565, London: Her Majesty's Stationery Office, 1961).

[14] Kitzinger, *op. cit.*, pp. 103 ff. For the economics underlying this reorientation, see Professor James E. Meade's important paper *UK, Commonwealth and Common Market* (London: Institute of Economic Affairs, 1962).

in these matters: namely a desire to link up both with Western Europe and with North America.[15] This frequently took the form of arguing that Britain's political institutions could not be amalgamated with those of the Continent.[16] Alternatively, one encountered the plea that the multiracial British Commonwealth, bridging as it does the gulf between advanced and backward countries (and between white and colored peoples), was greatly to be preferred to a "narrow" European grouping: though it was unexplained why a Europe closely linked to the former British and French dependencies in Africa should be "narrow." In fact, the real obstacle was that both Left and Right had grown accustomed to a situation in which Britain stood at the center of a world-wide Commonwealth, linking Ottawa with Delhi through channels ultimately controlled from London. It was only as the central factor within this global system (virtually synonymous—except for Canada—with the sterling area) that Britain could and did play a role independent of both Europe and the United States; and it was the discovery that the Americans increasingly sought partnership not with "Europe plus Britain" but with "Europe including Britain" that radically altered the picture.

This discovery was indeed more disagreeable for the Conservative Party, which had traditionally been the party of Empire, than it was for their Labour opponents. But then the Conservatives happened to be in office and so had to deal with the situation, while the Opposition could afford to be critical. The disappointment over the Free Trade Area thus involved, though in an indirect manner, the position of both the major political parties, which was the main reason why British politics became rather

[15] See R. W. G. Mackay, *Towards a United States of Europe* (London, 1961), pp. 117 ff. The author, one of the few influential Labour Party parliamentarians who actively backed the European cause, died shortly before the publication of his book in which he—an Australian by birth—took his colleagues to task for employing the Commonwealth solidarity argument as a justification of their rooted dislike of the European idea.

[16] See Pickles, *op. cit.*, *passim*, where great play is made with the clash between Continental legalism and Britain's "unwritten constitution": as though the Continent were not in this respect much closer to North America than is the United Kingdom! For a different view of what Britain's commitments might entail, see Pinder, *op. cit.*, pp. 80 ff.

disturbed in 1961–62, after the doldrums of the preceding years. If in 1962 there were mutinous stirrings in the Conservative ranks, while on the Labour side it could be claimed with some plausibility that the Opposition had a chance of sweeping the country on an anti-European and pro-Commonwealth platform, these tremors on the political surface translated into political terms the vague resentment of the public at the prospect of what looked like a wholesale abandonment of both national sovereignty and Commonwealth ties in favor of "Europe."[17] But although such sentiments reach down into greater depths than any merely rational arguments, the ultimate decision was certain to be made at a different level. Strategic and economic factors, as viewed through the prism of Whitehall (where the global balance of power has to be considered) would turn the scale, no matter what the precise state of popular feeling. If this required a voluntary renunciation of sovereignty in matters relating to the new supranational handling of Europe's economic affairs, Parliament's decision—whatever it might be in the end—would be determined by nonlegal considerations.

THE INSTITUTIONS OF THE EEC[18]

The purpose of the Rome Treaty being the establishment of a Common Market, or customs union, between the signatories, the legal documents outlining the Community's institutional framework are largely devoted to detailed provisions covering every aspect of economic policy. This, however, must not lead one to

17 At this stage only the Liberals were fully committed to entry into the EEC at almost any cost (and to abandonment of the British "nuclear deterrent" as useless and prohibitively expensive). The Government indeed stuck to its guns despite the almost unanimous disapproval voiced at a conference of Commonwealth statesmen in September, 1962, but Labour opposition to "entry into Europe" was hardening, and there were rumbles of doubt among Tory right-wingers.

18 For this and the following section, see in particular Robertson, *European Institutions*, pp. 148 ff.; Emile Benoit, *Europe at Sixes and Sevens* (New York, 1961), pp. 9 ff.; Jean François Deniau, *The Common Market* (London and New York, 1961), pp. 51 ff.; Paul Streeten, *Economic Integration: Aspects and Problems* (Leyden, 1961), *passim*.

treat the political "superstructure" of the Community as a mere means to an economic end. It would be truer to say that in the minds of its signatories the Common Market was envisaged as the material foundation of the future political union of Western Europe, with or without Britain. The governing bodies of the Common Market, officially known as the "institutions of the Community," have a political character in that they supersede some of the functions traditionally exercised by national governments and parliaments.

There are four such institutions: the Assembly (now self-styled the European Parliament);[19] the Council of Ministers representing the member governments directly as such; the Court of Justice, with powers to interpret the Treaty and adjust disputes over its clauses; and the Commission (the last-named being the true executive organ). In addition, there are two advisory bodies—the Monetary Committee and the Social and Economic Committee— and two outside bodies coordinated with the EEC proper—the European Coal and Steel Community (ECSC) and the European Atomic Energy Community (EURATOM). Lastly, the EEC has control over the financial resources of a European Investment Bank, a European Social Fund (mainly for industrial retraining and employment compensation), and an Overseas Development Fund, the last-named of special interest to the former colonial territories now indirectly associated with the Common Market.

The Assembly (whose functions are laid down in Articles 137– 144 of the Rome Treaty) corresponds in general to the now defunct Common Assembly of the ECSC, except that its membership is almost twice as numerous and the major countries are more heavily represented. Prior to Britain's decision to join it consisted of 142 members almost equally divided among 4 voting blocs, with France, West Germany, and Italy having 36 delegates each, and the Benelux group a total of 34 (14 each for Belgium and Holland, plus 6 for Luxembourg). Composed as it is of delegates nominated by the national parliaments from among their

[19] Except in the official French text, where it is known as the European Parliamentary Assembly.

members, it does not exactly reflect party line-ups at home, the Communists having been excluded. On the other hand, it has continued its forerunner's habit of forming supranational party blocs of Christian-Democrats, Socialists, and Liberals sitting and voting together irrespective of national origins. Since its inception in 1958, it has tended to develop in the direction of a true legislature, encroaching steadily on the executive, or rather on the two executives established by the Treaty. Only the Commission (which can even be dismissed by a two-thirds vote) is directly answerable to the Assembly; the Council of Ministers is not. This state of affairs is, however, likely to change when—as seems probable—the present Assembly is eventually succeeded by a true European Parliament elected directly by universal suffrage.[20]

Since the European Parliamentary Assembly—like the Common Assembly of the ECSC before it—meets in Strasbourg and functions as a quasi-legislative body, it has inevitably drawn a good deal of the limelight away from the Consultative Assembly of the Council of Europe referred to earlier. In the long run it appears likely that a true European Parliament—i.e., a body composed of elected members and possessing genuine legislative powers—will substitute itself for the present Assemblies, which will then appear as its forerunners. The problem lies in the future relationship of the Western European core—"Little Europe" as it is called by its critics—to the wider penumbra of NATO countries represented at Strasbourg. Conceivably, the original Council of Europe could become the precursor of an Atlantic Community Parliament representing North America as well as Western and Southern Europe, and Mediterranean

---

[20] The first overt move in this direction was taken on May 17, 1960, when the Assembly passed a resolution recommending that the member states take the necessary steps. The resolution was subsequently endorsed by M. Monnet's unofficial "Action Committee for the United States of Europe," the real motor of the whole integration movement. It is significant that, here as elsewhere, federalist and democratic forces have marched hand in hand. As the Chatham House organ *The World Today* noted in an editorial comment (May, 1962), "the Commission and the Parliament tend to regard themselves as allies in the process of furthering European integration against the sometimes laggard Council of Ministers."

countries like Turkey. Even so, it seems unlikely that the West Europeans will renounce their new-found unity and their common institutions. How fast and how far the economic community will transform itself into a political community is another question. For the present it must be emphasized that national sovereignty in matters relating to foreign affairs or defense is not affected by the Rome Treaty: The powers it delegates to the Community are exclusively economic. Any forward move to genuine federalism will require a new treaty. Neither the Council of Ministers, which normally decides by unanimous vote or by a qualified majority vote,[21] nor the Court of Justice (seven judges appointed by the governments for a maximum of six years), calls for special comment. There is, however, one noteworthy point: The regulations issued by the Council are binding in law from the moment of issue. This accords with Continental practice but conflicts with the British tradition of an unwritten Constitution which in principle reduces itself to the unrestricted sovereignty of the Parliament at Westminster. A treaty superseding national laws is easier to operate on the Continent than in Britain, where Parliament can in theory repudiate any obligations entered into on behalf of an earlier legislature, though in practice this is unlikely to happen. It may be said that any nation can "contract out" if it is really determined, but the principle of unfettered parliamentary sovereignty does make it somewhat easier to repudiate burdensome obligations—if the government of the day is so inclined.

The four bodies just named are of unequal importance. For practical purposes, the European Commission rather than the Council of Ministers seems likely to become the real executive organ—this despite the provision that the Council has the final word in policy matters. The mere fact that the nine administrators forming the Commission are appointed by the member gov-

21 Prior to the negotiations over Britain's entry, this meant twelve votes out of seventeen: France, Germany, and Italy having been allotted four votes each and Benelux five. It was thus possible for one big and one small country combined to muster six votes in opposition, thereby blocking proposals requiring a qualified majority.

ernments *acting in common* gives them a special status. They are, moreover, enjoined by statute to "exercise their functions in complete independence" of their respective national governments. In this they follow the example set by the High Authority of the Coal-Steel Community, except that the latter's powers are more far-reaching, since they are not shared with a ministerial organ.[22]

The Rome Treaty is too lengthy and complex a document for any summary to be given here, and some of the subsidiary bodies established under it—e.g., the Economic and Social Committee—may look more important on paper than they are likely to become in reality. But brief mention must be made of EURATOM, which was established parallel with the Economic Community. This was made the subject of a separate treaty for two reasons: first, the six governments had previously come to the conclusion that a joint effort was needed in this quite new field in order to harness Europe's nuclear energies and, if possible, render the area less dependent upon the United States. This called for state control, or even state ownership, and thus fell outside the general economic provisions of the Treaty, which aim at the reduction or elimination of governmental interference with the market economy—a point to which we shall revert. Secondly, it was necessary to stipulate that the military use of nuclear energy should be excluded. This was a condition of French assent, the French Government—even before the advent of the Gaullist regime—being determined to reserve its rights in this field. Since Western Germany had, under the Paris agreements of 1954, renounced the right to manufacture atomic weapons, and the other four participants had no intention of doing so, agreement was not difficult. EURATOM thus represents a "common market" in the field of nuclear energy for industrial and scientific purposes and a center for the coordination of national research, as

[22] See Articles 155–63 of the Rome Treaty; for an interpretation, see Robertson, *European Institutions*, p. 156. It may be noteworthy that in the Rome Treaty the term "supranational" (embodied in Article 9 of the ECSC Treaty, from which Article 157 of the Rome Treaty was copied) has been omitted; but this terminological concession to the antifederalists hardly affects the substance of the matter.

well as for cooperation with non-European countries. Like the Coal-Steel High Authority and the Common Market Commission, it is a Little Europe in miniature, its personnel being—in principle, anyhow—responsible only to the supranational institutions of the Community.[23]

The resulting institutional setup looks complicated. In practice it is simplified by the easy accessibility of the various centers of authority. With the European Parliament located in Strasbourg, the Common Market Commission and EURATOM in Brussels, and the Coal-Steel High Authority in neighboring Luxembourg, even the proposed establishment of a new Political Secretariat in Paris (hitherto still in the discussion stage) would not greatly complicate matters, the more so since the ambassadors of the member governments accredited to the EEC form a kind of unofficial link between Council and Commission. It is the latter that has become the real driving force. The reason is obvious: Unlike the Council of Ministers, which passes decisions unanimously or by a qualified majority, the Commission decides by simple majority vote. Its business is to execute the Treaty, which in practice means imposing its provisions upon recalcitrant interests, though in this it can be checked by the Council and the Court. It has powers to issue directives and decisions as well as recommendations and authorizations, and can thus specifically order a named country to take certain steps or desist from others. Lastly, it is both supranational and centralist, hence an ideal incorporation of the federalist idea, which envisages the gradual elimination of national obstacles to all-European planning and integration. For the same reason it has become the target of "states righters" worried over the erosion of national and parliamentary sovereignties.[24]

23 In practice, the French Government, under the impulsion of President de Gaulle, has somewhat circumscribed the independence of its representative on the executive body of EURATOM, currently located in Brussels.

24 See Pickles, *op. cit.*, pp. 19 ff., where considerable play is made with the bureaucratic character of the Commission. The argument would carry weight were it not for the fact that the democratic forces represented in the Parliamentary Assembly have generally been on the side of the Commission in its efforts to break down obstacles to European integration.

Federalism is in fact the counterpart of integration. This was so from the first behind-scenes steps taken by M. Monnet's Action Committee and has remained true during all the political fluctuations of the succeeding years. It is for this reason that the Commission has become the ally of those political forces on the Continent aiming at the establishment of a genuine European Government. Its bureaucratic—or technocratic, if the term is preferred—composition predisposes it in favor of supranationalism; so does its formal relationship to the Council of Ministers. The latter—in principle the ultimate political authority—can accept or reject the Commission's broad policies but may not alter them otherwise than by unanimous vote, which is seldom obtainable. This provision gives considerable weight to the Commission's activities, which cover the whole field of tariffs, agriculture, social policies and anticartel legislation, as well as financial matters affecting the Community's external balance of payments, and the control of investment policies. Lastly, as the official representative of the EEC in relations with non-European areas, it has taken the lead in negotiations with prospective members or associate members. With a staff of some 1,800 trained experts and civil servants, and a leadership dedicated to integration, the Commission is at the heart of the federalist drive for a United Europe. No one was surprised when its Vice-President (a Frenchman) committed himself in public to the statement that in the end it would be necessary to set up what he described as "a real government, and not merely periodic meetings of ministers."[25]

THE COMMON MARKET

Institutions draw their life from the aims they are meant to serve. The principal aim of the European Community institutions was and is the establishment of the Common Market. While this is widely understood, the originality of the Common Market conception is not generally appreciated. Even its supporters tend to be hazy about it, while its critics have not always taken the trouble to define their objections with sufficient precision. Talk

[25] Robert Marjolin, *Le Marché Commun et l'Unification de l'Europe,* (Brussels: Société Royale d'Economie Politique de Belgique, 1961), p. 11.

about "planning" and *laissez-faire*," or about the dangers of European protectionism vis-à-vis the backward countries (i.e., the primary producers), must remain vague, if not substantiated by an understanding of what it is that the members of the Economic Community have actually undertaken to do.

The simplest way to describe the Common Market is to call it a customs union, but that is only half the story, and perhaps the less important half. Tariff unification is no more than the indispensable means of establishing a true economic community; it is, however, the key to all the rest. A common tariff on imports from outside the Community, together with the gradual elimination of *all* internal tariffs and quotas among members, are the two basic provisions that from the start set the EEC concept off sharply from the British-sponsored Free Trade Area scheme. Part I of the Rome Treaty lays down detailed specifications in this field, the general aim being the attainment of complete internal free trade within twelve to fifteen years of the Treaty's inception. In practice, this program has been accelerated, so that by now 1970—or even 1967—is usually mentioned as the date for the disappearance of the last *internal* tariffs and quotas, including those on farm products, and the concurrent establishment of a common *external* tariff.[26]

Whereas the elimination of internal barriers might be regarded as a matter affecting only the European countries concerned, the adoption of a common external tariff clearly has implications for the rest of the world. Under the Rome Treaty, maximum tariff rates were specifically laid down, ranging in most cases from 3 to 25 per cent, although rising above this level for some products. A comparison of average external rates with previous national rates suggests that critics of the EEC who described it as a protectionist bloc were wildly mistaken. In fact, the common tariff under the Treaty works out at a considerably lower level than the average of national tariffs in force before the Common Market

[26] Imports into Britain from the British Commonwealth formed a special subject, which was still under negotiation when in January, 1962, the Six agreed on the alignment of their agricultural policies; though even here some important decisions, e.g., the fixing of grain prices, were left until later.

entered into operation: In the case of France and Italy it amounts to halving their old rates. It is true that Belgium, Holland, and Luxembourg would have to raise their previous rates, which were unusually low, but the total effect is nonetheless distinctly in the direction of freer international trade. In different terms, the European producer will obtain less tariff protection against non-Europeans, and of course none whatever within the Community itself, where he will for the first time be exposed to the full blast of untrammeled market forces.[27]

The customs union, however, is only envisaged as a means to a wider end, for which the phrase "economic union" is appropriate, though the Treaty avoids it. The term "Economic Community" was chosen to get around the difficulty of finding a common denominator acceptable to all the participants. As defined by the Treaty, the Economic Community is distinguished by the following aims going beyond a mere customs union: (a) free movement of capital and labor across national frontiers; (b) elimination of governmental measures (chiefly subsidies of all kinds) having the effect of restraining trade or distorting competition; (c) harmonization of social policies, i.e., chiefly wages, social-insurance benefits, and employment policies; (d) common agencies to coordinate investment within the Community and outside it, notably in formerly dependent overseas territories. The attainment of these aims—which have all been written into the Treaty—still falls short of a full economic union, in that they do not provide for a common currency and do not require national wages, investments, or employment policies to be identical. The Treaty merely asks for their "harmonization" to a degree that will enable the Community to function. Moreover, acceptance of these measures by the members is qualified in most cases, inasmuch as they cannot be simply decreed by the Economic

27 For details see Benoit, *op. cit.*, pp. 20 ff. With some exceptions, the common tariff is eventually to be set at a level representing an arithmetic average of the rates charged by the member countries on January 1, 1957—subject to reciprocal concessions negotiated by the EEC and its trading partners. In practice, this has meant a drastic lowering of French and Italian rates, a rise in Benelux rates, and no great change in either direction in the case of West Germany.

Commission but must be approved by the Council of Ministers, with its built-in veto. Even at a later stage, when the Council will in many cases be able to operate by qualified majority vote, a member state may still invoke various escape clauses alleging the priority of national legislation, or dangers to national security. In general one may say that these provisions correspond to a political relationship of the confederacy type, rather than to a true federal system. It was clearly felt that at this stage majority rule would have imposed too much of a strain, whether exercised through a supranational parliament with true legislative powers or through voting in the Ministerial Council. The result was a compromise, which at least had the merit of not alarming national sentiments to the point of endangering the whole scheme.

The provisions governing the free movement of capital and labor, and the setting-up of central funds to cope with transitional difficulties, call for no particular mention. On the other hand, two points are noteworthy because they are of more general import: The Treaty took account of the dangers that every customs union holds for the economically weaker members, and for the same reason it embodied special provisions for treating the whole field of agriculture on a supranational level and *removing it from the realm of the market economy*. Europe's agriculture is to be planned as a whole. This is not the least remarkable feature of an enterprise that has had the blessing of both liberals and socialists in Western Europe, including some last-ditch defenders of the pure market economy, who in this case tacitly agreed to compromise their principles.[28]

---

[28] Somewhat to the embarrassment of British socialist critics of the whole scheme. Thus Mr. Pickles, in the Fabian Bureau pamphlet already cited, concedes rather grudgingly that "one must recognise the merit of the idea of planning agriculture on a continental scale, even if one dislikes the methods used and is apprehensive about its probable results" (p. 25). His dislike of Continental Europe and its retrograde inhabitants wins out, however. Thus a little later he writes: "The way to reduce instability in Europe is to give whatever help we can from outside, not to sacrifice Britain to it. The sensible missionary does not jump into the cannibal stewpot in order to reduce its temperature" (p. 29). The "cannibals" in this particular case might perhaps retort that they are not keen on boiled missionary if the dish is to be as indigestible as this kind of talk would seem to indicate.

The connection between planning in general and planning for agriculture is not accidental. Every customs union carries with it serious dangers to its weaker members, and within their territories to those branches of the economy that are less productive. Far from helping them to overcome their disadvantages, it may cause them to fall further behind. In modern European history, the classic case is the unification of Italy a century ago, which left the agrarian and poverty-stricken South in worse condition than it had been before. Northern Italy obtained considerable benefits from the customs union then established to cover the whole country. Southern Italy got none, and its structural weaknesses were further aggravated, with long-term results which in the 1920's proved fatal to Italian democracy. This is the kind of problem doctrinaire free-traders and *laissez-fairists* either refuse to see or treat as a mere passing inconvenience. For an instance of this attitude one may cite a remark by a prominent economist who can stand for many:

> The removal of tariffs, and of other barriers to mobility following the unification of Italy, widened the range of alternatives open to the people of Southern Italy; and the extension of the range of choice normally benefits rather than harms a population.[29]

In fact, what the unification, and the simultaneous introduction of nationwide free trade, did to Italy in 1861—almost exactly a century before the Rome Treaty, fortunately drafted with greater wisdom by economists no longer wedded to *laissez-faire*—was to ruin the weak and unprotected industries of the South, while the change-over to industrial protection in the 1880's hurt its agriculture. The short-term result was to compel mass emigration to North and South America. The long-range consequences were more unpleasant still: The South temporarily pulled Italy down to its own sociopolitical level, for although the Fascist movement was born in the North, it battened on the backwardness of the countryside, the unsolved Southern agrarian problem, and in

[29] P. T. Bauer, "International Economic Development," *Economic Journal,* March, 1959, pp. 110–11 (quoted by Streeten, *op. cit.*, p. 54).

general the discredit that had been cast upon democracy by the ruling Liberals' obstinate adherence to their economic doctrines. In practice this meant ruining large parts of the country, or neglecting their development, in the interest of the few advanced industrial centers. In contrast to these exercises in economic orthodoxy, the Rome Treaty makes an attempt to correct regional inequalities through investment planning at the center. Socialists are entitled to argue that it does not go far enough. What they cannot honestly do is pretend that it is a *laissez-fairist* document.[30]

The place of agriculture in this picture is determined by its specific weight in the context of European economic life. Setting aside Britain, with less than 5 per cent of its population dependent on farming, as a special case, the West European countries are bound to protect the interests of producers who with their families account for 20 to 40 per cent of their populations.[31] The Rome Treaty consequently contains special provisions (listed in Annex II) that envisage what has been described as an "organized market" for European agriculture.[32] Their aim is officially described as being "to increase agricultural productivity, to ensure a fair standard of living for the agricultural population, to stabilize markets, to guarantee regular supplies, and to ensure reasonable prices in supplies to consumers." This language will be familiar to Americans. It is of course incompatible with nineteenth-century economic orthodoxy. One need only inquire what "a fair standard of living" is, or by what criteria it can be defined, to realize that these Treaty provisions by themselves undercut

[30] This is not to deny that many of its supporters—perhaps especially in the United States—are still wedded to a fairly simple-minded view of the economic universe. In these quarters, the ancient tautology "all legitimate interests are in harmony" may be interpreted to mean that complete free trade must benefit all sections of the community, except of course those whose interests are not "legitimate." But this kind of nonsense no longer enjoys much support, and in any case it has little effect on contemporary European politics.

[31] By 1960, the active population engaged in farming represented on an average less than one-quarter of the total, but the percentage was slightly higher for France and a good deal higher for Italy.

[32] Deniau, *op. cit.,* p. 68.

the assumptions held by the surviving doctrinaires of economic liberalism.

In quarters wedded to unrestricted free trade, this concern for farming and the farmer is frequently put down to ordinary political considerations: as though the agricultural population had any other means of making its weight felt than through the political process; or as though this were not a soundly democratic way of counterbalancing the greater economic pull of the urban industrial centers. But in fact the Treaty-makers had every reason, apart from political calculation and vote-catching (which of course played their part—but only by neutralizing other pulls), to take farming out of the area of unrestricted competition in which the Free Trade Area would have left it. To try to unify Europe industrially without paying attention to farming would have meant reproducing all the internal disharmonies already plaguing the Six individually at the higher level of the European Community. If French farmers in the summer of 1961 blocked the roads and threatened violence, they did so not because they resented the Common Market, but because they were restless over its failure so far to solve the problem of their unmarketable surpluses. The effect of their demonstrations indeed was to galvanize the governments of the Six into an effort to work out a joint policy for farming, complete with guaranteed prices (even if the principle was not spelled out in every detail when the ministers completed their exhausting labors the following January). National interests appeared to dominate the furious bargaining among the Six, with France, Italy, and Holland in particular insisting that if they were to lower their tariffs on industrial goods, the Germans must open their frontiers to farm surpluses. But what translated itself into conflicting national claims at the level of European politics was the underlying socio-economic problem of achieving a rational balance of industry and agriculture. That is why the eventual agreement was so important. Anyone could have foretold that governments dependent on electorates of which peasants and farm workers constitute an average of one quarter would be responsive to pressures from below.

What required proof was that the Six could agree on a joint policy—which is what in the end they managed to do.

This somewhat cursory discussion of the economic policies laid down in the Rome Treaty may be completed by a brief review of the measures already taken or envisaged to bring about a free flow of goods and services, as well as labor and technical skill, within the Community. These can be summarized under the following three heads:

A. *Internal trade barriers.* The first round of tariff-cutting among member states began on January 1, 1959, when all duties were lowered by the statutory 10 per cent, and this was followed by an equivalent reduction according to schedule on July 1, 1960. Since then, the tempo has accelerated and cuts have been made ahead of schedule. In January, 1961, industrial tariffs within the Community already stood at only 70 per cent of their 1957 level, and by July, 1962, they had fallen to 50 per cent of the base rate. It is now expected that the aim of total abolition of internal customs barriers will be achieved as early as 1967. Quotas have disappeared almost completely (except in foodstuffs, which are subject to the separate agreement concluded in Brussels in January, 1962). Among the consequences of this acceleration was a 50 per cent rise in intra-Community trade during the first two years after the round of tariff-cutting had begun.

B. *External tariffs.* In March, 1960, the lacunae of the Treaty were filled in and the final rates determined by the Council of Ministers. Allowing for a list of special products that called for higher rates, the common external tariff worked out at an average of 7.4 per cent (negligible for raw materials, 5.9 per cent for finished goods, 13.6–17.2 per cent for capital equipment and other manufactures). Thus a distinctly modest degree of protection was offered to European industrial producers; since then, negotiations with the United States have led to a further lowering.[33]

[33] See Deniau, *op. cit.*, p. 134. For details of the tariff-cutting procedure, and of the exceptions granted in respect of certain commodities (mainly in order to benefit overseas associated countries in Africa) see Kitzinger, *op. cit.*,

C. *Free movement of capital and labor.* The aim here was and is to treat all nationals of the member countries as though they were European citizens, i.e., to remove all statutory obstacles to the free movement of persons and properties across national frontiers. In fact this has been easier to achieve with capital than with labor, money being more mobile than people. Still, the principle of a European labor market for all wage earners in search of employment has been written into law, though with numerous exceptions and escape clauses relating, e.g., to public administration (states will continue to employ their own nationals for government services); public health and safety (limitless immigration of undesirable entrants continues to be barred); and short-term employment (work permits are renewable, but only after four years of regular employment do all discriminations on national grounds fall away completely). In practice, no mass movements have taken place, since all the Community countries except Italy suffer from a labor shortage, and even in Italy the industrial boom has almost done away with the unemployed hordes of the "reserve army." For the same reason, the complex provisions of the "Social Fund" set up to compensate workers for loss of employment have proved to be quite adequate. Lastly, there has been some progress with the promised harmonization of wages and social-security payments, a condition of France's entry, in view of French legislation stipulating equal pay for men and women and social benefits equal to almost 50 per cent of the basic wages bill.[34]

---

pp. 22 ff. In the spring of 1962, the six members of the EEC undertook to cut their outer tariff by 20 per cent on most manufactures, thus bringing it well below the British tariff against third countries. Once the Common Market enters its third stage (by 1966), further cuts need no longer be agreed on unanimously but can be decided by qualified majority.

[34] For details, see Benoit, *op. cit.*, pp. 33 ff.; Kitzinger, *op. cit.*, pp. 30 ff. In practice it has not proved easy to reconcile national planning and price-fixing policies with the provisions of the EEC and ECSC (Coal and Steel Community) rules, which forbid discrimination. For a particular instance arising out of the French Government's determination to control the level of steel prices, see *The Economist*, May 5, 1962. France has consistently been the most *dirigiste* and plan-minded of the countries concerned. The sociopolitical background of this difference will be examined later.

Planning and Freedom

"Planning" is a value term; so is "freedom." Both are invoked by critics as well as supporters of the European Economic Community, either with the aim of demonstrating that the Common Market is in reality a gigantic supercartel of big business interests and reactionary politicians in their pay[35] or with the object of showing that if the Common Market is to fulfill the stated aims of the Rome Treaty it will have to evolve away from classical liberalism towards a planned economy, without thereby becoming either exclusive or protectionist, and without toppling over into all-round state regulation. There are of course also old-fashioned *laissez-fairists* (liberals in European terminology)[36] who support the Common Market because they see in it a partial fulfillment of their long-standing aim to do away with all barriers to free trade. It is clearly a tribute to the ingenuity of its founders that the Community can attract support from conservatives, liberals, and socialists alike. Nonetheless, some degree of theoretical clarification seems called for. Agrarian conservatives, free-enterprise liberals, and plan-minded socialists may all have perfectly good reasons for supporting the aims of the Rome Treaty, but in the end the awkward question has to be faced: What sort of economic logic underlies the Treaty, and how can the Community be expected to develop? Is it simply a hotchpotch of compromises or does it correspond to a recognizable set of aims having their rationale in a coherent view of modern society?

Traditionally, European politics have revolved around the tripartite division of society into conservative defenders of the preindustrial way of life, liberal supporters of the market economy and *laissez-faire,* and socialist advocates of public ownership.

---

[35] The more frenzied propagandists of this school can be disregarded here. For a relatively moderate statement, see Pickles, *op. cit., passim;* for a less inhibited clarion-call from the far Left, see Michael Barratt-Brown and John Hughes, *Britain's Crisis and the Common Market* (London, 1961), pp. 12 ff.

[36] It is perhaps worth stressing that in Europe the term "liberal" does not signify what it often seems to mean in the United States: someone who favors more public control or an enlargement of the public sector. European socialists, even of the Fabian variety, still call themselves socialists, not liberals.

In the nineteenth century (and in a measure down to the 1930's) these divisions corresponded to the historic class conflict pitting landowners and peasants against the industrial and commercial bourgeoisie, and both against the rising working class. This is the line-up that underlies the familiar socialist view of European politics. In recent decades it has partly broken down, except in areas not fully transformed by the industrial revolution. But although the former class relationships no longer retain their previous significance, the three-party division persists. European politics rest upon a conservative-liberal-socialist tripod, with conservatives (at any rate on the Continent) generally defending the values of preindustrial society; liberals advocating a modernized ("managerial") form of capitalism, with built-in safeguards against depressions and mass unemployment; and socialists pressing for the fullest possible extension of labor legislation and the welfare state, plus over-all economic planning in the interest of the whole community. These aims are not incompatible, but they do conflict, thus giving the impression that society is still confronted with the class struggles of the nineteenth century. In actual fact the problem is one of compromise at an entirely new level. The extent to which public ownership and planning of economic resources are compatible with the operation of the market economy cannot be determined beforehand, and the debate thus gives rise to serious divergencies; but in principle all parties concerned are aware that it is a question of balance, not of substituting one social order for another. In this sense, the "mixed economy" and the "welfare state" may be said to have won general, if tacit, recognition.

But although political conflicts have lost much of their edge, theoretical disputes remain sharp and in some respects are clearly incapable of resolution because they relate back to different and conflicting ideals or "visions." It is perhaps easier for a conservative-socialist coalition government to arrive at a compromise over public ownership (Austria and Italy come to mind) than for conservative and socialist writers to agree on the respective values of an agrarian and an industrial way of life. Similarly, liberal and socialist economists in advanced countries such as Britain, Sweden, or Holland, may be on the best of terms and in agreement over nine-tenths of the field when it is a question of practical measures to finance the welfare state or to adopt Keynesian remedies against economic slumps. But agreement breaks down over the remaining tenth, which has to do with the rationale of economic planning. That this is not an academic issue must be apparent to anyone who considers what is implied by the term "planning" under conditions where governments—i.e., political authorities—increasingly make the basic decisions on which the whole life of the community depends. In this respect liberals have for decades been fighting a rearguard action, while socialists for their part have so far had to content themselves with a mere approximation to their final goal. A great deal depends on whether the European Economic Community is viewed as an institutional framework for classical liberalism, or as an instrument of more or less socialist planning, or as a balance of both (if it can be achieved); just as politically much depends on the uncertain attitude of the powerful Roman Catholic parties and trade unions when faced with these conflicting pressures. This is the real stuff of contemporary politics in Europe, compared to which all other issues appear increasingly trivial.

Matters would be considerably simplified if one could at least reduce the liberal-socialist dispute to a common denominator less vague than "private and public welfare." But notwithstanding some degree of mutual *rapprochement* compared with the prewar situation, the two sides to this controversy do not really talk the same language; each remains convinced that the other is wedded to an absurdly simplified, out-of-date, and unrealistic approach.[37] Keynesian neo-liberalism, while no longer *laissez-fairist* in the sense of placing all its faith in the market economy, concedes the necessity for state control only to the degree that is required to provide an institutional framework within which individuals may freely enter into economic relationships with each other. Antitrust legislation must preserve competition, taxation may

[37] For the following cf. in particular Streeten, *op. cit.*, pp. 13 ff. I make no apology for leaning rather heavily on this brilliant piece of analysis.

redress gross income inequalities, and monetary policy may do what it can to avert slumps. But the aim remains as before a society in which "buying in the cheapest and selling in the dearest market" is expected to result in a constant widening of economic opportunity for all. Competition and free trade are regarded as means to the end of rapid economic growth *and* growing equality of income for individuals and classes. The concrete specifications that flow from these assumptions are embodied in those provisions of the Rome Treaty which do away with internal tariffs and provide for the free flow of capital and labor from one end of the Community to the other. In this sense the Treaty is a document of classical liberalism. It is of course this aspect which has won for it the more or less wholehearted support of the business community.[38]

Unfortunately for the peace of mind of Keynesian liberals—not to mention pre-Keynesian *laissez-fairists* who still have a following in Western Europe and can occasionally exert political influence—these assumptions are disputed by socialists and supporters of economic planning generally.[39] The underlying philosophy of liberalism is not acceptable to those who remain convinced that—despite some concessions to reality—it remains fundamentally question-begging. Economic integration, when defined by liberals, takes it for granted that competition and free trade must in the long run bring about an allocation of resources such as to benefit all "viable" economic units, while remaining silent about the fate of the nonviable. It also disregards the fact that the *aims* of liberal economics—rapid growth and freedom of choice—may be achieved by purposive planning, while avoiding the haphazard and frequently catastrophic side effects of unregulated competition. The choice between reliance on the market mechanism, and over-all control by a central

[38] After some initial nervousness in France, which was overcome when French manufacturers, to their great surprise, discovered that they were fully competitive with the Germans.

[39] The distinction is a trifle tenuous, but the bureaucracy of the European Economic Community includes prominent people—notably French economists and administrators trained in the postwar school of economic planning from the center—who are *de facto* socialists, though they do not wear a party label.

planning authority relates back to different social priorities. Liberty and equality are not in principle incompatible, but they do conflict in practice. "Equality in the market, equality in the eyes of the law, equality of income and wealth, may or may not be expressions of the basic equality enshrined in the ideal."[40] In a scarcity economy—and even Western Europe has not yet risen above this level—clashes cannot be avoided, although their edge may be blunted by welfare measures. Moreover, the term "integration" says nothing about the relative weight given to workers' interests as against those of capital or management. In short, the political conflict goes on, as does the theoretical dispute.

All this may sound rather abstract, but it translates quite rapidly into practical politics when liberals and socialists, *laissez-fairists* and planners, are asked to state their views on the future shape of the Economic Community. The liberal belief in trade liberalization points to a conception of the EEC as a step towards an Atlantic economy—ultimately a world economy—from which all protective tariffs have disappeared and where economic rationality has at last come into its own. It is fair to say that such notions are viewed with distrust not only by tariff-minded conservatives anxious over the fate of agriculture and traditional ways of life, but also by plan-minded socialists who suspect that under such conditions purposive direction of economic life would become more difficult. The world of 1914, to which this kind of liberalism looks back as to a golden age, is not one that socialists contemplate with nostalgia. Moreover, it is arguable that the notion of restoring it is a fantasy. Full world-wide economic integration is not in any case seriously contemplated for the immediate future even by the most enthusiastic liberals. Meanwhile the present approximation—regional free trade—which in some respects looks like a first step, may actually interfere with the goal. To be viable, the Economic Community must promote a high rate of growth, which in turn depends upon an adequate volume of exports; yet the internal pull of full-employment policies drives prices and wages up, thus interfering with

[40] Streeten, *op. cit.,* p. 17.

the export goal. To keep a proper balance between external and internal requirements—which in practice means balancing the competing pressures of capital and labor—governments have to institute planning mechanisms which in turn acquire a momentum of their own. The conflicting claims of full employment and higher exports, faster growth rates and greater social equality, *can* in principle be bridged without state "interference," but only at the cost of violent ups and downs. Since in the struggle to determine the correct balance between long-term and short-term considerations each side can mobilize powerful social support, the State is compelled to step in and make itself the arbiter between competing pressure groups. In practice this tends to reinforce the role of the bureaucracy in general, and the planning bureaucracy in particular. There is no getting around this, once it is accepted that the determination of a rational policy is the task of the political authorities.

In the light of these considerations, we may conclude by saying that whereas the Free Trade Area represented the liberal solution of the problem, the European Economic Community—for all the political conservatism of the signatories to the Rome Treaty—points beyond liberalism. By setting up supranational authorities with power to plan investments, promote economic development in backward areas of Southern Europe and overseas, plan European agriculture and transport, break up cartels, and lay down a common external tariff towards the outside world, the Treaty overstepped the boundaries of classical liberal doctrine. It did so while at the same time satisfying the liberal demand for a clean sweep of internal barriers to free trade. The resulting compromise has left the meaning of "integration" undefined as between the liberal goal of free competition and the planners' belief in purposive direction. In practice the conflict translates itself into a pull between the true "institutions of the Community"—foremost among them the Economic Commission, EURATOM, the European Investment Bank, etc.—and the market forces let loose by the sweeping away of internal barriers.

A good instance of what supranational planning can signify

in practice was furnished in June, 1962, when the ECSC in Luxembourg approved what it called a "document of synthesis" on the creation of a common market in energy.[41] To arrive at this goal, the High Authority had to calculate the domestic energy supplies of Western Europe, as well as the sources of imported energy—primarily oil—and then consider the policies to be adopted in view of the probable closing down of uneconomic coal mines. It was assumed that by 1970 about half of Europe's total energy requirements would come from oil (as against 10 per cent in 1950) and about 35 per cent from coal (against 70 per cent in 1950). The key to energy prices will therefore be the cost of imported crude oil, which after 1970 will enter the Common Market free of restrictions, except for East European imports, which will be subject to a quota. The calculation envisaged a European energy demand in 1970 of 700 million tons of "coal equivalent" a year, against a current 500 million, most of the increase being made up of imported oil. Now a common energy market, with imports of crude oil kept free of duty, has obvious implications for the European mining industry, as well as for such oil suppliers as Algeria. This is the type of decision-making which, by its very nature, compels liberal and socialist theorists to grope for a common platform. It is also part of the answer—though only part—to the insistent question of what is meant in practice by "planning." Every government is now more or less deeply involved in all kinds of planning—fiscal, industrial, balance of payments, and so on—and it is easy to become lost amidst the rhetoric of competing interests intent on dignifying their particular claims by pinning this fashionable and popular label to it. In principle this could also happen—and doubtless will—at the European level. It is all the more important to have before one a clear case of the much-maligned "Eurocrats" trying to impose a rational pattern upon Europe's energy resources. Needless to say, the particular solution chosen by them can be challenged. It can be criticized, for example, on the grounds that it is uneconomic for Europe to produce so much of its own

[41] See *The Economist,* June 16, 1962.

energy; but that is another matter. If one happens to be interested in the question how far "planning" can become a rational exercise in conscious control of the economic environment, the experiments now carried on in Western Europe must rank among the major innovations of our time.

It is important to realize that this type of supranational planning has grown out of the more familiar national policy-making in which some leading Western European countries began to engage after 1945, when the planners were swept into office. Most of the fundamental thinking that underlies the European Community has so far been French, and France has since 1945 been committed to *dirigisme,* though with varying shades of emphasis depending on changing political constellations. Nothing is sillier than the notion that the Community—because some of its rules militate against national protectionism—is thereby committed to reliance on market forces. West Germany's well-advertised opposition to planning—in part an understandable reaction against the shattering experience of National Socialism—is usually cited in evidence when it is argued that the only kind of economic control operative in the Community is one that masks the activities of cartels. What these critics overlook is that Bonn's doctrinaire attitude (which has recently been wilting a little, with the "economic miracle" plainly coming to an end and giving way to the familiar anxieties about inflation and price rises) has not prevented France from dominating the Brussels Commission; and France—by way of trying to solve her own problems of growth— has become Europe's greatest planner. Nor has it prevented the more recent Italian moves in the direction of greater public control over the economy, starting with the nationalization of energy supplies.

Planning has a logic of its own, which starts with the decision to take an over-all view of the economy. As has rightly been remarked, the European Community is *dirigiste* by nature.[42] It is

---

[42] S. C. Leslie, "Competition in the New Europe," *The Listener,* August 16, 1962: "For years its leaders have devoted themselves to bringing about a desired end by deliberate contrivance. It has lived to plan and lived by planning."

dominated by men who are aware that the day of unregulated liberal capitalism is done; and it has already established a framework within which competition acts as a spur to efficiency only as an aid to over-all central planning. This is most notable in agriculture, which indeed is now being "planned" in response to socio-political objectives laid down from the top. It is less visible in industry, because cartelized big business offers enough resistance to the controllers to create the illusion that competition has not really been transcended. Yet the essential fact is that here, too, the central decisions are being taken on political grounds. The growing clamor about "technocracy" and the excessive powers of the Brussels Commission is evidence that the business world does not share the naïve notion that the Treaty of Rome has made Europe safe for *laissez-faire*.

The danger, insofar as there is one, lies in another direction. Economic logic dictates not only a measure of central planning by governments; it also dictates a growing concentration of power at lower levels. Whether state controlled or in private hands, the bigger and more efficient enterprises tend to assume a monopolistic structure. Public and private planning combine to bring about a state of affairs where genuine competition shrinks in importance and is increasingly relegated to minor industries and to the fringes of economic life, while the basic sectors of the economy are dominated by state-owned industries and private monopolies of varying size and efficiency. At the end of this process there lies a stable compromise between public and private planning, the latter either cartelized or in corporate hands. In practice this must take the form of an increasingly close partnership between governments and big business. Under given political circumstances, with the corporations dominating the state, this could result in the emergence of a corporate structure of society, with liberal democracy going by the board alongside competition and free enterprise. There are elements in Europe's social make-up which favor such an outcome. After all, it very nearly happened in some important European countries as a reaction against the economic breakdown of the 1930's.

But to see this danger is not to say that it is bound to materialize. Whether it will or will not depends on a balance of social forces that shifts with the growth or decline of countertendencies. There are at least two identifiable factors that militate against big-business domination and the corporate state: democracy as such, and the drive to plan the European economy in terms of social goals set by the "technocrats" of the Brussels Commission, who are also the most convinced "Europeans" of all. Democracy will continue to find its bulwarks in the national parliaments, in labor movements and other popular organizations, and in the remnants of the older liberalism insofar as it is not simply a convenient instrument of big business. The moral authority of the Brussels Commission will, one hopes, be backed not only by national governments—with the French in the lead—but by the growing political consciousness of the "technical intelligentsia," which is beginning to emerge as the key stratum of the new society. It is going to depend on the political orientation of this stratum whether the balance of forces shifts in the direction of democratic, technocratic, or corporate planning—the latter presumably finding its political counterpart in some form of fascism. A European government not sufficiently controlled by the residual democratic forces could indeed degenerate into an oligarchy of bureaucrats manipulated by the great corporations and their political spokesmen. It is precisely because this danger is real that Europe's labor movements and socialist parties have from the start tried to control the European bureaucracy and establish strategic positions inside the political structure: so far with success.

The alarming vision of a Europe dominated by big business and uncontrolled bureaucrats has just enough reality to mobilize the countertendencies inherent in modern society. Since the growth of centralized decision-making cannot be avoided, the democratic forces will have to make sure that the process is kept under control, and that government by consent, and the rule of law, are strengthened rather than weakened. They will be the more successful the less they allow themselves to be deflected into mere vote-catching, defense of sectional interests, or academic disputes over the respective merits of parliamentary or presidential types of government, such as have recently absorbed some of their energies in France. It would be absurd and dangerous to tie the democratic cause to such side issues. Ultimately what counts is the ability of the democratic forces to develop elites capable of mastering the complexities of the postliberal age. If they fail, they will not escape their responsibility by declaiming against semi-authoritarian solutions of the Gaullist type that predictably fill the void left by the collapse of traditional parliamentary authority. The democratic response to the challenge inherent in such situations lies in a reconsideration of what is meant by popular control over the executive. This need not be limited to the familiar interplay of government and parliament. It can also take the form of associating responsible democratic bodies—with the trade unions in the lead—more directly with the formulation and execution of four-year or five-year national economic plans. Nor is it impossible to reorganize the structure of representative assemblies so as to give due weight to corporate interests: the danger of "corporatism" as an alternative to democratic control arises precisely where such interests are not properly integrated into the fabric of representative government. A modern pluralist society which frankly acknowledges the need to balance conflicting interests is not for that reason obliged to make an unreal choice between authority and democracy. With a modicum of luck and good sense it can have both.

III

THE STRUCTURE OF
WESTERN EUROPE

GENERAL FEATURES

The "Europe" with which this chapter is concerned comprises twenty countries. In alphabetical order they are: Austria, Belgium, Britain, Denmark, Finland, France, Greece, Iceland, Ireland, Italy, Luxembourg, the Netherlands, Norway, Portugal, Spain, Sweden, Switzerland, Turkey, West Germany, and Yugoslavia. This is not the geographer's Europe, nor is it the "Little Europe" of the Rome Treaty. With the exception of Finland and Yugoslavia, all the countries in the above list are members of the Organization for Economic Cooperation and Development (OECD) set up under a Convention signed in Paris on December 14, 1960, with Canada and the United States joining their European partners in what was largely the economic counterpart of the NATO alliance (although it also included the perennial neutrals—Austria, Sweden, and Switzerland). The fact that Finland and Yugoslavia did not go in for clearly political reasons, while on the other hand Canada and the U.S.A. belong to it, makes it impracticable to discuss West European economics in OECD terms, though it is necessary to do so when one considers the Atlantic Community. Here as elsewhere one has to make a choice and clarify one's terminology, which is best done by deciding what it is one wants to talk about. If one's subject is the economic geography of Western Europe, then the fact that Spain has been ruled by a Fascist dictatorship since 1939, while Yugoslavia has been under a Communist regime since 1945, should not prevent one from considering their economic structures alongside those of their neighbors. On the other hand, a line must be drawn somewhere if the discussion is to remain realistic. One cannot ignore the fact that most of Eastern Europe constitutes a coherent regional bloc, of which Eastern Germany, e.g., forms part, whereas Yugoslavia does not.[1] Historically, this division is new and therefore apparently senseless. It does not take much thought to perceive that Austria and Hungary, although divided by an almost impassable frontier, have more in common with each other than with most of their respective associates. But although both belong to the Danubian basin, they also adhere to self-contained regional economic blocs which are steadily developing in different directions. In what follows we simply take it for granted that, as a political and economic unit, Central Europe has—temporarily or permanently—disappeared, and that the present division into Eastern and Western Europe corresponds to economic orientations which, in practice, amount to the emergence of two different types of society.[2]

For practical purposes we can ignore both Turkey and Yugoslavia as being on the fringe of the West European area, while Spain, Portugal, and Greece (with or without Cyprus) fall into a clearly defined subgroup of their own. If Algeria, Tunisia, and Morocco are excluded, one cannot speak seriously of a Mediterranean economy. There may be a case for grouping these three North African countries with Turkey, Greece, Spain, Portugal, and Yugoslavia, in which case it could be argued that Egypt and Israel should be included as well. But where is one to stop? Clearly all these groupings intersect. All one can do is to try

[1] If Belgrade were to become a member of the COMECON organization, which coordinates the economies of all the Soviet-controlled East European regimes, it would then rank, according to this classification, as East European. This is the only relevant criterion if one thinks of current political realities. The fact that a country has a Communist government and a planned economy is neither here nor there. Geographically and in terms of socio-cultural development, Yugoslavia is anyhow closer to Greece and Turkey than, say, to East Germany.

[2] For this and the following, see in particular J. Frederick Dewhurst *et al.*, *Europe's Needs and Resources* (New York, 1961).

not to confuse the issue by introducing irrelevant criteria, such as the balance between market forces and public planning. This balance is anyhow a shifting one, even within a single country. It is not necessarily true that there is a correlation between economic liberalism and adherence to democracy. The most one can say is that backward countries tend to evolve authoritarian forms of rule and planned economies to match. But their "planning" is quite different, in intention and technique, from that of a highly developed industrial country such as France, which adopted a semiplanned economy after 1945. Again, one cannot well exclude Spain from Western Europe on account of its current political orientation, yet its claim to be regarded as a "free" country is worse than Turkey's. The rational procedure is to disregard all such considerations. Once this is done, the definition of "Western Europe" offers no particular problem.[3]

With or without the doubtful cases, this western part of the geographer's Europe comprises the greatest concentration of economic strength outside the United States. Certainly its economic resources are out of proportion to its size. With only 3 per cent of the world's land surface and little more than 10 per cent of its population, Western Europe accounts for some 25 per cent of the world's total output, 20 per cent of its food supply, and 40 per cent of its trade. Its 320 million people[4] inhabit one of the most densely populated and highly industrialized regions of the globe, and their economic intercourse with the rest of the world places them in the peculiar position of a "workshop" processing imported raw materials. Setting aside trade *within* Western Europe, the area's position as the chief "workshop of the world" is disclosed by the fact that almost 80

[3] The Twentieth Century Fund *Survey,* which excludes Turkey and Yugoslavia (the latter on political grounds), makes room for Spain, presumably because it is one of the "noncommunist Western-oriented countries of Europe, the economies of which are largely responsive to the free play of market forces rather than government fiat" (p. xxi). All classifications are arbitrary; a classification which makes a fetish of "market forces" displays the cloven hoof of partisanship rather more blatantly than most.

[4] In round figures and bearing in mind the problem of defining the area. For details, see Dewhurst *et al., op. cit.,* chap. 2, pp. 32 ff.

per cent of its imports are primary products and only 20 per cent manufactures, whereas for exports the percentages are almost exactly reversed.[5] With the prospect of growing dependence on non-European sources of fuel (especially oil), this contrast is likely to become more pronounced. It has been estimated that by 1970, Western Europe's imports from the outside world are likely to be some 45 per cent above their 1955 total of $18 billion, with fuels, ores, and other minerals rising a good deal more rapidly than foodstuffs and agricultural raw materials. Despite a slight decrease in the proportion of imports in relation to gross output, this will leave Western Europe in the position of being the largest single importer of primary products. Intra-European trade, which now accounts for about half the total trading activity of the West European countries, is likely to increase even more rapidly.[6]

These over-all remarks must be qualified by a reminder that Western Europe includes large regions of what it is now fashionable to call "underdevelopment"—a blanket term which conceals the fact that in some cases intensive "development" along the wrong lines has been going on for centuries, with the result that soil erosion and crop exhaustion have added themselves to poverty and overpopulation. These stagnant and backward areas comprise much of southern Italy, most of Spain and Portugal, parts of Greece and Turkey, and some areas of Ireland. Taken as a group, the 100 million or so inhabitants of the Mediterranean lands (including Turkey, Greece, and Yugoslavia, as well as the poorer parts of the Italian South) do not participate in the customary advantages of belonging to an industrial civilization— a circumstance amply demonstrated by the fact that their average income is only one-third that of the inhabitants of the wealthy Northwest European group. (In the case of southern Italy this is now being slowly remedied through Italy's postwar industrial boom and its membership in the EEC.) Western Europe in fact compromises two distinct "civilizations," of which the southern and more backward is characterized by heavy dependence on

5 *Ibid.*, chap. 28, pp. 889 ff.
6 *Ibid.*, p. 890. As noted above, this *Survey* excludes Turkey and Yugoslavia.

agriculture and related activities. There is extensive, though largely "invisible," unemployment on the land, mostly of unqualified labor that cannot be quickly absorbed into industry, even if the economic resources were available. In the past, these countries have typically attempted to solve their problem of excess population by sending emigrants abroad, chiefly to the United States and Latin America; they are currently obtaining relief through the industrial boom in northern Italy, France, West Germany, and neighboring areas. This is part of the answer to the question why "Europe" is not doing more to assist the backward countries. Europe has its own backward regions and is far from having solved the problems they represent.

Even with this important proviso, Western Europe taken as a whole remains one of three great concentrations of economic power in the modern world, North America and the Soviet Union being the other two. The following observations are intended as a brief summary of some of the principal features common to the region, leaving for later a series of thumbnail sketches of its chief national constituents.

By any standard proper to the writing of history, Europe reached the peak of its power and wealth, relative to the other continents, in the early years of the present century. Yet those writers who around 1950 saw an absolute as well as a relative decline[7] clearly underrated the recuperative powers of modern society. Ten years later, it was possible for a group of American economists to note with satisfaction that "the more than 300 million people of Western Europe enjoy average incomes with purchasing power more than one-third higher than the per capita incomes of the 260 million who lived in the same region on the eve of the most devastating war in history. Industrial production, in this birthplace of modern industrial society, has more than doubled over the past two decades. Agricultural output—with fewer men on the farm—is over a third larger than in the imme-

---

[7] M. R. Shackleton, in *Europe: A Regional Geography* (p. 1), thought it "certain that the two great recent wars have seriously impoverished the continent."

diate prewar years."[8] Moreover, while this advance was uneven and left some of the backward areas almost unaffected, "the rates of growth of nearly all European countries for the 1950's alone surpassed those of the U.S. and Canada."[9] Between 1950 and 1959, the combined gross national product of the eighteen member countries of the OEEC (later the OECD) increased by 46 per cent, or $80 billion (measured in 1954 market prices). This was equal to an annual compound rate of over 4.3 per cent— enough to bring about a 100 per cent increase over 1950 by 1967. These are figures for *total* output. Industrial production rose a good deal faster.[10]

Some subsidiary points are worth noting. First, by 1950, Western Europe had already made good much of the war damage and attained a larger gross national product—total and per head of population—than in the last prewar year, 1938, which admittedly was not a very good one. Secondly, a much larger share of the bigger output was being invested, i.e., used for capital formation. This was true both of countries like France, Italy, Holland, and Norway, which after 1945 adopted extensive governmental planning, and of free-enterprise areas like Germany. Thereafter, the advance was uneven but spectacular. Between 1950 and 1960, Germany, Austria, and Greece (laggards in 1950, when they were still struggling with heavy war damage) made very swift progress in gross output (Germany by almost 90 per cent). Italy came next, with a 64 per cent rise in total output by 1959, and an even more rapid rise thereafter. France, Holland, and Switzerland gained some 50 per cent during the decade; the Scandinavian

8 Dewhurst *et al., op. cit.,* p. 3. By a somewhat different reckoning the same authors calculated that the West Europeans in 1960 were consuming "nearly 60 percent more goods and services than the 15 percent fewer people who lived in the same territory just before World War II" (p. 862).

9 *Ibid.*

10 *Ibid.,* pp. 16 ff. For details, see *OEEC General Statistics* (Paris, January and March, 1960); *Europe and the World Economy,* 1960. In the *Economic Survey of Europe in 1949,* the staff of the Economic Commission for Europe, looking ahead for ten years, foresaw a 40 to 60 per cent rise in industrial output by 1959. In fact, the 40 per cent increase was achieved by 1954, and 60 per cent by 1956. Yet even the 1949 estimates assumed an industrial growth rate that Europe had not known since 1913!

countries about one-third, Belgium-Luxembourg about one-fourth, and the United Kingdom one-fifth. In Ireland, where the population was falling, output expanded only 10 per cent. Overall, Germany and Italy made the fastest progress, though in Italy the advance was concentrated in the heavily industrialized North, thereby widening the disparity with the rest of the country. On a larger scale, this pattern was reproduced in the widening gap between the poorer Mediterranean countries and the wealthy northern group, though among the former Greece made striking progress and there was some advance even in Spain. Within the Common Market group of the Six, Belgium lagged behind the others, while among the Seven, Austria and Switzerland were ahead, with the Scandinavian countries making satisfactory but unsensational progress, and Britain coming last. The relatively poor performance of Britain and Belgium seemed to reflect the structural problems of countries that had pioneered the industrial revolution and had difficulty adapting their aging industrial and transport systems to modern demands. Almost everywhere, industrial output rose faster than total production, and by 1957 only five countries—Denmark, Portugal, Spain, Ireland, and Greece—obtained less than 40 per cent of their gross domestic product from industry; they included, however, one of the wealthiest (Denmark) as well as the four poorest (not counting Turkey and Yugoslavia, which fall in the same category).[11]

The obvious conclusion—that the West European boom of the decade was linked to the area's growing industrialization—has long-range implications for Europe's relation to the other continents. Overall, the region stands in somewhat the same relation to the rest of the world as does Switzerland to the remainder of Europe. As it becomes wealthier, it also becomes more vul-

---

[11] *Ibid.*, pp. 21–22. The fact that Denmark draws so large a share of its gross domestic product from farming does not, of course, mean that the country can be classed with the Mediterranean group. Within the latter, the most striking change has come in Italy, where in 1950 industry accounted for only a third of total gross product at factor cost, while by 1957 it provided 44 per cent and in 1961 about 50 per cent.

nerable, and this growing dependence on foreign trade goes far to explain the increasingly pacific character of West European politics in the present era. Nations that depend to an increasing extent on commercial ties with the outside world are less inclined than large "autarchic" countries to incur major political risks. In this respect, West Germany has now caught up with an evolution characteristic of the smaller West European countries ever since they ceased to count on a world scale. The political implications of this change will be discussed later.

Setting aside minor fluctuations (such as a brief recession in 1958, which was hardly more than a pause for breath) Western Europe can be said to have had a permanent boom ever since American aid in the immediate postwar period (1946–49) sparked off the initial reconstruction. If these early years are discounted as being mainly a period of recovery from war damage, a twelve-year period of uninterrupted and almost unwavering economic growth is an impressive phenomenon, especially when contrasted with the slower and more cyclical development of North America during the same period. Expansion was virtually continuous everywhere, though most rapid in the industrialized areas (other than Belgium and the United Kingdom). There was a regular year-to-year expansion in Germany, France, and Italy, though France suffered a brief setback in 1958, and Germany seemed to falter early in 1962. The governments concerned on the whole put expansion ahead of price stability and were rewarded by an investment boom, which by 1962 had brought about something approaching full employment not only in the traditional industrial centers but even in Italy (despite continued unemployment on the land). In general it may be said that France, Austria, Finland, Norway, and Greece paid for their expansion by a fairly rapid price rise and some devaluations; Germany, Italy, and Switzerland scored a very large growth in output with relatively modest price increases; Britain on the whole chose deflationary measures to limit the wage-cost effects of full employment, failed to achieve price stability, and got the worst of both worlds; in only one country, Portugal, was there almost complete price stability, and significantly it stayed near the bottom of the growth list.[12]

It remains to be added that the U.S. Government, for all its commitment to the ideology of free enterprise, was instrumental in enabling the West European countries to adopt and enlarge the post-1945 pattern of "planned" saving and investment. Marshall Plan aid and other forms of assistance were indeed crucial in carrying Europe through the transition period without upheaval, but these forms of aid were made dependent on the adoption of planned investment programs by the recipients, and thus enhanced a tendency—already strong among political leaders, administrators, and economists who had emerged from the (mainly left-wing) Resistance movements—to plan their economies on a national, i.e., governmental, level. This tendency was partly counteracted by the free-trade provisions of the Rome Treaty and the ECSC, but at the same time planning was institutionalized at a European level—with the full support of the U.S. Government. This may be described as a case where economic rationality (and of course political pressure and fear of the Soviet bloc) won out over ideological commitments. That the resulting picture was tolerated in Washington may have been due to the fact that West Germany was expected to set the "planners"— most influential in France, Holland, and Norway, less so in Italy—a sound example. In the event, French notions of planning, being more in tune with economic realities and European requirements, penetrated even into liberal-conservative strongholds such as Germany, Britain, and Belgium.[13]

---

12 Dewhurst *et al.*, *op. cit.*, pp. 27 ff., 111 ff., 443 ff. "The general picture that emerges in Western Europe in the decade following World War II is one of a great volume of investment resulting more from political decisions than from individual economic decisions. . . . In classical theory the sort of inflation which Europe experienced almost steadily in the period . . . would have been expected to dry up the flow of private saving in its traditional forms. The fact that it did not do so has yet to be explained satisfactorily . . ." (*Ibid.*, pp. 461–62).

13 For the British discussion, see in particular *Economic Planning in France* ("PEP Report" [London, August, 1961]), and *The Growing Economy—Britain, Western Germany, and France* ("PEP Report" [October, 1960]). For a significant editorial comment see "Planned Europe?" *The Economist*, May 5, 1962, where some interesting conclusions are drawn from the link between

What has been said so far relates either to Western and Southern, i.e., Mediterranean, Europe as a whole, including the laggards (Greece, Turkey, Yugoslavia, Spain, Portugal), or to industrialized Northwestern Europe, plus or minus the Italian South. To single out the Six of the Rome Treaty is to adopt a different perspective, but the resulting picture merely serves to emphasize the dimensions of the post-1945 expansion and its dependence upon the hard core of highly industrialized countries. The European Economic Community of the Six, with its heavy investment commitments in Africa and its dependence on imported fuel (including Sahara oil), duplicates some of the major problems of the whole area, but it also displays much of its underlying strength. Trade among the six countries of the EEC has increased even faster than intra-European trade in general. Output has likewise grown at a more rapid rate, even before the Common Market came into operation: Between 1949 and 1957, gross domestic production (at factor cost and 1954 prices) for the Community as a whole rose from $75 billion to $122 billion, an increase of 63 per cent in eight years, or 6.3 per cent annually at compound rate. Admittedly this includes the early years of recovery from war damage, when Marshall Plan funds were made available, and to that extent the growth rate was untypical. The fact remains that during this period gross national product (GNP) *per inhabitant* (at 1954 market prices and exchange rates) rose almost twice as fast as it did in the United States, namely at an annual compound rate of 5.4 per cent as against 2.5 per cent.[14] In the four-year period 1954–58, the per capita rate of in-

---

center-left political currents in France and Italy, and the drive for "planning on a European level." By 1962, the contrast between planned expansion and unplanned stagnation had indeed become so glaring that a Conservative Government in Britain was induced, after many hesitations, to set up a simulacrum of a planning body.

[14] See Dewhurst, *et al., op. cit.,* pp. 842 ff. Increase in GNP *per worker* and *per inhabitant* has not differed much for the United States during this period, but there is a difference if GNP is calculated *per man-hour,* since working hours shortened. For the whole 1947–60 span, the increase in productivity per worker has been independently estimated at about 2.3 per cent, and at about 2.9 per cent per man-hour. There has been a steady tendency for unemployment to rise in the United States—a trend not paralleled in Europe.

crease in GNP (at constant 1954 prices) was still 4.3 per cent
for the whole EEC: a significant slowing-down, but still a very
respectable achievement.[15] On the basis of a compound rate of
4.3 per cent, GNP per inhabitant (measured in 1958 prices) would
increase from $950 in 1958 to $1,580 in 1970. Assuming that GNP
in the United States continued to rise during this period at the
annual compound rate registered in the 1949–58 period, the
corresponding advance between 1958 and 1970 would be from
$2,550 per inhabitant to $3,120.[16] Thus by 1970 the member countries of the European Economic Community would have a per
capita income of slightly more than half that of the United
States, whereas in 1960 it was not much more than one-third.[17]
To that extent the gap tends to close, while at the same time it
becomes more pronounced between Europe's industrialized core
and its backward hinterland. But this is simply an instance of
uneven progress. Whether it is beneficial for the backward areas
depends upon the policies adopted by the more advanced ones.

What cannot be doubted is that the formation of the EEC
introduced a new impetus just when the original drive was
beginning to slacken. Since the Common Market came into operation, its member countries have more than maintained the rate
of growth achieved by the mid-fifties. Indeed, 1960 was a boom
year, with industrial output rising by 13 per cent and total output
by perhaps half that figure. Though the advance slowed down
in 1961, when industrial production rose by only 6.5 per cent,
the EEC Commission in April, 1962, foresaw a 4.5 to 5 per cent
expansion in 1962 for the Six as a whole, while the French Four

15 *Ibid.*, p. 842. Germany had the highest rate, with 5.2 per cent, followed by Italy (4.9 per cent), France (3.9 per cent), Holland (2.6 per cent),
and Belgium (1.6 per cent).

16 *Ibid.* The annual compound rate of 1.7 per cent, on which this rise is
calculated, is based on a different calculation and thus diverges from the 2.5
per annum rate mentioned earlier.

17 Britain's entry would make no fundamental change, since its basic
income structure is today no different from that of the six original EEC
members. Popular notions to the contrary notwithstanding, Continental living
standards in the 1960's are no longer significantly behind Britain's.

Year Plan for 1962–65 operates on the assumption of an annual 5.5 per cent growth rate.[18] For Western Europe as a whole, a 4 per cent rate of expansion was assumed by the Economic Commission for Europe.[19] These forecasts are substantially in tune with the longer-range projections previously cited for the period ending in 1970. Beyond this date, projections become too uncertain to have much value. In particular, it is impossible to forecast the extent to which growing wage pressures—which were already marked throughout the EEC area in 1961–62—will lead to a shift from investment to consumption and a consequent slowing-down of the growth rate. For Western Europe as a whole, the outlook is even less measurable. Projecting the 4.3 per cent annual increase that occurred over the 1950–59 period to 1970 would give a very satisfactory result: an 88 per cent gain over 1955, when Europe had already fully recovered from the war. But shortages of labor and critical raw materials may intervene to slow the growth rate down.[20] Even at an annual growth rate of 3 per cent (higher than the estimated 2.5 per cent rate achieved between 1870 and 1913, when Western Europe was the world's principal industrial region), gross national product in 1970 would be 55 per cent above the 1955 level. And since—in contrast to the pre-1913 period—Western Europe's population is now growing very slowly, per capita gains will be almost as large as gains in total GNP. Standards of living, in other words, can be expected to mount fairly rapidly. In our age of "population explosions," this places Western Europe in an almost unique position. The region is in fact completing a long-term demographic transition from high levels of birth and death to near-stability on the basis of small families and low death rates. During the 1950's, its population was growing at about 2 million a year,

[18] See *The Economist,* May 5, 1962. Since then, the 1963 estimate has been pushed up to 6 per cent.

[19] See its annual *Report* (Geneva, April, 1962).

[20] Dewhurst, *et al., op. cit.,* p. 865. This growth rate for eighteen West and South European countries must not be confused with the increase of GNP per inhabitant in the smaller EEC area.

and the projected population for 1970 is 320 million—only 8 per cent more than in 1955.[21]

If current projections for population growth, the size of the labor force, and greater productivity (i.e., output per man-hour) are accepted as valid, the estimated rise of 55 per cent in total gross national product works out at an increase of per capita GNP from $747 in 1955 to $1,067 in 1970 for the 320 million inhabitants of eighteen West and South European countries (slightly less if Turkey and Yugoslavia are added to the list).[22] Within the region, relative progress is likely to be fastest in Italy, where substantial labor reserves still remain to be drawn into industrial production, and slowest in Ireland, despite constant or shrinking population figures. If one assumes a rate of growth substantially larger than 3 per cent compound per annum, the resulting picture still leaves unaltered the two basic traits already mentioned: a striking growth in the relative weight of industry as against agriculture in nearly all the countries concerned, and a substantial disparity between the fully industrialized group and the rest. The problem then becomes one of directing surplus capital from the advanced to the backward regions; in other words, it becomes one of European planning, and hence a political question, since the relevant decisions can only be made at the center.

Notwithstanding this cautionary observation, it will be necessary to say something about the outlook for the chief national entities concerned. But first let us try to meet two possible criticisms that bear upon the principle of European economic integration as such: its irrelevance to built-in socio-economic inequalities, and the misleading nature of quantitative measurements

21 *Ibid.*, p. 866. This does not include Turkey and Yugoslavia, of which the former at least is now undergoing a genuine and rather alarming "population explosion." But even so, the total figure for all the twenty countries should not exceed 370 million by 1970.

22 *Ibid.*, p. 869. The striking disparity between this figure and the amount of $1,580 per inhabitant for the EEC countries (see above) reflects the gap that still divides Europe's industrial core from its backward southern hinterland.

when applied to trade between countries of roughly comparable economic structure.

As to the first, it can plausibly be argued that a mere increase in the gross revenue of the countries concerned says nothing about living standards as they affect the majority. Just as the gap between advanced and backward members of the European family will tend to widen in the absence of deliberate countermeasures, so it is arguable that a rise in average incomes for the West European countries to something like half the U.S. standard would leave the gap between rich and poor in Europe not merely unaltered but even more pronounced than it is today. The commodities that weigh heavily in the budget of the working classes and the salaried lower-middle classes—food purchased in groceries, working clothes, heating materials, etc.—are relatively cheaper in the United States than in Europe, which is another way of saying that the living standard of the American workingman is higher than that of his European counterpart. Supposing then that gross national incomes rose, while social disparities remained unchanged, the gap between rich and poor would by 1970 have become wider than it is today, the more so since luxury goods and services consumed by the rich are cheaper in Europe than in the United States. The rich would have become richer, and the poor at least relatively poorer, though actually somewhat better off. This is true and important, but it only amounts to saying that economic growth by itself does nothing to alter social inequalities. From a democratic standpoint, this is an argument against the market economy, not against European integration. The conclusion it leads to is quite simply that in an integrated Western Europe, socialists—and democrats in general—will have their work cut out trying to prevent the possessing classes from monopolizing the fruits of progress.

The second difficulty is more serious, and there is perhaps no wholly acceptable solution. European union does imply a certain degree of protectionism, and to the extent that it does so, it obviously hinders the optimal allocation of world resources. A Europe that tried to become almost wholly self-supporting in foodstuffs would cease to be a market for countries that depend on export of food against import of manufactures. In practice, this affects the producers of temperate foodstuffs more than it does the tropical and subtropical countries, which of course are the genuinely poor ones; but there is clearly a danger in such bizarre exercises in protectionism as the artificial stimulation of European rice and sugar-beet production at the expense of tropical and subtropical suppliers. Perhaps the most effective counterweight to such tendencies lies in the political association of Western Europe with its former African and Asian dependencies. So far from being a species of "neocolonialism," this association serves to give these countries a guarantee against the latent menace of European protectionism. It is less easy to see what Europe can do to assist Australia or Canada without ruining its own farmers. In purely economic terms, and setting aside the catastrophic effect on the Continent's peasant farmers, the European consumer would gain more from the adhesion of Canada to the Common Market than from British membership, since he would then get low-cost Canadian cereals and minerals free of duty. But such paradoxical exercises in economic logic merely serve to underline the irreality of all abstract reasoning. In practice, European union, though it has an economic logic of its own, involves some additional burdens; it is arguable that no sacrifices should be demanded from the really poor countries, but this is the only major qualification most Europeans are likely to accept. For the rest they will have to bear, with whatever fortitude they can muster, the charge that in fusing their not very dissimilar economies, they are subordinating economic rationality to political goals.

NORTHWESTERN EUROPE

Politically and economically, the Common Market area is dominated by Germany and France, with Italy following at some distance, and the Benelux group forming an entity of its own, which for some purposes acts as a link between the Franco-German group and the United Kingdom. Conversely, among the Seven of the still-born EFTA partnership, Britain clearly stood out as the major unit. These internal divisions, which at times assume major political importance,[23] appear secondary when considered against the background of the more lasting structural disparity between the two halves of Western Europe: the northwestern and the Mediterranean. The former covers all the Six and the Seven, except for Portugal and possibly the Italian South. The second group comprises a number of countries that clearly have more in common among themselves than with the members of the northwestern region. For our purpose it is immaterial in what form countries like Sweden, Switzerland, and Austria may eventually adhere to a politico-economic union of Western Europe. Structurally they form part of the "advanced" group. These subdivisions are relevant if one is trying to make sense of the realities underlying the flux of political events.[24]

A. For simplicity's sake, let us start with the United Kingdom of Great Britain and Northern Ireland (excluding Eire, which from the geographer's viewpoint is nonsense, but cannot be helped); and again for the sake of elementary order let us begin with a few basic statistics, as provided by the OECD *Economic Survey* of March, 1962. As noted before, economic growth in Britain during the 1950's was slow: about half the rate achieved by the members of the EEC. Industrial production rose fairly rapidly in two brief spurts, from the end of 1952 to mid-1955, and again from the end of 1958 to early 1960, but for the rest of the time was more or less stagnant: a condition that still obtained in the first half of 1962, though exports had improved over

[23] E.g., during the European union negotiations of April–May, 1962, when M. Spaak on behalf of Belgium tried to mediate between the British and French viewpoints and inevitably attracted criticism from both sides; see *The Guardian*, May 16, 1962. Prior to this, the Benelux group had temporarily refused to proceed with the talks on Western Europe's political future until a decision had been taken on Britain's membership. The French viewpoint was set out with considerable effect by General de Gaulle on May 15.

[24] Gottmann, in *A Geography of Europe*, limits Western Europe to Britain, Ireland, Scandinavia, the Benelux group, France, and Switzerland, while Germany (East and West) is assigned to Central Europe, as is Austria, and Italy is grouped with the Mediterranean countries. Today this seems less plausible than perhaps it did a decade ago.

the preceding year. Although the U.S.A. and Canada have over the past decade stayed at the bottom of the poll, this is no consolation for the British policy-makers, since the more relevant comparison is with the countries of the Continental European group. For the 1950's as a whole, the rate of growth of GNP in the United Kingdom was about half the rate achieved in the EEC area.[25] Moreover, U.K. exports rose only half as fast as imports between 1955 and 1960, while in the EEC area exports gradually overtook imports so as to constitute a surplus. On balance, the lower rate of growth would seem to have been a consequence of the fact that foreign trade did not play a major role in stimulating demand, while on the Continent the industrial boom was fed by a much more dynamic export drive: typically during the 1950's in the case of West Germany, latterly in Italy and France as well. Whether this sluggishness was primarily due to the upward trend of costs and prices, to labor immobility, or to poor industrial relations and managerial conservatism was a subject much debated in Britain. On the face of it, what stood out was the relatively fast growth in money incomes, and consequently in unit costs, compared with the industrialized Continental countries, though from 1960 onward this difference tended to narrow consequent upon the more rapid rise of real wages on the Continent. The notion that wages were rising too fast in relation to productivity was widely accepted in British official quarters, leading to an unpopular "wage pause" in 1961–62, whose chief effect perhaps was to erode the Conservative Party's electoral support. The pressure of home demand upon exporters was also blamed, although it was noted by critics of official policy that periods of mounting domestic demand in 1955 and 1959 were accompanied by rising exports. This threw some doubt upon the notion—popular in Treasury circles—that exports would benefit from deflationary measures designed to limit home demand. Economists and businessmen critical of official policy thought it likely that deflation was having a depressing effect upon the entire economic climate. It also seemed probable that in overseas sterling

[25] *OECD Economic Survey of the United Kingdom*, March, 1962, p. 10.

markets, which expanded slowly for quite other reasons (e.g., the gradual erosion of tariff and quota preferences favoring Britain as against European, Japanese, and American competitors), costs were not the main hindrance. At any rate it was noteworthy in 1961–62 that British exports to Western Europe and North America expanded fairly rapidly, while sales to the overseas sterling area were stagnant, having previously declined from 49 per cent to 38 per cent of the total between 1954 and 1961, while the share of exports going to Western Europe and North America rose during the same period from 38 to 46 per cent.[26] A growing export surplus on current account has been required since 1958, when for the first time net receipts from "invisibles" (banking, shipping, foreign investments, etc.) were insufficient to cover overseas government expenditure (mainly military) and net capital exports abroad. The resulting balance-of-payments problem has been the principal preoccupation of the authorities in recent years, leading to violent fluctuations in the gold reserve and consequent manipulation of the interest rate, with disconcerting effects upon foreign sterling holders and domestic producers alike. The decision to seek membership in the EEC sprang largely from these difficulties and the resultant loss of faith in the effectiveness of traditional commercial arrangements, which seemed to make the country dependent on the sterling area at a time when West European markets were (a) expanding more rapidly, (b) threatening to become integrated behind a common tariff wall unless Britain could join the Common Market. It could of course be argued that, even without being a member of the EEC, Britain was, in 1962, doing pretty well in exporting to Western Europe.

From a long-term viewpoint there was some doubt whether explanations fastening upon post-1945 weaknesses were relevant to the country's unsatisfactory economic performance. Investigations into Britain's economic growth rate for the past century suggest that the pace has in fact been slow in relation to other

[26] *Ibid.*, p. 22. For an official analysis, see the Government's own *Economic Survey* of April, 1962 (Cmnd. 1678), especially pp. 29 ff.

countries for a very long time.[27] There is then not much justification for compiling economic "league tables" for the 1950's, since
these comparisons assume that all the West European countries
started level around 1950, or at any rate in 1955, when war damage had been repaired. If the lag in Britain's growth rate goes
back to the early years of the century, or to an even earlier date,
this procedure becomes questionable. On the other hand, it becomes even more urgent to adopt a long-term strategy for accelerating the rate of growth. Early in 1962 a step in this direction
was taken with the establishment of a National Economic Development Council to advise the Government on measures to promote faster growth consistent with financial stability. Unlike its
French counterpart, the Commissariat du Plan (whose success in
stimulating France's postwar economic growth had clearly in-
spired its authors), the NEDC appeared to have been conceived
as a purely advisory body with very limited opportunities for
escaping from Treasury control (not to mention the control of
the principal vested interests whom it would have to override).
Perhaps its establishment marked above all a change in the
mental climate. At any rate it brought the term "planning" back
into favor, after ten years of Conservative reliance upon market
forces, following in turn six years of rather halfhearted planning
under the 1945–51 Labour Government.

In the atmosphere created by a decade of conservatism it was
perhaps not surprising that this innovation should encounter a
defensive attitude on the part of economists who had previously
belabored the planners for trusting too much to their own forecasts. This rather overlooked the difference between mere guess-

---

[27] See in particular the July, 1961, issue of the *National Institute of Economic Research Review;* for a brief discussion of the subject see *The Guardian,* May 9, 1962: "the best measures available . . . show that the lag in our
growth rates was much the same in 1950–59, 1922–29, and 1900–38. . . . If
our performance has been bad, it has apparently been bad for a long time,
and there is no evidence that it has become in any way worse since the
Second World War." For some of the institutional causes of the trouble, see
Michael Shanks, *The Stagnant Society* (London, 1961); Graham Hutton, "Evolution or Revolution?" in *National Provincial Bank Review* (London), May,
1962.

ing and genuine decision-making. At any rate, some experts still felt quite satisfied in 1962 that the record was not too bad. "Contrary to another popular misconception," one of them wrote, "our rate of growth in the supposedly stagnant nineteen-fifties has not been low by historical standards, or by comparison with the rate of growth in countries such as Scandinavia, which started the decade from roughly comparable positions."[28] This ignored the relevant comparison with the German, and lately the French, performance. As shown before, such comparisons are unfavorable to Britain, although it is difficult to say to what this is due. In 1960 it had been suggested by a group of investigators that the British investment rate "expressed as a percentage of gross national product has been significantly low compared with that of most other countries in Western Europe, just as the rate of growth of production has been low . . ."[29] But the authors hastened to add that a higher rate of investment was no automatic solution. In fact, investment subsequently crept up to a more respectable percentage without seeming to make much difference. Inevitably this led the *laissez-fairists* to proclaim that what was really lacking was not fixed capital formation but a proper competitive atmosphere. "To do significantly better . . . we would have to create a much more ruthless, competitive, materialistic society."[30] Others might be pardoned for believing that the same result could be attained with the help of a little more ruthlessness at the center of decision-making. Among those who took this view were not only the Socialists, who traditionally set a low value upon competition and market forces, but the reorganized Liberals, who in 1962 seemed to have shaken off their Gladstonian inheritance and were gaining election victories on a platform

[28] John Brunner, "The Flight from Reality," *The Listener*, May 17, 1962. The argument is valid enough if one accepts the writer's own yardstick. One detail it overlooks is that the Scandinavian countries are not trying to maintain the trappings of a great power position, notably in such matters as military expenditure overseas. Nor are they expected to contribute heavily to the development of backward countries.

[29] "The Growing Economy—Britain, Western Germany and France," *PEP Bulletin*, October 17, 1960, p. 289.

[30] Brunner, *loc. cit.*

calculated to alarm old-fashioned free-enterprisers. In the words of a slightly puzzled commentator,

> The historical principles of the Liberal Party, individualism, economic laisser faire, free trade, are (except for the first) scarcely visible beneath the surface of Mr. Grimond's refurbished modern party. Laisser faire has given way to an appetite for economic planning *à la française:* free trade is suspended by enthusiasm for a common European tariff . . .[31]

This outlook seemed to correspond to social changes that were propelling Britain—notably its suburban middle class of salaried and professional people, who were prominent in flocking to a Liberal Party clearly modelled upon the "New Frontier"—in a direction already taken by some of its European competitors. Here was an aspect of "Americanization" not usually associated with the United States, and fundamentally unacceptable to the Conservative Party, since it led away from reliance upon the market. "Planning *à la française*" was at any rate an alternative to the "social market economy" of Dr. Erhard, hitherto held up as a model to the British public by so many of its spokesmen. It had latterly become a habit to compare the British with the German, and thereafter with the French, performance. Such comparisons were rendered easier for the layman by the Development Council's formal commitment, in the spring of 1962, to a fairly ambitious target for the country's economic growth over a five-year period ending in 1966.[32] If this aim could be attained it would record an advance beyond any comparable period in Britain's experience, the more so since it assumed a very sharp rise in productivity growth per worker.[33] Though the target figure was

---

[31] *The Times,* April 19, 1962, editorial.

[32] See *The Economist,* May 12, 1962. The growth rate was fixed at a cumulative average of 4 per cent for the 1961–66 period, or nearly 22 per cent altogether. This still contrasted unfavorably with the 24 per cent target of the French Plan for a shorter period (1962–66), which assumed an annual rate of 5.5 per cent, since then tentatively raised to 6 per cent.

[33] Allowing for population growth, the 4 per cent target figure represents a 3.3 per cent annual improvement in output per worker. This is rather more than double the figure for the pre-1939 period, and a good deal more

hedged about with reservations, it appeared to commit the Government—which was ultimately responsible for the Council's statements—to an expansionist policy whose success depended *inter alia* on something like a national wages policy. By the end of 1962, there were reasonable grounds for doubt whether these targets could be reached without either a far higher degree of central planning or a truly Germanic outburst of productive and competitive mania, which in turn might promote inflation and balance-of-payments trouble rather than orderly expansion. In any case, the controllers of Britain's economy appeared to have decided that, whether or not the United Kingdom joined the Common Market, it must approximate the more rapid rates of growth on the Continent; and from this judgment there was for once hardly any articulate dissent, though skeptics might question whether such a break with tradition was likely under a Conservative, or indeed a Labour Government, neither party having in the past placed all its weight behind expansionism, though each now seemed eager to assert that expansion was indeed its foremost aim, to which all other considerations must be subordinated.[34]

In the latter half of 1962 it was still possible for economists critical of Britain's past performances to doubt whether the Development Council was more than an elaborate piece of whitewash. Such critics might note that most authorities had not yet modified their curious habit of calculating British GNP at *factor cost,* whereas Continental countries—and the United States—habitually reckoned gross output *at market prices.* If British output in 1961–62 were presented in the standard European and American manner, it would appear significantly larger—by some

---

than the 2 per cent achieved in the 1950's. The NEDC report also called for an annual increase of 5.7 per cent in exports—double the rate achieved in recent years. Investment is to climb by 6.2 per cent a year. So far it is not clear how these desired aims are to be reached.

[34] See Mr. Douglas Jay, M.P., in *The Statist,* May 18, 1962: "Expansion must be the overriding aim of the economic and social policy of the next Labour Government." The pronouncement gained weight from the fact that its author had himself helped to shape the financial policies of the postwar Labour Government.

£3 billion. It may seem odd that the official figures should under-estimate the size of the national "cake," but there is a reverse side to this modesty: If the national product is larger, the proportion taken by investment—i.e., addition to capital—is smaller than appears in the official statistics. Specifically, if the British national product at market prices in 1961 worked out at £26.7 billion (some £3 billion over the official figure), the share of gross fixed investment at £4.53 billion was only 17 per cent, as against the official claim of 19 per cent, and against an estimated 25 per cent in Germany (calculated on a German GNP of £27.7 billion at market prices and current exchange rates). Moreover, when deduction is made for the cost of renewals, net investment in Britain appears at the modest figure of about 9 per cent, against an estimated 17 per cent in Germany—almost twice the British figure. This comparison goes some way to account for the difference in economic performance, since after all what matters is net annual addition to the country's stock of fixed equipment. This is not to say that the British economy has not been suffering as well from other factors, e.g., shortage of skilled labor, but the insufficient investment rate must probably be given pride of place.

A word remains to be said about the alleged handicap Britain is supposed to have been suffering in consequence of strikes and other labor troubles, an explanation much fancied in business and managerial quarters, where until quite recently it was also maintained—against all the evidence—that Britain was more heavily taxed than Germany (in actual fact the reverse is the case). Here it will be sufficient to cite some statistics compiled by the International Labour Office in Geneva, which place the matter in perspective.[35] It appears that during the period 1953–60, the United States lost six times more working days than Britain, though the U.S. wage-earning population is only two and a half

[35] See *The Statist*, May 18, 1962, pp. 499–500, and June 8, 1962, pp. 710 ff., for this and the argument of the preceding passage. It is noteworthy that the NEDC blueprint for progress from 1961 to 1966 breaks with tradition in giving figures for gross domestic product at market prices. National product so defined is estimated as £26.486 billion for 1961 (not counting imported goods and services of more than £4 billion), and is expected to grow to £32.225 billion by 1966 (£37.310 billion including imports).

times greater and the number of organized workers is less than twice those in Britain. There were 3,333 strikes in the U.S. in 1960, involving 1.32 million workers, and 19.1 million working days were lost, compared with 2,832 British strikes involving 818,800 workers and costing 3.024 million working days. The American figures were among the best in recent years, comparing most favorably with 1959, when 69 million working days were lost, against 5.27 million in Britain. Japan, one of Britain's most serious international trade competitors, also has a markedly worse strike record. With an urban and industrial labor force of more than 17 million (of whom about 7 million are trade unionists) Japan lost 4.8 million working days annually between 1953 and 1960, 1 million more than Britain with her larger labor force. France and Italy, with less than half the number of wage earners in Britain (11.5 million and 9 million respectively, excluding agricultural workers), each suffered from a higher proportion of disputes than Britain. These cost France nearly 3 million working days annually and Italy more than 5.5 million, again worse than in Britain. France has approximately 3 million trade unionists, about half of whom are estimated to belong to the Communist-controlled General Confederation of Labor.

B. There is comparatively little to be said about the Federal Republic of Germany. For one thing, its economic record is well known and represents no particular problem; for another, its general socio-political climate is distinguished by a dullness only surpassed by the mental atmosphere of Belgium. The Federal Republic is the most prosperous and most heavily industrialized country in Western Europe today. In other respects it is far from fascinating, and perhaps not even very significant. West German political life, since the collapse of nationalism and the gradual disappearance of the lingering belief in the reunification of the Eastern and Western halves of the country, has resolved itself into a thoroughly parochial tug between the dominant coalition of Christian-Democrats and so-called Liberals, and the Social-Democratic opposition. This makes it easy to summarize the present state of affairs: There is really nothing to talk about except economics, and the figures speak for themselves. At the end of 1960, the population of West Germany (excluding West Berlin) was estimated at 53,756,000, against 52,676,000 in the United Kingdom.[36] The shares of the main sectors of the economy in the value of total output are very similar in Germany and Britain; in fact, the two economies are now very alike in structure, the chief difference being that West Germany still has 17 per cent of its population employed in farming, against a mere 4 per cent in the United Kingdom. There is no need to recapitulate the German productive achievement. Suffice it to say that between 1953 and 1960, industrial production rose by 80 per cent (against 30 per cent in Britain) and that industrial productivity, i.e., output per worker employed, was estimated in 1958 to be 50 per cent higher than before the war.[37] Living standards tended on average to remain below the British level, but were catching up for the urban population. In general, West Germany had improved much more on its prewar level of output per head than had the United Kingdom, largely owing to enforced modernization and the influx of millions of refugees from the lost territories.

It is hardly possible to abandon this subject without noting that West Germany's labor record is the stablest of any major industrial power. With an estimated paid working population (less agricultural workers) of 21 million, its industry lost just under 1 million working days a year during the 1953–60 period, about one-quarter of Britain's loss. An average of 140,000 workers went on strike annually, seven times fewer than in Britain. This state of affairs—much envied by industrialists elsewhere— evidently resulted from exceptional conditions which reduced labor until recently to a much more pliant force than in other countries: vast wartime destruction of industrial centers and thus the urgent need to rebuild the foundations of economic life in order to survive; weak trade unions; several years of heavy unemployment; and—until August, 1961—a ceaseless flow of hundreds of thousands of refugees from East Germany that helped

36 *OECD Economic Survey*, December, 1961; for the East German economy, see *The World Today* (London), June, 1962.

37 *PEP Bulletin*, October 17, 1960, p. 293.

to keep down wages. The situation has been changing recently, following the rapid growth of the economy in the past few years and the tightening of the labor market. In February, 1962, the metal workers' union, the largest union in Western Europe, with 1.7 million members (total West German union membership is just over 8 million), won a 6 per cent wage increase after a threat of strike action backed by a high union poll. More recently, the chemical workers won an 11.5 per cent increase, the miners 8 per cent, and members of the public services and transport unions 12 per cent. Overall, industrial wage rates rose by more than 12 per cent in the first half of 1961 compared with 1960, when (according to the December, 1961 OECD *Survey*) average wages and salaries per employed person had risen by 8.9 per cent; in May, 1961, average hourly earnings in industry were nearly 11 per cent higher than a year earlier, and since the beginning of 1960, the rise in industrial hourly earnings has outstripped the advance in output per man-hour, with a sharp increase in unit costs. In general it is now accepted that there is less physical scope for expansion than in the past; capacity and manpower are generally fully employed, and the labor supply is henceforth likely to grow more slowly. The natural growth of the labor force will be small, the influx of workers from outside the Federal Republic is declining, and working hours are being reduced. Investment is likely to become increasingly concentrated on rationalization, encouraged by the shortage of labor, the revaluation of the currency, and rising wage costs.

These developments represent an acceleration of tendencies already visible in the 1930's, when Germany was the most highly industrialized country on the continent of Europe but suffered from heavy unemployment and balance-of-payments difficulties. Contrary to a widespread notion, the postwar "economic miracle," which followed the amputation of the Eastern provinces, did not constitute a complete novelty but rather speeded a trend of development that in the prewar period had been artificially held back by political and social factors stemming in the last resort from the backwardness of the country's Eastern half. Unlike postwar France and Italy, the Federal Republic has not had to undergo an economic transformation. Instead, it experienced a political upheaval that resulted in the belated emergence, for the first time in German history, of a fully capitalist society. In consequence of the traumatic experience they underwent during the Hitler period, the West Germans are today integrated in the Western world, from which they had tried to escape under National-Socialism. The "social market economy"—a meaningless cant phrase currently employed to describe what is elsewhere known as the market economy *tout court*—corresponds to the structure of a society which has become fully "bourgeois" and now rivals Belgium in its political conservatism and in the predominance of middle-class values. From a structural viewpoint, West Germany as such has changed less than might be supposed, since its basic features were already evident in the 1930's, though for political reasons they did not at the time obtain adequate expression.

By way of comparison it may be pertinent to say a few words about the East German performance. For most purposes, comparisons between Eastern and Western Europe are pointless, if only because the two sides operate with different statistical procedures, and because East-bloc figures are known to be unreliable. Moreover, the East European countries grouped in the COMECON organization now have regional problems of their own. But since East Germany retains important trade links with the Federal Republic, and may conceivably one day be reunited with it, there is some sense in asking how it has been performing in recent years. The answer is that its economy is in a pretty bad state, and has been for some time. When the economic plan for 1961 was presented in the spring of that year, it had been known for some months that the economy had progressed at a much slower rate than in 1958 and 1959. The year 1960 had, in fact, been the turning point. Industrial output has increased at a steadily declining rate of growth, namely in 1959 by 13 per cent, in 1960 by 8 per cent, and in 1961 by 6 per cent. These are the official claims. Even the reduced rates might seem high, but it must be borne in mind that they are inflated by statistical padding and multiple counting at fictitious prices. Although the concept of gross industrial production is known to be faulty, it continues to remain in use in the Soviet orbit. The gross national product figure, which eliminates some of the statistical errors, has not been published for 1961, but an increase of 3.5 per cent is thought to have been achieved, compared with 8.5 and 6 per cent in 1959 and 1960, respectively: again a steadily declining rate.

The year 1961, moreover, brought the worst harvest since 1953. Farming seems to be a child of sorrows wherever Communists are in control, and in East Germany it is in a particularly bad state. Forced collectivization is largely responsible for the continued crop failure. Output of grain and sugar beet has been estimated at 15 per cent less in 1961 than in 1960. The shortfall of grain and potatoes amounted to 2 million tons of grain equivalent, and thus more than doubled East Germany's traditional grain deficit. Even in more normal years, the area's output is unsatisfactory: Grain yields are usually about 15 per cent below those of West Germany. An equal quantity of farm output thus requires a greater number of workers and animals than in the West. It seems likely that East Germany will remain dependent on large-scale Soviet aid. In May, 1961, a loan covering the years 1961 to 1965, and equivalent to more than $500 million, was made available, while additional supplies on credit during 1962 amounted to more than $300 million. East Germany will thus move still farther in the direction of an "economic community" with the Soviet Union. Of the country's total external trade, which is equivalent to $4.5 billion, the Soviet Union's share amounts to 45 per cent, and that of the Soviet bloc to 75 per cent, another 10 per cent being interzonal trade between East and West Germany, and the remainder East-West trade (excluding interzonal transactions).

When the Berlin Wall was erected in August, 1961, the East German population suffered its greatest psychological blow, but the Party leaders were given little time to enjoy their newly gained freedom of action, for when Mr. Khrushchev announced, at the Twenty-second Congress of the CPSU in October, that he would no longer insist on December, 1961, as the deadline for the signing of a German peace treaty, it was the turn of the East

German functionaries to suffer a shock. Since then, confusion has been permanent and has left its mark on the performance of the economy, thus in turn promoting the renewed drive to gain international standing through a "peace treaty" signed by the U.S.S.R.

C. If forecasting were simply a matter of extrapolating present trends, one would have to conclude that West Germany is likely to dominate the West European economy of 1970. In actual fact the Federal Republic may already have neared the limit of its capacity for rapid expansion, while countries like France and Italy are still far from having exhausted their reserve potential. This is especially true of France, with a land area twice the size that of West Germany or Britain, and with about a quarter of the occupied population working on the land and thus constituting an important labor reserve for industry.[38] Considering France's geographic location, "the importance of her natural resources, still scarcely exploited but now being prospected; the great possibilities of improvement in her agricultural yields; her demographic rejuvenation; the size, dynamism and modernity of her great industrial enterprises; the intellectual vigor of which she has shown proof for some years past . . ."[39] it is not surprising that the traditional notion of a Europe dominated by Germany has in recent years given way to the more realistic picture of an EEC grouped around the Franco-German axis. Setting aside political factors, which are partly counterbalanced by the pro-British orientation of the German business community and the future role of Britain in an integrated Europe, a certain degree of German-French fusion within the Common Market seems likely, if for no other reason than that the EEC embodies a built-in compromise between German industry and French agriculture. Two factors, however, serve to make the French situation more closely comparable to the British than to the German. The first is the burden of arms expenditure and the evident intention of

[38] See Lucien L. Sermon, "Dynamics of European Integration," in *Europe's Needs and Resources,* pp. 818 ff., especially 853 ff.

[39] Sermon, *op. cit.,* p. 853.

the Gaullist regime (which is unlikely to be abandoned by its successor) to equip France with an independent nuclear striking force. The second is the orientation of French economic policy. France, like Britain, carried through extensive nationalization measures after 1945, resulting in a public sector which in 1957 already claimed 25 per cent of total gross fixed investment (against 30 per cent in Britain), and has since expanded further. France has also, since 1947, been officially committed to a planned economy, and (contrary to some expectations) this commitment has become increasingly important to the policy-makers, with the result that French political life is now largely dominated by the quadrennial struggle over the official Four-Year Plan. Under the Gaullist regime, which reinforced these trends, planning and "technocracy" entered the public consciousness—so much so that a return to muddling-through and reliance on market forces seems excluded. France not merely has a welfare state: It has a government that fixes the goals of economic policy and the level of total demand. In this respect it is now a very modern country indeed.

Economically, the boom of the later 1950's started from a low level, having been preceded by a partial stagnation in 1950–53, when the first postwar modernization plan was being extended to replace war damage and catch up on the arrears of the 1930's. Looked at in this light, the rapid progress since 1953 appears less remarkable, being partly a belated attempt to catch up with Germany. The fact remains that growth has been rapid and sustained, apart from minor fluctuations, with top priority being given to industry. Unlike the Germans, the French planners pursued their goal at the expense of price stability; unlike the British, they ruthlessly sacrificed their balance of payments. The result, by 1958, was a situation that called for drastic measures of devaluation and deflation to right the payments balance, stimulate exports, and hold wages down. The cure having been administered by the Gaullist regime through a series of emergency decrees in 1958–59, the patient responded to the shock treatment by entering upon another (and more firmly based) period of expansion in 1960, greatly helped by the discovery that French industry was fully competitive within the Common Market and even able to undercut the Germans. This expansion, which currently aims at an almost 25 per cent rise in total output between 1962 and 1965, has come in the nick of time, for owing to the demographic recovery of France since the late 1940's—the birthrate has been rising steadily and there is now a much larger intake of young workers—industrial capacity had to be enlarged to ensure full employment. On top of this there is now considerable migration of labor from farming to industry, owing to the rapid mechanization of agriculture since the 1950's. In sum, France is becoming a modern country. This achievement—for which the Fourth Republic must be given much of the credit, although in the end its political institutions proved unable to stand the strain—is not significantly lessened by the fact that it was paid for by repeated devaluations and violent price increases, both of which have now come to an end. It was a case of having to choose between inflation and stagnation, and the planners rightly chose inflation. Moreover, for all the rise in prices and the temporary wage pause of 1958–59, the real income of wage and salary earners may have risen by as much as 50 per cent during the decade, though admittedly from a rather low level.[40]

Investment in the years since the political upheaval of 1945 (when the Left was for the first time able to impose some of its ideas) has been more centrally planned than in Germany, or even in Britain under the postwar Labour Government. In general it was recognized even by liberal economists that the state had to take over more of the financing of investment, and this led to a degree of central planning that has now been institutionalized. The "Monnet Plan" of 1946 was the first of four on which postwar investment policy was based. It concentrated upon the basic industries: fuel and power, transport, steel, cement, and agricultural equipment. It was successful in that by 1950 the supply of these basic goods and services had caught up with the demand.

[40] See *Le Monde*, April 15–16, 1962, for current wage and salary levels. For a detailed comparison with living standards in other European countries, see "Niveaux de vie et coopération économique dans l'Europe de l'Ouest," in *Etudes Economiques Internationales* (Paris, 1962).

Later plans switched attention to manufacturing industry, housing, and agriculture. The production targets set in these plans have been achieved with remarkable accuracy. Real investment at constant prices increased by 38 per cent between 1954 and 1958, and its share of the national product rose from 16.2 per cent to 18.5 per cent.

The key organization in the planning of investment has been the Commissariat du Plan de Modernisation et d'Equipement, first established with M. Monnet as Commissaire Général in January, 1946. In drawing up the plans, the Commissariat makes use of Commissions composed of civil servants, industrialists, trade unionists, and experts. The plan is then forwarded to the Economic Council for recommendation and submitted to Parliament for approval. The Commissariat is responsible for seeing that the plan is put into effect and for drawing up annual plans within the framework of the long-term program. Its central office, which does not have a large staff, works through the other departments, bringing to the notice of the government any factors that might prevent the implementation of the plans. The practice of working through existing institutions, and not usurping their functions, has made possible the combining of a high degree of flexibility with a firm general intention. The Plan Office indeed owes part of its strength to its nondepartmental position in the administrative machine. At first it was a branch of the Prime Minister's office. It seemed desirable, however, though the Minister of Finance in France does not have the wide powers of the Chancellor of the Exchequer in Britain, to bring planning closer to his department. The Commissariat Général now comes under the Minister of Finance and Economic Affairs, but it has not been incorporated into his department, and its position remains extradepartmental. The main strength of the Commissariat Général is that it is a permanent meeting place for the exchange of information and discussion of the plans, both of the administration and of the business world. The main agent for such cooperation has always been the "Modernization Commission." This consists of thirty to fifty people, seldom more, who are not paid for their work and who are appointed by the government on the Commissaire Général's initiative.

So far as the technique of planning is concerned,[41] work concentrates on the shape of things at the end year of each plan, i.e., for the Fourth Plan, 1965. For such a short period, available manpower may be taken as given; and since major social changes are not considered, great shifts in the distribution of income, or a revolution in the pattern of consumption, can be ruled out. The preliminary work for the Fourth Plan was, however, accompanied by a long-term projection up to 1975, in order to pick out important developments that might otherwise be missed. Use is not made in preparing the projections of a formal growth model, partly because the available data on national accounting are insufficient, and partly because useful inferences could hardly be drawn from the recent disturbed economic history of France. Instead, alternative rates of over-all growth (5, 5.5, or 6 per cent) are selected, whose implications on the different, but interdependent, sectors of the economy are then studied. For each hypothetical rate of growth a pattern of final expenditure is selected. This is based on numerous long-term studies of demand—though sometimes a straight extrapolation of past trends is all that is possible. The rate of investment compatible with the increase in consumption is then estimated for each of the producing sectors. Foreign trade is the most uncertain field and is now complicated by the Common Market. There is some hope that econometric studies may help in this field. Experience has shown that a rapid rate of economic growth tends to be associated with a foreign trade imbalance: Too high a rate of investment is likely to require substantial imports of capital. These considerations led to the acceptance of a rate of growth of 5.5 per cent a year for the Fourth Plan, which was later revised upward.

Statistics released by the OECD in July, 1961, indicated that for the latter part of the Third Plan the official target was attained. Gross National Product increased in volume by 6.3 per

41 For details, see *Economic Planning in France* ("PEP Report No. 454" [London, August 14, 1961]).

cent from 1959 to 1960, compared with an increase of only 2.3 per cent from 1958 to 1959. The results in fact exceeded the targets fixed in the interim Two-Year Plan (an increase of 5.5 per cent in Gross National Product in 1960 and in 1961), and the delays in carrying out the Third Plan in 1958 and 1959 were to a large extent made good. Nevertheless, the rate of growth was not as high as in other European countries, and the available resources were not used to the maximum. The Fourth Plan consequently fixed a bolder target, though still not bold enough for the taste of socialists and others committed to maximum expansion. Disputes over the rate of growth were in fact becoming the main subject of political differences among writers concerned with public affairs. *The Economist* (May 5, 1962) commented on these trends as follows:

> While the British are trying to learn from the planning structure the French set up in 1947, the French are considering how to adapt it to the nineteen-sixties. With resources under strain, the choice of various alternative policies becomes more important and more difficult. Last year the French planners began work on forecasts of growth up to 1975, to give depth to their forecasts for the four-year plan which came out in January. In preparing the fourth plan, they worked out not one but three different estimates for growth, so that the implications—for investment, foreign trade and so on—could be seen clearly, before the choice of a certain rate of growth was made. Eventually the middle estimate—an increase in national product of some 5.5 per cent a year—was chosen, with special emphasis on public investment in such things as schools and roads. Even the minister of finance seems to be catching a little of the new mood of *gaullisme social*. . . . His tone sounds different from the high orthodoxy of his predecessor, who once dismissed talk of inputs and outputs in the committee of national accounts with a brusque: "Tell the gentlemen to speak French."

Bolder thoughts on the future of French planning were thrown out in three articles in *Le Monde* in March, 1962, by M. Gilbert Mathieu. The first plans, he pointed out, had been empirical devices thought up by the technocrats for breaking through certain bottlenecks in the investment industries and getting businessmen used to growth. Now that the choices had become so much more complex, there was need for more effective democratic control. Parliament should be able to choose which of several objectives should be followed, and whether to go for more leisure or more consumption, more public investment in schools or more private investment in the television industry. Planning, in short, should have social objectives in whose determination the popular voice should be heard. In the fall of 1962, M. Mendès-France, challenged to outline an alternative to the Gaullist regime that did not involve reverting to the discredited parliamentary system, enlarged the area of debate by putting forward a more ambitious project: The entire framework of government and parliament should be reorganized around the Plan, so as to make French democracy conscious of the need to supervise its execution. Significantly, the proposal called for such drastic constitutional innovations as the replacement of the Senate by a Second Chamber representing economic and social organizations rather than localities. Since similar proposals were coming from the Gaullist side, the debate appeared to resolve itself into a choice between "technocratic" and "democratic" forms of planning. Both sides, however much they might differ over other matters, clearly took for granted the need to adapt France's traditional political structure to the exigencies of the postliberal age.

What stands out from this glance at French postwar economic history? Despite setbacks, of which the most important was the currency crisis of 1957–58, gross national output after 1950 rose at an average rate of more than 4.5 per cent per year. More particularly, the doubling of industrial production in ten years is evidence of a real change. On the debit side, while GNP in 1961 rose by 6 per cent to an estimated NF260 billion ($52 billion), a sharp rise in wages and salaries led to some pressure on profits and a consequent drop in self-financing. In 1962, wages continued to increase at an annual rate of 8 to 10 per cent, thus accentuating the profits squeeze. Even so, the outlook remained substantially unaltered, and at the end of the year the authorities forecast a 6 per cent increase in GNP for 1963 to keep pace with the absorption of North African repatriates and the extra cost of the Algerian settlement.

D. The Benelux group, the Scandinavian countries, Austria, and Switzerland share common features both among themselves and—with the partial exception of Italy—with the major countries of the Common Market group as well as with Britain. This is the justification for treating them jointly, notwithstanding the fact that in 1962 their membership was still distributed between the Six and the Seven, the Benelux countries belonging to the former group and the others to the latter. The artificial character of all these arrangements is sufficiently indicated by the fact that the Seven also included Portugal. In what follows we abstract from the distinction between the EEC and EFTA groupings. For the rest, it is worth noting that the authors of the Rome Treaty had in mind the possibility of a free-trade area being set up for the whole of Western Europe, and that Article 238 of the Treaty does not rule out free-trade arrangements between the European Economic Community as a whole and one or more nonmember countries.[42] The EEC-EFTA distinction is in any case dependent on Britain's future relations with the Common Market, which at the time of writing have not been finally settled. Again, countries like Luxembourg and Iceland are going to have their economic future decided for them by their larger neighbors: There is no point in considering them separately.[43] Belgium, the Netherlands, and Luxembourg represent no particular problem. As members of the EEC they share the latter's general prospects in world markets, while their social structure may be described as a cross between the French and the German. Economically, Belgium has been marking time for some years, but of late has made somewhat better progress, with GNP increasing in 1960 by more than 5 per cent in volume, as against a mere 2.4 per cent in 1959. Lux-

[42] For the position of these countries, see in detail the special study published by the Secretariat of the Council of Europe under the title *European Economic Relations* (Strasbourg, November, 1961).

[43] *Mutatis mutandis* the same applies to Cyprus in relation to Greece. Israel is a special case, but it clearly belongs to the Mediterranean group.

embourg is virtually an appendix of Belgium. Holland, which in some respects is closer to Britain than to her Continental neighbors, has consistently made fairly rapid progress, its 1960 record being particularly striking, with an 8 per cent rise in GNP. A full enumeration of national statistics would be tedious and purposeless. It is enough to say that with a combined population of slightly more than 20 million people and a heavy dependence on foreign trade (varying from 33 per cent of GNP for Belgium to over 50 per cent for Holland), the Benelux group exhibits in an extreme form some features that are becoming characteristic of Western Europe as a whole: a high degree of industrialization and specialization, and a consequent movement towards economic interdependence, at any rate within the European area. Holland has gone further in the direction of a planned economy and has reaped the corresponding benefit of faster growth. All three countries have been foremost in promoting European integration and have set an example in the treaty instituting the Benelux Economic Union, which came into force on November 1, 1960. Since then, they have virtually completed the transformation of their national trade agreements into common Benelux agreements. As pace-setters of European unification in the political field as well, their public men have become the chief advocates of European federalism and of abandonment of national sovereignty in as many fields as possible, a tendency still resisted by their larger neighbors. Indeed "Benelux" and "federalism" are now virtually synonymous. It is fitting that Brussels and Luxembourg were chosen as headquarters of the EEC and the ECSC, respectively, and that federalist meetings commonly take place at The Hague. When the history of European federalism comes to be written, the Benelux group is clearly destined to occupy the place of honor. Institutionally and ideologically, Western Europe has since 1945 organized itself around these small, civilized, and democratic countries, with their semiplanned economies and their Catholic-Liberal or Catholic-Socialist coalition governments. Since the fortunate loss of their former colonial empires, they have been able to concentrate their energies wholly on European affairs, thereby providing their neighbors with a yardstick whereby to measure their own advance towards a higher form of organization.

Economically, however, there is a considerable difference between the Belgian and the Dutch performances. Since 1950, Holland has progressed at a rate exceeded only by that of West Germany, while Belgium has consistently been near the bottom of the scale. It would be tempting to attribute this wholly to different economic policies, were it not for the fact that Belgium's faithful adherence to economic liberalism has been matched by that of Germany. Yet while the rate of growth in free-enterprise Germany and in semiplanned Holland has been startling, Belgium has lagged behind. Perhaps the absence of a fresh start had something to do with this. In contrast to Germany and Holland, war damage hardly touched Belgian industry. Is destruction through damage then the best means of disposing of outdated capital equipment? It would perhaps be truer to say that Belgium already suffered from an insufficient rate of growth, with a consequent unbalance in favor of the old as against the new, and that there was no external shock to precipitate new attitudes. Actually, the phenomenon of economic old age, from which Belgium is suffering, can easily be diagnosed: a lack of capital accumulation. Between 1948 and 1957, Belgium annually invested an average of only 11.3 per cent of its gross national product in fixed capital (excluding housing)—a rate which, although roughly the same as that of Britain, is nonetheless insufficient in comparison with other countries in Western Europe. Moreover, investment has largely been in old and declining industries. In short, national planning has been sorely lacking in the Belgian economy. There are always various reasons for investing, but they are not equally valid. Planning consists in drawing up a list of priorities.

When one turns to the members of the EFTA group, including both the so-called "neutrals" (Sweden, Austria, and Switzerland) and the two NATO members (Denmark and Norway), one runs up against the international uncertainties already referred to: Their economic outlook depends on the future amalgamation of the EEC and EFTA blocs, or failing that, on the conclusion of separate association agreements under the free-trade-area formula, or possibly the customs-union formula.[44] The point here is that, short of complete membership, association with the EEC leaves the way open for gradual harmonization of tariffs and economic policies while making hardly any change in the political status of the associate country. The arrangement may therefore be thought to fit the requirements of at least the "neutrals." Associate status, whether in a customs union or a free-trade area, must carry with it substantial economic obligations in the form of timetables for dismantling trade barriers.[45] Institutionally and politically, there need be no change, and of course an associate country would not be committed to common policies decided by majority vote. On the other hand, it would have little or no influence over such decisions, and in many cases would probably be faced with a *fait accompli*. It would also be excluded from the benefits of the European Investment Bank and other common institutions. On balance, it seems plausible that the decision to apply for associate status would be taken for political reasons, i.e., in order to safeguard national independence in all fields not covered by the treaty of association. Economically, the associate country would probably be better off as a full member, at any rate if it were highly industrialized and competitive. To take one example, the dependence of the Danish economy on exports of agricultural products to the U.K. and Germany makes Denmark one of the countries that would be most seriously affected by a lasting economic division in Western Europe along the present lines. While the level of Denmark's tariff is below that of the U.K. and the common external tariff of the Six, there is no doubt that many Danish industries, because of their relatively small size, would be likely to be adversely affected by unrestricted competition from the industries of the Six.

Swedish industry and agriculture are in general modern and efficient: Sweden should therefore be in a position to benefit from the advantages of a large free market in Europe. On the

---

44 See the Council of Europe study already mentioned, especially pp. 17 ff.
45 In the case of a mere free-trade-area agreement, there is in principle no commitment with regard to tariffs towards third countries, but in practice some harmonization with the EEC tariff is likely.

other hand, close integration on the lines of the Rome Treaty would present difficulties in some commercial, economic, and social fields. The External Tariff of the EEC raises difficulties for Sweden both on account of its level, which is considerably higher than that of the Swedish tariff, and because its specific incidence on various items is different. Sweden is by tradition a low-tariff country, and the economy is therefore adapted to a low or negligible duty element in the cost of most imported raw materials and fuels, of many semimanufactures, and even of certain manufactures. This is considered to have been an advantage to Swedish industry in general, and not least to the export industry.

As regards Austria, traditionally a large percentage of her exports go to Germany. In the normal course of events it might have been expected that this factor would have led Austria to seek to join the Six. However, there were difficulties of a political character, and she joined EFTA as a means of developing alternative markets. The volume of Austrian exports going to Eastern Europe (some 13 per cent) is higher than that of any other EFTA country. For long-standing reasons, Austria has a trade structure involving links with many of the countries of Eastern Europe, and this will no doubt continue.

Switzerland also presents difficulties. The existing equilibrium of the Swiss economy is the result of extensive trade with the rest of the world. Over 40 per cent of Swiss products sold abroad go to destinations outside Europe, being widely scattered over all continents and countries. There is no economic obstacle that would make it difficult for Switzerland to join the EEC. The Swiss economy is competitive, and specialized in relation to the country's natural and human resources by reason of the long-standing low-tariff policy pursued. Nevertheless, should Switzerland join or become associated with the Common Market, problems would arise. The maintenance of Swiss exports outside Europe is bound up with the existence of low customs duties on imports into Switzerland. Hence, if Switzerland were to enter a European grouping having a common external tariff, it would prefer the average level to be lower than the present common tariff of the Six.

It is, however, the political problem that is most important. Switzerland considers its neutrality the foundation stone of its policy and the guarantee of its survival. It is extremely cautious about subscribing to any condition likely to prejudice its neutrality. The authorities reject the notion that majority decisions may be imposed upon Switzerland either by other governments or by a European community. It is to be observed, however, that Switzerland did not make its neutrality a reason for not joining the OECD.

SOUTHERN EUROPE

There is no need to recapitulate what was said earlier about the disparity between the advanced and backward—or "developed" and "underdeveloped"—halves of Western Europe. That the region does in fact comprise substantial areas of backwardness has long been common knowledge, but it took the formation of Continental economic organizations to ram the truth home so far as the general public was concerned. Even today it is doubtful whether the average inhabitant of Northwestern Europe has fully accepted Greeks, Turks, Spaniards, or even Southern Italians, as fellow Europeans. Within the EEC, the contrast is veiled by the fact of Italian membership, and by the tacit understanding that the South is a problem for the Italian Government rather than the Community as a whole. As long as one thinks in national terms, regional disparities within a single country are a matter for the country concerned and for no one else. Within Europe, this is ceasing to be the case, but the process of integration has only begun. The notion that the Mediterranean countries ought to pull themselves up by their bootstraps, and that it is their own fault if they do not succeed, still has much unconscious support. In fact, they cannot do so unless they hitch themselves to a more developed organism. Italy really contains two different civilizations; Spain, Portugal, Greece, Yugoslavia, and Turkey plainly belong to a regional group with common characteristics. An evaluation that delves below the political surface would have to take account of geographical and

climatic factors, as well as of a historical background linking
these countries to the vanished world of antiquity.[46]

The most important of these countries—Italy—is fortunately
also the most advanced. Indeed its northern half has a typically
modern structure, and the country's membership in the Common
Market group testifies to its industrial competitiveness. But for
the persistent lag of the South, Italy as a whole would take rank
among the fully industrialized countries. Even as matters stand
today, it is in a different category from Spain—a circumstance
adequately reflected in their respective political systems. Authoritarianism may not be the inevitable consequence of backwardness,
but a military-*cum*-clerical despotism of the Iberian type is certainly not possible in an advanced country. *Mutatis mutandis*
the same applies to the Yugoslav and Turkish dictatorships, for
all the radical incongruity of Francoist, Titoist, and Kemalist
ideologies. This implies that until Spain shakes off its present
rulers, it must rank politically with Turkey and Yugoslavia,
rather than with Italy and Greece. Yet from a socio-economic
viewpoint these distinctions are secondary. A successful democratic revolution in Spain or Portugal could not precipitate these
countries into the modern world straightaway, though it would
remove the worst institutional obstacles. Neither authoritarianism
nor liberal democracy supplies a ready-made solution for inherited problems of rural poverty and overpopulation. Yugoslavia and Turkey, under different forms of authoritarian rule,
experience similar problems of agrarian backwardness and lagging industrialization. Spanish, Greek, and Southern Italian
agriculture have many features in common. Climate and soil
conditions render the existence of small farmers and landless
laborers in Greece more precarious perhaps than in any other
European country with the exception of Sicily. National policies
have as yet not inaugurated a rate of development permitting a
genuine industrial take-off: always excepting Italy, where since
the 1950's a take-off *has* occurred, and which is now at last beginning to solve its inherited structural problems.

[46] See *Europe's Needs and Resources,* pp. 712 ff., for economic data on
Southern Europe (other than Turkey and Yugoslavia).

A. Italy's record in recent years indeed has a better claim to the rather absurd term "economic miracle" than the frequently cited West German experience, which—as remarked above—required no basic structural changes and was largely a continuation of prewar trends. Italy, by contrast, has undergone a genuine transformation and, for the first time, become a modern country, i.e., an industrialized country with a rapid rate of capital accumulation. Between 1951 and 1961, the country's gross national income increased at an average rate of over 5.5 per cent a year. Since the population increased by less than 1 per cent annually, most of the new capital was available for investment based on savings. After allowing for the increase in population, the rise in consumption per head worked out at rather less than 4 per cent per annum, whereas the increase in investment came to nearly 9 per cent. Without resort to forced savings, the proportion of internal resources devoted to fixed capital investment went up from one-fifth to one-quarter. This rapid accumulation of capital through internal savings provides one of the keys to Italy's economic record since 1950. The phenomenon is even more remarkable if the comparatively low level of average individual incomes is borne in mind, and if one adds that since the end of the Marshall era, investment has had to be financed from internal savings alone.[47]

During the decade 1950 to 1960, the Italian economy in fact grew at a more rapid rate than that of Western Europe as a whole—almost 6 per cent as against 4.5 per cent—while industrial production rose so fast that in 1960 it stood at 85 per cent above the 1953 level, having grown by 11 per cent in a single year

[47] For some of the relevant indexes, see the special supplement to *The Statist* of April 6, 1962. With a pardonable touch of satisfaction, the Minister for the Budget, Signor La Malfa, was able to tell readers of that journal: "During the last ten years, the national product has risen by 5.8 per cent each year, per capita consumption has increased by over half, and total investments have more than doubled. The larger resources thus created have been accompanied by a high degree of internal financial stability and a substantial surplus in the balance of payments. Today Italy has accumulated a reserve of nearly 3,000 million in US dollars. Three million new jobs have been created outside agriculture, i.e., in trade and services, against an increase in the labor force, net of emigration, amounting to 1.4 million."

(1960).[48] Compared with 1950, the volume of imports in 1960 had more than doubled, while exports had nearly trebled. With the northern industrial areas taking the lead, Italy for the first time established itself in the world market as a major exporter of manufactures. Meanwhile, the share of agriculture in the gross national product, which stood at around 27 per cent in 1948–53, declined to about 20 per cent in 1961, though almost as many people are still employed in farming as in industry. Paradoxically, however, this rapid advance accentuated rather than diminished the historic contrast between North and South, for although both made progress, the North inevitably reaped the greater share. It is doubtless to the advantage of the country that the unemployed should be able to find jobs in Milan and Turin instead of having to emigrate abroad (industrial unemployment has in fact virtually disappeared, though rural *underemployment* has not), but as long as the South does not participate in the growth of industrialization to a larger extent than it currently does, the benefits will continue to be unequally distributed (and the Communist Party will continue to be the only genuine opposition party south of Rome). Italy is not the only European country where farming continues to lag behind the general rate of progress (30 per cent of the population producing less than 20 per cent of the country's wealth).[49] It is, however, peculiar in that this disparity is reflected in a regional contrast, which admittedly has deep historic roots. After ten years of unparalleled progress, the OECD experts in 1961 were constrained to summarize the achievement in words that injected a note of caution:

> The Italian Government is at present according a high priority to measures designed to improve the efficiency of the agricultural sector; but any radical progress in the field is dependent on progress towards other major objectives of public policy, i.e., the absorption of the surplus agricultural labor force and the industrialization of the Southern provinces.
>
> The broad objectives of approaching the full employment of the

[48] *OECD Statistics*, February, 1961.
[49] *Ibid.*, p. 30.

available labor force, and of narrowing progressively the differentials in production and income levels between the Northern and Southern regions of Italy, remain as major aims of public policy. . . . Considerable progress has been achieved in the South, both in terms of living standards and of an expansion of infrastructures; but directly productive investment has not been impressive so far, while the rapid progress attained by the industrial regions of the North has meant that the relative lag of the South has not been reduced. On the other hand, the high rates of growth in investment and industrial production were accompanied by increases in employment lower than those foreseen in the Ten-Year Plan drawn up in 1954.

The report recommended "a decisive effort to create new industrial centers in the South" and hinted broadly at the need for more public planning to channel investment into key sectors. Since then, political changes in the direction of a Center-Left coalition have seemed to indicate a conscious effort to break through the remaining crust of stagnation. When it is borne in mind that this stagnation benefits both the country's two largest parties—Christian-Democrats and Communists—inasmuch as it perpetuates the sterile pattern of Southern politics and the consequent polarization of factions, it will be appreciated that "modernization" is not simply a matter of economics. Least of all does it serve the "harmony of all legitimate interests," for to industrialize the South means upsetting its traditional way of life. In their own way, the Italians in this decade are making the discovery that modern capitalism imposes something like a social revolution.

In 1962, at least one prominent Italian industrialist in charge of a state-controlled monopoly had no doubt what this revolution signified in terms of public policy:

The Italian recovery, called by some people a "miracle," has been made possible because there has been a profound transformation in the productive, social and political structure of our country. Especially is this so in the economic field, where new ideas have been propounded and acted upon. It is certainly sigificant that the much-debated principle of the State's responsibility for economic progress has in the end prevailed.

In my opinion, two fundamental economic-political choices have been the determining factors in this brilliant recovery. The first is the implicit repudiation of protectionism by the courageous acceptance of international competition, the liberalization of trade, and the integration of the Italian economy within the larger orbit of a European market through unification. The second . . . is the decision to launch a program for the economic and industrial development of the most backward areas, with the objective of absorbing the unemployed and the underemployed, and of remedying the still striking contrast between the income levels in various zones of the national territory. . . .

The difficulties and resistance which had to be overcome to gain acceptance for these fundamental choices are well known. . . . It is a fact—and this is fundamental for a correct evaluation of the forces which today drive our economic system—that the initiative in the matter of choice and in its application came from the State; that is to say that in many cases it was imposed. . . .

Amongst other prejudices that have crumbled in Italy, there is also that ancient bugbear that saw State management in industry as unfailingly inefficient and uneconomic, as compared with dynamic and competitive private industry. But the past 15 years have shown us how publicly-owned industrial enterprises, adjusted to the demands of the economy, give an impetus to the process of development in areas and sectors which private enterprise has for so long neglected.[50]

B. By comparison with Italy, the Mediterranean group properly so called—Spain, Portugal, Greece, Turkey, Yugoslavia, Cyprus—constitutes a socio-economic whole. A discussion of the various economic ills and social maladjustments of the individual countries would be tedious and pointless. Portugal presents an image similar to that of Spain, though what is tragedy in Spain tends to become seriocomic in the neighboring country. Yugo-

[50] Signor Enrico Mattei, as quoted in *The Statist*, April 6, 1962. Six months later, Signor Mattei's sudden death in a plane accident drew attention to the unusual career of this modern "technocrat" who combined the authoritarian management of a gigantic state monopoly (ENI) with active participation in public affairs as a left-wing Christian-Democrat, plus involvement in international oil politics. Prior to his death, the great oil and hydrocarbon concern over which he presided had to be reckoned a major political force supporting the current experiment in Catholic-Socialist coalition rule (and the Italian Government's nationalization of the electric-power industry).

slavia hovers on the borderline of Eastern and Southern Europe, and this circumstance—rather than the imposition of a planned economy—makes it questionable whether there is much point in discussing its problems within our present context. Cyprus is partly an extension of Greece and partly an offshore island of Turkey. Greece is close in social structure to its Balkan neighbors, but has recently developed an economic dynamism that holds promise of a genuine take-off. It has also become an associate of the Common Market group.[51] Turkey, on the borderline between the Balkans and the Middle East, represents a cross between their respective social structures. Instead of wasting time on all the members of the group, let us single out Spain and Turkey. These two are respectively closest to, and farthest away from, the Western European core. After all, it would only take a political upheaval to raise Spain (and Portugal) to the Italian level, while Turkey, with the best will, cannot shake off the Islamic heritage. As for Yugoslavia, its problems are in some respects also those of Hungary or Bulgaria, to name only two members of the Soviet bloc. Until the Yugoslavs themselves have made up their minds, there is no certainty whether their country will eventually form part of Eastern or Southern Europe. It can, of course, be argued that Turkey likewise is torn between two different allegiances.

The Spanish economy presents all the features of a backward and predominantly agricultural country. Thus participation in European integration would raise serious problems. It seems likely, judging from the present state of Spanish industry, that it will still be some considerable time before Spain is able to dispense with protection against competition. Spanish duties are much higher than the EEC external common tariff. For historical reasons, due partly to the attitude that other European countries

[51] The Association Agreement of July 9, 1961, establishes a customs union, covering both industrial and agricultural products, based on the common external tariff of the Six. The removal of tariffs will in general take place over a twelve-year transition period, but for a number of sensitive products Greece is allowed twenty-two years to dismantle protection. Social policy and capital movements are not covered by the agreement, but transport and movement of labor are.

have since 1945 adopted towards Spain, the Government has followed a policy of avoidance of commitments. It seems unlikely that the present regime will agree to any surrender of sovereignty, the more so since considerable differences exist between the common standards and policies outlined in the aims of the Rome Treaty and the economic policies and practices currently followed in Spain. On the other hand, it may be just as difficult for Spain to remain aloof from the movement towards European economic integration (which will lead to the fusion of the principal Spanish export markets) as to accept the obligations that membership of the EEC would involve. Some form of association might be the most acceptable arrangement for both sides, on condition that the political structure can be reformed.

To meet the cost of imports necessary for development, Spain relies chiefly on two sources, namely revenue from tourism and agricultural exports. From both aspects, the countries that would constitute an enlarged EEC are far and away Spain's biggest customers. The policy followed by other Western European countries tends to favor the expansion of Spain's tourist traffic, but the same cannot be said for agricultural exports. If Spain stayed out of the wider Common Market, the country's agricultural exports might find it difficult to compete with Italy and Greece. The trend of agricultural policy within the EEC is consequently decisive in determining Spain's future attitude.

The population of Turkey is 28 million and is increasing at the very rapid rate of 3 per cent per annum. National per capita income is lower than in most European countries. Three-quarters of the working population are engaged in agriculture, which supplies the greater part of the country's exports. A considerable investment effort has been made over the last ten years, and is still going on, with the aim of accelerating the process of industrialization, but Turkey is now suffering from a degree of urban stagnation, combined with growing pressure on the land.

There is no problem of a political nature militating against Turkey's participation in the EEC. On the contrary, Turkish leaders are anxious for the country to take part in the work of European integration. On this point the existing political parties are in agreement, and the change of regime in 1960 has not altered the views of the authorities on this subject. Opinion in political circles is favorable to joining the Common Market, not only for economic reasons but also on political grounds. However, Turkey's economic situation is not such that an immediate accession to the EEC can be contemplated, since the country cannot fulfill the obligations of membership. The Government has therefore been trying to negotiate an association agreement that would pay due regard to the country's economic difficulties.

Lastly, there is Greece. When fifteen years of American aid to Greece came to an end in July, 1962, the country had devoured $3.42 billion, of which a third was spent on keeping it on this side of the Iron Curtain. The search for fresh sources of financing is now being actively pursued. Greece spends $170 million a year on defense, and all but $20 million of this comes from internal revenue. If this money went to development, Greece would be able to finance its ambitious five-year plan for rapid industrialization. The NATO ministerial meeting in Athens in May, 1962, advocated the establishment of a consortium for aid to Greece, and promptly laid the problem in the lap of the Organization for Economic Cooperation and Development. The OECD is now examining the basic outline of an accelerated development plan until 1966, which carries a domestic and foreign payments deficit of $800 million. The plan is still, unfortunately, no more than an outline. Moreover, most of the consortium members will also be required to contribute funds for Turkish aid. There are also psychological difficulties: Although it has reached the take-off stage, Greece has remained a poor country where pressures for social equality have had to be resisted for the sake of economic development. National income has steadily grown at an annual average rate of 6 per cent during the last fifteen years, but Western Europe has also advanced by 6 per cent, and in consequence the "prosperity gap" has remained.

This summary of the economic problems confronting some of the smaller European countries will have served its purpose if it has clarified the reasons why these countries originally grouped themselves in two rival economic blocs, the Six and the Seven. It is plain enough that these reasons were political. From a structural viewpoint, the economies of the Benelux countries and the Scandinavian group belong to the same type. That Sweden and Denmark should at first have chosen to group themselves with Portugal is comprehensible only in terms of Britain's long-standing relationship with that country. EFTA could not be a purely regional bloc. There is of course an argument in favor of uniting dissimilar economies that can complement each other; just as on the other side one may legitimately question the value of promoting a flourishing exchange of British and German motorcars, on the grounds that it contributes little or nothing to general well-being. Fortunately the argument works both ways: Denmark is a food producer, and economically its inclusion in the Common Market makes good sense, as does the association of Switzerland and Austria with the inner core of the Community.

For all that, it cannot be denied that European economic union means the joining together of economies whose structures are rather similar, and thus not complementary. At any rate, this argument applies to the industrialized regions of Northwestern Europe. Its force is weakened if account is taken of the longer period, for in this perspective the joining together of the very dissimilar structures of Northern and Southern Europe appears among the prime goals of union.

IV

THE ATLANTIC COMMUNITY

SOME BASIC FACTORS

In the preceding chapters attention has been mainly focused on the countries forming the European Economic Community, plus Great Britain. It is not by accident that these regions constitute the historic core of Western Europe; they are, moreover, a powerful economic and political bloc in themselves, aggregating as they do some 170 million people (over 220 million on the assumption of British membership) with combined resources not markedly inferior to those of the U.S. and the U.S.S.R. Yet there is some inconvenience in singling them out. In the first place, the need to differentiate between Britain and the Six imposes a tiresome complication. Reckoning British economic resources together with those of the original members does not altogether help either: On the one hand, it tends to obscure the unity of the Continental bloc, which is bound to retain its cohesion for some time even if the British prove unexpectedly willing partners in the common European enterprise; it also ignores the problems of the nonmembers, or associate members, from Finland down to Greece and Turkey. There is, after all, a sense in which all West European countries, when contrasted with the U.S. and the U.S.S.R., form a bloc. As against this, it has been shown that to talk about "Western Europe" in general is to overlook the quite fundamental cleavage dividing its industrially developed northern half from the backward Mediterranean regions. To an economist, the dividing line running through the middle of Italy is certainly more real than any political frontiers. How is one to take due account of all these different criteria? There is a further complication: Trade negotiations in which the United States enters the picture are of major relevance only if they involve the EEC (with or without Britain). Yet the whole of Western Europe must be reckoned in if one thinks in terms of an Atlantic Community. In what follows we proceed somewhat illogically by considering first the EEC and the British Commonwealth before turning to the wider question of economic relations between the two halves of the Atlantic world.

As constituted in 1958, i.e., before Britain had applied for membership, the EEC represented a total population of 167 million and a working population of 74 million, against 178 million and 69 million, respectively, for the U.S.[1] In that year, the six countries produced 58 million tons of steel (U.S. 77 million), and their total power consumption—including all forms of energy— could be reckoned as corresponding to 416 million tons of coal in 1956 (U.S. 1.356 billion). National income figures were appreciably below the American level, and gross national product in 1957, with an aggregate of $156 billion, stood at about 40 per cent of the corresponding U.S. figure. On the other hand, the Six together occupied a bigger place in *world trade* than the U.S., underlining Western Europe's greater dependence on outside resources. For 1959, the balance stood as follows:

| | *In billions of dollars* | |
	Imports	*Exports*
World total	104.4	99.9
U.S.A.	15.0	17.4
EEC	24.1	25.2
Britain	11.2	9.3
Sterling area (including Britain)	24.8	21.5 (1958)*

* Deniau, *op. cit.*, p. 109.

[1] Deniau, *op. cit.*, pp. 108, gives the following population figures for 1958, which are somewhat below the present actual level: Federal Republic of Germany, 52.5 million; France, 44.8; Italy, 48.9; Holland, 11.3; Belgium, 9.1; Luxembourg, 0.3; total, 166.9. The somewhat larger working population compared with the U.S.A. is presumably due in part to the absence of unemployment (except in Southern Italy) but may also reflect the lower school-leaving age.

As importers of foodstuffs and raw materials, the Six in 1959 accounted for some 31 per cent of world trade, the United States for 16 per cent, the United Kingdom for 18 per cent. Thus the Community offered a market for these products almost twice the size of the American, and two-thirds larger than the British, although the United Kingdom continued to be the largest single importer of raw materials and foodstuffs. As an exporter of industrial goods, the EEC accounted for almost exactly 33 per cent of world trade, against 26 per cent for the U.S. and 16 per cent for Britain. It was already noteworthy in that year that the Six traded extensively with each other, so that there was something slightly deceptive about their share of world trade properly so called, but the market for overseas producers was nonetheless very large and growing. The United States appeared to offer very little in the nature of a market for the EEC's farmers and other primary producers. In manufactures, the Six were doing better, but they nonetheless sold almost four times more to each other than to the United States.

It will have been noted that the EEC's share of world trade in 1959 was almost exactly equal to that of the sterling area, i.e., Britain and the Commonwealth minus Canada. This was the economic fact underlying the then popular (in Britain, anyhow) argument that North America, the sterling bloc, and the EEC formed three approximately equal segments of world trade that were obviously destined to come together at the level of a truly world-wide system. Here was a thesis that appealed to free traders, especially in the United States. From a different standpoint it could be argued that this threefold division offered Britain an alternative to joining the Rome Treaty, inasmuch as the sterling area constituted a ready-made market for British goods. This latter argument lost a good deal of plausibility with the relative stagnation of sterling-area markets, compared with the rapid expansion of British exports to the EEC countries. But as late as 1962, it was possible for a distinguished British economist to stress that the Commonwealth (i.e., the sterling area plus Canada) took almost 50 per cent of Britain's total exports, as against the 15 per cent sold to the Six.[2]

The Commonwealth is so large, and its future importance as a trading partner for the reorganized EEC (with or without Britain) is so considerable, that something must be said about it, although strictly speaking it is external to the problem of Western Europe's economic resources. Historically, it is the product of British overseas expansion since the early seventeenth century. Viewed from London it represents an amalgam of territories stretching from North America via the Mediterranean to the Far East, and ranging in population from India (about 450 million) and Pakistan (nearing 100 million) to Malaya (6.5 million) and New Zealand (2.3 million); plus, in Africa, such former colonies as Nigeria (nearly 40 million) and Ghana (6 million), among several others. There is clearly some sense in which all these formerly British-ruled territories form a kind of community. It is, however, becoming increasingly difficult to view it as a unit in either political or economic terms. When one considers that Canada is constitutionally a member of the Commonwealth without belonging to the sterling area, while South Africa retains its sterling-area membership although having withdrawn from the Commonwealth, it is clear enough that centrifugal tendencies are getting the upper hand. No one can say how long India and Pakistan (both officially republics within a Commonwealth supposedly headed by a monarchy) will care to retain their membership in the association, though one may suppose that Australian and New Zealand loyalties will not be affected. Economically, the Commonwealth is not a unit, as is evident from the fact that Canada forms part—geographically and for monetary purposes—of the North American economic complex.

---

2 Meade, *op. cit.*, p. 12. "Association with the EEC instead of the Commonwealth means *perhaps* association with a more rapidly growing market; it means *certainly* association with what is at present a much smaller market." There is of course the further argument that trade between countries with greatly different economic structures is more beneficial than trade between economies that resemble each other.

The Ottawa Conference of 1932 tried to impose a unified tariff system, which is now seen to have failed in its main purpose, if that purpose was to create a world-wide trading system based on mutual preferences.[3] Commonwealth trade with the United Kingdom continues indeed to bulk large, but it is also subject to a certain optical illusion. If Canada is treated as part of the North American area, and Britain as part of Western Europe, it is at once apparent that the remainder of the Commonwealth (and/or sterling area) does not take a very big slice of total world trade.[4] Perhaps the strongest argument in favor of the Commonwealth–sterling-area grouping is that it bridges the gap between advanced and backward countries. It is also of course a multiracial association that offers its industrialized members a chance of promoting economic development in the new Asian and African territories, now politically sovereign. But it is not clear why these various relationships should be profoundly affected—except in the case of Canadian and Australian exporters who are well able to stand the loss—by Britain becoming a member of the EEC. In any case, we are not here concerned with the future of these countries, or with the question to what extent they may choose to group themselves politically around a new Atlantic axis.

If one abstracts from the Commonwealth problem, whose significance in the context of the British debate over European union is perhaps not primarily economic, the link between economic and political factors in promoting the British Government's decision to seek membership in the EEC is plain enough. It can be spelled out in figures showing the relative growth of production and trade in the EEC countries and in Britain during the 1950's, i.e., during a decade when war damage had

[3] See in particular *The Economist*'s comments on the Commonwealth conference of September, 1962.

[4] For 1957, the respective export-import figures were: U.S. and Canada, 26.2 and 19.5 per cent; Europe and U.K., 40.5 and 43.2 per cent; other British Commonwealth countries, 12.3 and 12.9 per cent; Latin America, 8.7 and 8.7 per cent. See Mackay, p. 57.

largely been repaired and all the West European countries were participating in the general upward movement:

ECONOMIC RECORD
OF THE UNITED KINGDOM
AND THE EUROPEAN ECONOMIC COMMUNITY

1950–60

	1950–55		1955–60	
	United Kingdom	EEC	United Kingdom	EEC
Gross National Product	+15	+34	+13	+27
Employment	+4.5	+5.9	+1.7	+6.1
GNP per head of employed population	+10	+27	+11	+20
Industrial production	+21	+52	+14	+40
Volume index of imports	+26	+56	+26	+66
Volume index of exports	+6	+76	+13	+63
Change in the visible trade balance (million dollars, current rate)	—756	+1,392	+72	+1,464
Change in official gold and foreign exchange holdings (million dollars, end of period)	—120	+5,002	+518	+5,975

SOURCE: *Economic Surveys by the OECD* (Paris, March, 1962): *United Kingdom*, p. 11.

From these figures it is evident that throughout the 1950's Britain lagged behind her rivals. Economic growth, whether measured in absolute figures or in terms of productivity, was significantly slower than on the Continent. After allowance is made for the fact that employment grew more slowly in Britain (where labor reserves were not replenished by movements from the countryside as in France and Italy, or by mass migration as in the case of West Germany), the growth of national product per head of employed population was two-and-a-half to three times faster on the Continent up to 1955, and twice as fast subsequently. Nor was this slow growth counterbalanced by price stability. On the contrary, prices in Britain rose faster than in any of the EEC countries with the exception of France, where a very rapid pace of expansion was paid for by two devaluations. Britain thus combined the disadvantages of relative stagnation—notably in exports, as compared with the EEC—with those of price instability. What a leading British periodical described as "The dreary story of Britain's record in the 1950's—of inflation without expansion, inadequate investment in the wrong industries, and an overstretched labour force glued like discarded chewing-gum to the places where it is least needed"[5] was made even more striking by the fact that during the second half of this period imports rose twice as fast as exports, thereby aggravating a balance-of-payments problem which, by the early 1960's, had come to be recognized as the chief obstacle to faster economic growth. Over the decade, the gold and foreign-currency reserves held by EEC members rose by $11 billion, while British reserves stagnated, and even this result was only secured by deliberately holding down the level of production. Every time something like a boom threatened to develop, it was promptly brought to a halt by a payments crisis and a resolute throttling of imports and internal consumer demand.

In trying to discover why Britain throughout this decade of general trade expansion managed to get the worst of both worlds —price inflation plus relative stagnation—attention naturally riveted on the slow growth of exports. Whereas the Continental countries were helped by their booming export trade—though in France this factor entered the picture rather later than it did in Germany and Italy—British exports rose very slowly and thus

5 *The Statist*, London, April 6, 1962. In the July 6, 1962, issue of the same periodical, Professor Frank Paish, the distinguished economist and British Treasury consultant, pointed out that the same period witnessed a further shrinkage in Britain's overseas investment and capital-lending to other countries; such investments now average around 1 per cent of net national income, against 8 per cent in 1913. Over the past half century, Britain has ceased to be a major capital supplier to developing countries. That investments abroad should aggravate a perennial balance-of-payments problem is remarkable when one considers that during this period the terms of trade have almost consistently favored British exports.

failed to play a major role in the growth process. It was home
demand that spearheaded developments and through successive
balance-of-payments crises regulated the trade cycle in such a
way that productive resources were never fully employed.[6] The
contrast became particularly glaring in 1961–62, when the United
Kingdom underwent another payments crisis and suffered almost
complete industrial stagnation for over a year, while on the Continent national output continued to rise, with an average increase
in 1961 for the more industrialized countries of just under 4.5
per cent, following a sensational leap of 6.5 per cent in the boom
year 1960, when exports rose to record heights. While the drop
reflected a less favorable export situation, and thus underlined
Western Europe's continued dependence on external factors, no
country save Britain had an actual payments problem. The
United Kingdom thus continued to be the odd man in the picture, and it was this unfavorable contrast that, by 1962, had
turned a majority of academic economists in Britain into reluctant converts to Europeanism.[7]

The fact that the whole of Continental Western Europe—not
only the EEC bloc—was making more rapid progress could of
course be treated as an argument against joining the EEC, the
more so since British exports to the EEC countries (as well as to
the rest of Western Europe) rose quite sharply in this period
while sales to overseas markets declined or stagnated. It could
thus be argued that Britain might get the benefit of greater
prosperity on the Continent without being obliged to adhere

[6] *OECD Report* (March, 1962), p. 13. "The picture was, repeatedly, one
of home demand rising faster than output, with exports insufficiently dynamic
to look after the balance of payments. . . . The external payments position
was further complicated by the relatively large burden of defence expenditure and, later, of overseas aid."

[7] The new mood was reflected primarily in Liberal organs such as *The
Guardian,* and in the traditional City papers, led by *The Financial Times,
The Economist,* and *The Statist.* But it could also be sensed on the left wing
of the Conservative Party, as represented by the so-called Bow Group—an
association of "modern" young managerial elements. At this stage, the Labour
Party—with some significant exceptions on its right wing—was almost alone
in giving the impression that it would really prefer the United Kingdom to
turn its back on Europe.

to the Rome Treaty; and needless to say, this argument was employed by all those critics of the Common Market who were hostile to it on other grounds. But doubts were also expressed by economists who on general theoretical grounds favored the Common Market as an approximation to free trade. Apart from questioning whether the faster rate of growth in the six countries was really due to the formation of the EEC, these writers emphasized the disadvantages to Britain of diverting some of its trade from the overseas countries to Europe.[8] They also stressed the undesirability of imposing duties on Commonwealth goods which had hitherto enjoyed free entry to the United Kingdom. Lastly, the argument was put forward that international tariff-cutting could be promoted by better methods than joining a West European bloc, even though its common external tariff might be low.[9] The debate thus reverted to what has in fact been the fundamental issue in British postwar politics: the choice between a European and an Atlantic (i.e., Anglo-American) orientation, with the tacit proviso that if the Americans could be induced to bypass the Common Market and come out for Atlantic free trade, Britain could turn her back on the Continent and resume her traditional role. In the end, therefore, the decision would (as usual) fall in Washington.

Yet to say this is not to minimize the gravity of the problem facing both the United Kingdom and the British Commonwealth on the eve of the historic decision to "go into Europe." Preferences on British goods in Commonwealth markets are the less important half of the matter. The real difficulty has always concerned the free entry of Commonwealth products—notably temperate-zone foodstuffs—into Britain. In a completely tariff-free world it might matter less if Britain no longer offered a preferential market for these goods, but what British membership in the

8 Meade, *op. cit.*, pp. 11 ff.
9 Meade, *op. cit.*, p. 16. ". . . joining the EEC is not the only way of reducing duties on the import of manufactured goods into the UK. . . . If President Kennedy's attempt to gain substantially increased powers from Congress to bargain reductions in the US tariff is successful, we shall have even better opportunities in the future."

EEC really implies is the replacement of one set of preferences for another. Malayan tin, Australian wool, and Rhodesian copper are fairly safe, but other staples are not. Where previously Australian wheat, New Zealand butter, and Indian textiles entered the British market duty-free, they will encounter a barrier of tariffs or quotas, while French wheat, German or Italian textiles, and Danish butter will come in free. Discrimination would persist, but its edge would be turned against the Commonwealth countries, some of which—though plainly not Canada or Australia—are among the poorest in the world. There is in fact a perfectly good argument against this kind of policy. It has been forcefully put in words that deserve to be quoted:

The underdeveloped, overpopulated countries of Asia should be able, as Japan has been, to produce and to sell abroad the cheap labour-intensive manufactures which will enable them to buy capital equipment, foodstuffs, and raw materials from the developed countries of Europe, North America, and Australasia. . . . The future welfare of the poorest countries is at stake. The heavily populated underdeveloped countries can in many cases achieve reasonable progress only if they can find rapidly expanding markets. . . . The sensible development of trade patterns is that the highly developed, industrialised countries of Western Europe should produce and export more of the capital goods and consumption goods that require much technical know-how, skill, and specialised equipment, and should import more of the easily made manufactured consumption goods from the industrialising overseas countries.[10]

The same argument is applicable to the Atlantic Community as a whole, a subject to which it is now necessary to turn.

[10] Meade, *op. cit.*, pp. 28–29. For details, see among others *The Commonwealth and Europe*, published by the Council of Europe (Strasbourg, March, 1962); "Australia, Britain, and the Common Market," *The World Today* (Royal Institute of International Affairs, London, April, 1962). That Britain's interests are likewise affected is evident from the fact that under the Ottawa arrangements she had access to suppliers whose costs, for temperate-zone foods and raw materials, were and are greatly below those of Britain's own producers. Any preference extended to European suppliers will benefit producers whose costs are roughly equal to Britain's.

ATLANTIC FREE TRADE?

The Atlantic Community, however defined in political terms, contains three major economic areas: the dollar area, the sterling area, and Continental Western Europe. Irrespective of Britain's future relations with the EEC, this threefold division is likely to persist as long as the sterling area holds together.[11] It is sometimes argued that Britain's entry into the EEC should pave the way for a gradual amalgamation of Western Europe and the sterling area, on the analogy of the associate status granted by the Rome Treaty to France's former African territories; but the comparison is spurious. Arrangements can perhaps be made in favor of some formerly British-controlled African territories, but to talk of the sterling area as a whole amalgamating with Western Europe is to depart from reality. The Six cannot throw open their markets to the free entry of Commonwealth products without ruining their own farmers, and it is one of the underlying aims of the Rome Treaty that Europe's peasant agricultures should *not* be ruined but, on the contrary, protected from the market mechanism and helped to adapt themselves to changed conditions over a lengthy period. Moreover, free entry of Commonwealth foodstuffs and raw materials into Europe would amount to discrimination against competing American exports, and this is something the U.S. Government can be expected to resist with the utmost energy, in its own name as well as in the name of such Latin American countries as Brazil, whose European markets would disappear if the enlarged EEC admitted tropical and subtropical foodstuffs from all of Europe's former overseas colonies free of duty, while placing tariffs on comparable South American goods. There may be some juggling with quotas, but in the long run the rational solution clearly lies in reducing tariffs all round, with the industrialized countries taking the lead.

[11] As of now, the area comprises the United Kingdom and the British Commonwealth except for Canada, plus such independent countries as Ireland, South Africa, Burma, and various Middle Eastern territories chiefly remarkable for their oil royalties and the consequent accumulation of sterling holdings.

The proper procedure would be for the enlarged EEC and the United States to reduce their barriers, but on a most-favored-nation basis, so that any concessions they gave each other would be automatically extended to imports from all other areas. This done, such industrialized countries as Canada, Australia, and Japan might then join the agreement on the understanding that they would not ask for much in return from the underdeveloped countries, which at the present stage are bound to protect their infant industries and must be permitted to do so. Any other arrangement can only result in the Atlantic Community becoming a rich-man's club and a ready target for Communist-*cum*-nationalist abuse and hostility.[12]

Judging from official statements made in Washington and elsewhere, general free trade is more or less accepted as an aim by the Kennedy Administration, notwithstanding some vague talk about the U.S.A. "joining" the Common Market—talk that to Europeans sounds both fanciful and alarming. There appeared to be some genuine ground for such alarm towards the end of 1961, when various unofficial voices in Washington hinted that U.S. policy might evolve in the direction of turning the Atlantic Community into an exclusive customs union of the industrialized countries.[13] Fortunately, these siren songs were resisted by the Administration and publicly disavowed by President Kennedy himself. Speaking before the National Association of Manufacturers on December 6, 1961, Mr. Kennedy said:

> I am not proposing, nor is it either necessary or desirable, that we join the Common Market . . . create an Atlantic free-trade area, or impair in any way our close economic ties with Canada, Japan, and the rest of the free world. . . . We do not want Japan left out of this

[12] Meade, *op. cit.*, pp. 30 ff.; see also Oscar Gass, "The Crusade for Trade," *The New Republic* (Washington), March 19–26, 1962.

[13] See, e.g., Walter Lippmann, "A Giant Step," *New York Herald-Tribune*, November 2, 1961. This followed the publication of a joint statement issued by Christian A. Herter and Will Clayton, and published as a Congressional document, which seemed to foreshadow an American exercise in the Free Trade Area formerly sponsored by the British (though of course on a larger scale).

great market, or Latin America, which has depended so much on the European market.[14]

The same note was struck in the President's formal "Message on Trade" sent to Congress on January 25, 1962:

> We must make certain that any arrangements which we make with the European Economic Community are worked out in such a fashion as to insure nondiscriminatory application to all third countries . . . the United States and Europe together have a joint responsibility to all of the less-developed countries. . . .[15]

It is true that these sensible principles were not spelled out very precisely. In particular there remained an uncertainty—not quite removed to this day—whether the policy-makers had grasped the need to *discriminate in favor* of the backward countries, a matter that goes rather beyond reciprocity. If the industrialized countries throw open their markets to the products of poorer areas, it does not follow that this entitles them to insist on reciprocal freedom to overwhelm their weaker partners with a flood of costly manufactures, or useless luxury goods, in the name of free trade. These distinctions go rather against the logic of liberalism, but they are essential to an understanding of the relationship between advanced and backward countries. The latter are inclined to sport national-socialist regimes[16] intent on planned economic development, and the East-West conflict being what it is, they are not

---

14 Cited by Gass, *loc. cit.*

15 *Ibid.* It may be worth noting that the President's proposals (now adopted with minor changes) envisaged two different sets of tariff-cutting measures: powers to reduce U.S. duties by 50 per cent, and bargaining powers to reduce such duties to zero in cases where the U.S.A. and the EEC together account for 80 per cent of world exports (not counting exports to or from the Soviet bloc). As a practical matter, this second clause only becomes important if Britain joins the Common Market.

16 The term carries no pejorative meaning; it simply takes account of the fact that modern nationalist movements in backward countries are necessarily socialist, and vice versa. Some of them may also be cryptocommunist, but that is another matter and really irrelevant to the issue. It would take a Byzantine logician to distinguish between the national-socialist and the communist strands in the complex personalities of some contemporary African politicians.

obliged to turn themselves into guinea pigs for Western *laissez-fairists*. It remains to be seen how far these truths have been grasped in Washington, and still more whether the policy-makers are able and willing to depart from economic orthodoxy. Still, so far as it went, Mr. Kennedy's statement indicated a healthy degree of realism.

It also disposed of another fear, one held by the Europeans themselves: namely that Washington would upset the delicate balance of the European Economic Community by, so to speak, trying to join the club. For the United States to adhere to the Rome Treaty—supposing such a thing to be economically feasible—would be to destroy the whole carefully built edifice of European political integration. The absurdity of the idea was brought out by the Brussels official who, on hearing of it, asked: "How can an elephant get into a bathtub?" But it is not just a matter of size. The Common Market was deliberately set up to serve as the economic framework of a future united Europe. It cannot be enlarged to include the U.S.A. without losing its original purpose. Even an "association" on the lines of Britain's original Free Trade Area scheme—i.e., with Europe and the U.S.A. retaining their tariff sovereignty in respect to third parties —would weaken its purpose, to say nothing of the fact that an Atlantic Free Trade area that practiced free trade only among its members, while retaining customs barriers against the outside world, would—as remarked before—hurt all the backward countries and formally separate the rich from the poor, the white from the colored, nations. A preferential trading community of the Western world makes sense only on the assumption that the Cold War has been lost and the backward countries have gone over to Moscow.

To say this is not to argue against the general concept of an Atlantic Community, still less against Atlantic free trade, provided it is compatible with the aim of aiding the nonindustrialized countries. For such purposes, however, the term "Atlantic" is plainly a misnomer.[17] Japan is not part of the "Atlantic"

[17] See William Diebold, Jr., "Britain, the Six, and the World Economy," in *Foreign Affairs*, April, 1962, pp. 407 ff.

world, nor are some of the most important British Commonwealth countries. If Western Europe and North America take
steps to create an Atlantic free-trade area, they will simultaneously have to protect the interests of these outlying areas either
by stabilizing world prices, or by providing guaranteed markets,
or both. The problem is particularly serious for non-European
temperate-zone food producers, who are already being discriminated against by the Common Market, and quite properly so,
since it is one of the purposes of the European Economic Community to plan its own farming on a continental scale. In principle, there is only a step from national to international—or
from continental to intercontinental—planning, but the step
is a long one. At any rate this is an area in which tariff reductions will not help, nor will the formation of an Atlantic free-
trade bloc. A solution may emerge along the lines of an agreed
world price based on the present French or American level (the
two are fairly close). This would tend to increase food production, but in a world two-thirds of whose population still go hun-
gry that would hardly be a disaster. It would mean, however,
that food "surpluses" would have to be taken right out of the
market economy, and distributed below cost wherever they are
most needed.

Public opinion has not yet caught on to the fact that the leading industrial countries are also the major food producers.[18] The
world's greatest industrial center, the U.S.A., is also the greatest
exporter of surplus foodstuffs. Canada, Australia, and New Zealand, with living standards higher than any West European country except Sweden and Switzerland, rely heavily on food exports
while building up their industries. In Europe itself, the Common
Market Six already cover nine-tenths of their food requirements
and may soon become completely self-sufficient, if not exporters
of some products such as coarse grains. Britain, on the other
hand, imports about half its foodstuffs, thus providing a market
for North America and Australia–New Zealand which will be
partly thrown open to West European producers if the United

18 See *The Economist*, December 30, 1961.

Kingdom joins the EEC. These producers may, however, find that the removal of preferences is not the whole answer: Wheat is grown in Canada and Australia at half the French cost not because of subsidies, but because of the vast scale of its cultivation. There are thus two different sets of problems: how to reconcile the interests of European, Commonwealth, and American producers, and what to do with the West's genuine over-all surpluses. The second is perhaps the easier to solve. After all, food need only be given away to the developing countries. The fact that the surplus producers are also the leading industrial countries of the West should in principal make an agreed politico-economic solution easier. In a rational world it doubtless would: What could be simpler than to pool the surpluses and then give them away or sell them below cost?[19]

Although the backward countries—the fashionable term "underdeveloped" hardly takes account of the actual *overdevelopment* many of these countries have suffered through monoculture, soil exhaustion, and overpopulation—are generally short of food, they are beginning to produce a surplus of marketable consumers' goods, especially textiles. An Atlantic Community that discriminated against them could hardly expect to find a welcome. The emerging countries of Asia and Africa have to find markets for manufactures into which a great deal of human labor has gone, and the advanced industrial countries dare not shut them out completely for political reasons alone. In this respect Britain, which imports 30 per cent of its consumption of cotton textiles from regions like India and Hong Kong, is better placed than the Continental Six, which import only 5 per cent from all the backward countries combined. An Indian might be forgiven for re-

[19] See U. W. Kitzinger, in *The Guardian*, April 17, 1962 for some of the problems connected with plans for stabilizing world food markets and the reasons for British opposition thereto. Generally speaking, the EEC currently protects its farmers by an average 20 per cent tariff wall, while Britain has hitherto subsidized local food producers by payments equivalent to some 40 per cent of gross output. A higher world food price would seriously unhinge the British balance of payments, which currently profits from the low cost of food imports. It can of course be argued that British policy has resulted in keeping world food prices artificially low.

garding this as a more important matter than the future trade in high-cost manufactures between the European and American halves of the Atlantic Community. This consideration serves to place Washington's current trade proposals into proper perspective. With the passage of its legislative proposals, the Administration is now committed to tariff-bargaining procedures whereby the United States and Europe would negotiate for the reciprocal elimination of tariffs on goods in which the Six, Britain, and the U.S.A. together carry on 80 per cent or more of world trade. These happen to be mainly high-cost industrial products—motorcars for example—which in 1960 accounted for $2 billion worth of U.S. exports to the EEC countries and $1.4 billion worth of U.S. imports from them.[20] Concessions obtained in this way would be nondiscriminatory, i.e., they would be extended to the other trading partners of the United States, such as Latin America or Japan. This sounds very impressive until one realizes that the list of goods in question "has been devised, frankly, to cover those capital-intensive industries—chemicals, vehicles, parts of engineering—where the removal of tariffs by America and Europe would not lead to a massive influx of goods from low-wage Asia."[21] No wonder a well-known American economist commented: "We are prepared to buy other peoples' resources, but not their labor. . . . Our barriers are highest against those who have nothing to sell except their skill and their work."[22] Countries falling under this latter description,

20 *The World Today* (London), March, 1962, p. 97.

21 *The Economist*, March 24, 1962, p. 1,094. It is true that in asking for powers to negotiate such tariff cuts, President Kennedy also urged steps to reduce or eliminate restrictions on the import of tropical foodstuffs; but most of these were on the American free list anyway, and the President's proposals were moreover made contingent on the EEC doing the same and thus lessening the preferences given to its former African colonies—clearly a case of being liberal with other peoples' property.

22 Gass, *loc. cit.* It is only fair to add that the European authorities are busy subsidizing their expensive domestic sugar-beet production while ignoring the urgent need of poor tropical and subtropical countries that could supply all of Europe's needs at considerably lower prices than those now charged to the domestic consumer. There is also the curious case of rice, where a high import duty has been planned in Brussels, apparently in order to enable Italian producers to expand their high-cost output.

it might be noted, include Italy and even Switzerland, as well as India and Japan. On the other hand, some leading raw material suppliers—e.g., Canada and Venezuela—pay hardly any customs duties on their exports to the United States. It is probably useless to cast blame on these tariff policies. They are to some extent imposed on the U.S. Administration by the need to discriminate in favor of marginal producers at home. But it is as well to recognize that the chief beneficiaries from lowered tariffs—not to mention Atlantic free trade—would once more be the heavily capitalized industries—motors, machinery, metals, chemicals—which are already doing quite well.

From the American viewpoint this preoccupation with Atlantic free trade is indeed understandable and even commendable. It is after all preferable to a "fortress-America" policy of trying to shut out European imports, or to a pseudo-Machiavellian policy of keeping Europe weak and disunited. By taking a gamble on the Common Market, Washington has shown its willingness to risk tougher competition in future, and even some degree of West European resistance to American pressures, political or economic. The unspoken assumptions underlying the Common Market are not anti-American, but they are opposed to American hegemony within the Western world: Western Europe is to become master of its own fate, so far as that is possible. One may suppose that in the long run this attitude will be shared even by the British, once they have got over their lingering attachment to the myth of Anglo-American partnership. European independence—within reasonable limits—from both America and Russia is a relatively new theme, but given time and an economic foundation it could become a focus of political loyalties. An Atlantic Community spanning America and Europe thus offers an emotional counter to European isolationism. For Britain it has the additional attraction of making "entry into Europe" more palatable while at the same time presenting British statesmanship once more in the role of mediator between America and Europe. A possible foretaste of this exercise in triangular loyalties may be found in a statement made by a British Cabinet spokesman before a European audience last spring, when the question

of British membership was about to be settled. Addressing six
other Ministers of the Western European Union (who were also
the six of the EEC) in London on April 10, 1962, the Lord Privy
Seal, Mr. Edward Heath, said (according to *The Times* of April
13):

> We quite accept that the European political union, if it is to be
> effective, will have a common concern for defence problems and
> that a European point of view on defence will emerge. What is essen-
> tial, however, is that any European point of view or policy on defence
> should be directly related to the Atlantic alliance. We must make it
> clear beyond all doubt that the object of our common policy is to
> defend and strengthen the liberties for which the Atlantic alliance is
> the indispensable shield.
>
> But of course as the European Community develops, the balance
> within the Atlantic alliance is going to change. In the course of time
> there will be two great groupings in the west: North America and
> Europe. The growth of this European point of view in the defence
> field will not, we believe, be long in making itself felt. Already we
> have seen the signs. We have the Western European Union itself, and
> we have the beginnings of cooperation in joint defence projects.
>
> There is no doubt in my mind that, with the closer integration of
> our industries which will follow British accession to the European
> Economic Community, we shall see great advances in European co-
> operation over defence, production, research and development.

As breezes of this kind begin to flow across the Atlantic, Americans in responsible positions may well begin to feel that an
Atlantic free-trade area will tend to make the Europeans less
inward-looking. This doubtless accounts for some of the enthusiasm with which trade-liberalization programs are greeted in
internationalist quarters where concern over America's export
performance mingles with genuine apprehension lest Western
Europe turn itself into a protectionist area, leaving the task of
assisting the undeveloped countries to the United States. In
actual fact, the West Europeans have not done so badly in recent
years, both in importing more from other areas and in assisting
the emergent countries. Between 1957 and 1961, monthly imports
by the Six from countries outside the OECD region (Western

Europe and North America) rose by 13 per cent, from $777 million to $857 million—hardly evidence of inward-looking protectionism, especially when contrasted with the British performance during the same period, which resulted in imports from these countries (mainly the backward) remaining stagnant at $510 million per month.[23] Where direct aid to the "underdeveloped" is concerned, the picture is no different. Between 1957 and 1960, total contributions in gifts and loans by the United States fell from $4.1 billion to $3.781 billion, and by Britain from $910 million to $857 million, while in the same period the Six raised their contribution from $2.077 billion to $2.626 billion.[24] In 1962, the Six of the European Economic Community provided one-third of all Western aid to backward countries, and Britain one-ninth. This suggests that in future Western Europe's share is likely to equal that of the United States; in other words, the burden of helping the undeveloped countries to industrialize will be shared more or less equally by the two halves of the Atlantic world.

Transatlantic trade raises an entirely different set of issues and one that must not be confused with the essentially political objectives involved in Western relations with the backward countries. No amount of common understanding about aiding the undeveloped can enlarge the European market for American farm

[23] *The Guardian,* April 17, 1962. In his article referred to earlier, Professor Paish points out that the terms of trade have consistently favored Britain, except during the war years. Since 1951, average prices of British imports have fallen by nearly 20 per cent, while export prices have risen by over 10 per cent, so that the terms of trade are today nearly back to their 1938 level. At present import-export levels, this change is worth about £1.5 billion to Britain. This is among the reasons why the British Government has hitherto been cool to French proposals for the regulation (i.e., cartelization) of world trade in temperate-zone foodstuffs. Such plans might benefit the producers, but would inevitably drive up Britain's import bill.

[24] *Ibid.* It is interesting to find that over the past five years France has devoted something like 2.7 per cent of her national income to such aid, against 1.3 per cent for Britain; though this figure of course includes Algeria. Aid figures tend to be inflated by such devices as counting commercial loans on the plus side while failing to subtract repayments; but this is true of all countries, including of course the U.S.S.R., and does not account for the trend reflected in the figures cited above.

surpluses, or make the Europeans more enthusiastic about schemes for the United States to drop its tariffs and "join the Common Market." Nor can it eliminate the need for Europe to coordinate the policies of its member states so as to guard against balance-of-payments troubles. With the current outflow of gold and dollars from the United States this is not an immediate problem, but it could easily become one. How near the Community will come to genuine integration will depend on the strength of its supranational institutions, such as the Economic Commission. The stronger they are, the more they will impose their own solution of the perennial problem of balancing economic against social considerations: free trade against full employment, plentiful reserves of foreign currency against higher living standards, larger imports against stable prices. By making this a matter of supranational concern, the Economic Community undercuts both national parochialism and *laissez-faire*. The European market may or may not become more attractive for U.S. exporters.[25] The prime purpose of European integration in any case is not to help American exports, but to enable Europe to overcome its inherited handicaps in a world where the nation-state of limited size and unlimited sovereignty is rapidly going out of fashion. It is to the credit of American public opinion that this prospect has on the whole been accepted with remarkably little protest or resentment.

EUROPE AND AFRICA

Not a great deal can or need be said about the economics of Europe's relationship with its former colonial hinterland in Africa, but the little that must be said has a close bearing upon the questions discussed in the previous section. European trade with Africa does not indeed differ in principle from European trade with Asia or Latin America, but the political framework differs. A glance at the map is sufficient to show why. It is useless to argue that politics should be irrelevant: They are not. West-

---

[25] For the probable difficulties, see Gass, *loc. cit.;* for an analysis of the U.S. payments problem prior to 1962, see Benoit, *op. cit.,* pp. 125 ff.

ern Europe's connection with Africa is closer than its connection with Asia or South America. The traditional relationship has been of a different order, and the economic provisions written into the Rome Treaty are the consequence of that fact. Even without the sizable amounts of "conscience money" that countries like Algeria are plainly due to obtain, the politico-economic links are strong. The former British, French, and Belgian colonies differ among themselves about the wisdom of close association with the European Economic Community; they do not differ about the importance of securing access to European markets and investment funds, even when their requests are phrased in the menacing language of African socialism. The hands are the hands of Esau, but the voice is the voice of Jacob, and Jacob is secure in the knowledge that his claims will not be ignored.

The political map of Africa discloses a tangle of more or less accidental frontiers and some enduring geographical contours upon which the colonial regimes in the past superimposed their economic and linguistic patterns. As now constituted, independent Africa—setting aside the Portuguese enclaves and the European-dominated Republic of South Africa—is articulated into no fewer than twenty-six precariously independent states, plus nine or ten colonial territories (all British-ruled) due to become self-governing within a few years. Singly, they cannot each devote enough resources to industrialization, or indeed provide markets for any but the smallest and least efficient units. Together, they could pull themselves up by a joint effort, if aided by the West, and especially by the European Economic Community. This calls once more for supranational planning, and above all for an effort to overcome the linguistic and political barriers dividing the formerly French from the ex-British territories. The latter are numerically preponderant (Nigeria plus Ghana having almost twice the population of all the ex-French states) but in size the "French" bloc plus the vast ex-Belgian Congo forms the bulk of the West and Central African land mass. On the other side of the continental divide, an English-speaking association of East African territories seems about to emerge. The political alignment between so-called "moderate" and "radical" groupings cuts across these geographical and cultural boundaries, linking English-speaking Ghana with French-speaking Guinea (plus, incongruously, Egypt and Morocco) as against Nigeria, the Congo, and most of the ex-French territories. It is the latter that form the hard core of what is currently known as "Eurafrica"— the beginning of a permanent association between Western Europe and its former colonies.[26]

Economically, these political and cultural divisions are largely irrelevant, which is not to say that they are unimportant. If one looks at the matter from the economist's angle, it seems clear enough that industrialization cannot proceed effectively unless it is undertaken jointly and with the help of the Atlantic nations, or at any rate the EEC (with Britain inside it). Unfortunately, independence has been achieved at the cost of regional cohesion. The fragmentation of the former trading union between the French-controlled territories of West and Equatorial Africa has not helped, and the failure of the English-speaking states to cooperate among themselves, and with the ex-French states, is an ominous sign. The rational solution clearly is a threefold grouping of West, Central, and East African countries, ignoring language barriers. If coordination is not achieved at an early stage, economic frontiers will harden, and industrialization will be launched by "national" units too small and weak to achieve significant results. It is the first step that counts.

Where does the EEC stand in this? It has hitherto been dominated by France's desire to promote development on a bilateral basis, i.e., by associating the former colonies as closely as possible with Europe. In practice this has meant that the formerly French

26 See Barbara Ward Jackson, "Free Africa and the Common Market," *Foreign Affairs,* April, 1962; J. R. Lambert, "The E.E.C. and the Associated African States," *The World Today,* August, 1961. "Eurafrica" was formally launched at a Parliamentary Conference meeting in the Maison de l'Europe in Strasbourg from June 19–24, 1961, with a hundred delegates from the parliamentary assemblies of sixteen African states and Madagascar (now the Malagasy Republic) sitting side by side with the same number of delegates from the European Parliamentary Assembly. Most of the African delegates came from formerly French territories assembled in the so-called Brazzaville bloc.

territories have obtained free entry for their products into the markets of the EEC countries. In accordance with the Rome Treaty, these territories also obtained massive direct grants from the EEC and the right to protect their infant industries by levying duties on European imports. These duties must be nondiscriminatory. Thus an "associated overseas territory" is now entitled to export and import freely to and from France, Germany, Italy, and the Benelux countries, whereas under the colonial regime its exports were directed to France and its home market virtually reserved for French goods. This makes a considerable and welcome change. Yet in 1960, France still conducted about 30 per cent of her foreign trade with her former colonies and protectorates, although the proportion was declining.[27] For France's partners in the EEC, these "associates" are considerably less important, which may be among the reasons why Germany and Holland were unenthusiastic when, at a conference of European Ministers and African representatives in Brussels, in April 1962, the French proposed to increase the aid allocated by the EEC institutions to these Community associates, over the five years from the beginning of 1963, to about $1.2 billion, or more than twice the amount allotted to them for the five-year period ending in December, 1962.[28] The same cleavage appeared over the proposal (fervently supported by the United States in the name of free trade) for a scaling-down of European tariff preferences granted to France's African associates. The French were willing to lower the preferences granted to African countries under the Common External Tariff of the European Community, but they balked at the notion of a 50 per cent cut. For the future, the odds are that all such disputes will be settled by a substan-

[27] *The Statist*, April 13, 1962, p. 110.
[28] *Ibid.*, p. 111. Under the Rome Treaty, France secured a total subsidy of $581 million for the (mainly ex-French) Associated Overseas Territories during the five-year interim period ending in 1962, as well as free entry into the Common Market customs area, and tariff protection for their industries against European *and African* competitors. In July, 1962, the six EEC members provisionally committed themselves to an amount of $780 million (later raised to $800 million) in aid to eighteen associated African states for a five-year period beginning in January, 1963.

tial tariff reduction, coupled with an equally substantial rise in development funds, as compensation. This conflicts with Washington's desire to get rid of "tied" aid funds, but the benefit of such aid to the new African countries is too great for them to renounce it on doctrinaire grounds alone. For the same reason, of course, most of these new regimes have shown themselves relatively indifferent to anti-Western propaganda, though willing enough to accept aid from the Soviet Union and even from China.[29]

The immediate advantage to the African countries of close cooperation with Western Europe can be spelled out in figures. It is most obvious in the case of the formerly French territories, which are now among the most heavily subsidized areas in the world. Although the "closed circuit" of the franc area, whereby the metropolis and the colonies formed a monetary and economic unit, has been broken, French investments have been stepped up. Over the past decade, the amount of *public* capital alone that France has poured into her former African colonies south of the Sahara—i.e., leaving out Morocco, Tunisia, and Algeria—has reached the remarkable figure of $300 million per year.[30] At the same time, the fall in world prices for tropical products has made all these territories doubly dependent on the guaranteed markets and prices made available to them under the Rome Treaty. Ultimately, the common external tariff of the EEC will give them a competitive advantage over Latin American and other suppliers. Not surprisingly, most of the ex-French territories have remained remarkably loyal both to France and to protectionism (now known as planning).[31] British West Africa, hav-

29 Colin Legum, "Economic Commission for Africa: Progress Report," *The World Today*, July, 1961; Walter Kolarz, "The Impact of Communism on West Africa," *International Affairs* (London), April, 1962.

30 Jackson, *loc. cit.* This does not include the steadily growing sums made available by the joint Common Market Fund for Development (FEDOM); over the past five-year period these latter payments averaged $100 million annually for the ex-colonies, nearly all of them French. This was part of the bargain France extracted from her partners before signing the Rome Treaty.

31 The two well-known exceptions are Guinea, which in September, 1958, flounced out of the (then-existing) French Union in a huff, and Mali, (the former French Sudan) which followed the example a little later; and there

ing been encouraged to "stand on its own feet" economically and do without subsidies, was never subjected to similar temptations and has consequently shown greater skepticism of the value of European entanglements.[32]

Eurafrica in fact is a French concept. It has few supporters in Bonn, where Dr. Erhard and his friends share Washington's anxiety that Latin American products shall not be permanently disadvantaged by preferences granted to France's former African colonies. (It so happens that Latin America is an important German market). Nor does it rouse much enthusiasm in London, where it is correctly felt that following the French example would mean incurring very heavy expenditure in capital grants and technical assistance. Even in France, the mounting cost of aiding these territories through direct grants, price supports, and subsidies of all kinds encounters some resistance, at any rate on the parliamentary level. Eurafrica also has the disadvantage of suggesting to many African nationalists—with or without Communist prompting—that Africa is intended to remain the poor relation in an alliance in which the European countries will draw on its raw material reserves for the benefit of their own

---

are signs that both are having second thoughts. At any rate, the so-called "union" of Ghana and Guinea, to which Mali later adhered, has never risen above a phantom existence, and Guinea has lately given signs of being willing to revert to its old allegiance, while Mali has signed the EEC association protocol.

[32] Jackson, *loc. cit.* "Since the ultimate aim of British colonial policy was to produce self-governing and finally independent territories, countries such as Ghana or Nigeria were not drawn into a centralized economic system directed by Britain. They had to balance their own books and cover their own expenditure. Membership in the sterling area gave no guarantee that internal overdrafts and external imbalances could be covered by London. Welfare and development funds remained small. . . . Britain granted some imperial preferences on tropical products . . . but received no preferences in return except in the two very small territories of Gambia and Sierra Leone. As a result, British Africa traded widely with the rest of the world. . . . In 1957, on independence, Ghana's reserves reached $700,000,000. But these reserves were not grants from the metropolitan power. They had been truly earned . . ." It might be added that they have by now been well and truly squandered. Whether starving the public sector in the name of free trade is the best way to promote development in backward countries might make a fascinating subject for a doctoral dissertation.

industries. The best way to overcome these suspicions is for the European Economic Community to step up its direct grants and for the African states to pool their industrialization plans. It is obviously senseless for twenty-six—soon there will be more— different territories to promote such plans in isolation. But though the principle may be conceded on all sides, it is not easy to coordinate the policies of areas like Mauritania, "where 600,000 people depend on an iron mine and a railway," with those of Nigeria, the giant of West Africa with a population nearing 40 million.[33]

Counting the United States in, the West still has an overwhelming economic preponderance in trade with Africa. Guinea apart, where the Soviet bloc has won a foothold (but perhaps a shrinking one), all the West African countries conduct over 80 per cent of their foreign trade with Europe and America, and the share of the former metropolitan power is usually about 50 per cent; indeed, in some of France's ex-colonies it is still around 90 per cent.[34] In Central and Eastern Africa, including the turbulent Congo, the pattern is the same. All these countries draw heavily on Western expertise, notably in education, and their intellectual elites, however radical their thinking, still look predominantly Westward. The trouble hitherto has been that the European powers have tended to project their differences into the African context. This has been true even after the formation of the EEC, for France's aid to her former colonies has been on such a colossal scale as to cut across their trading relationships with the ex-British territories. This was doubtless among the reasons why late in March, 1962, the twelve states of the "Brazzaville group," at a conference in Bangui (Central African Repub-

[33] *The Economist*, January 20, 1962: "In wealth the scale runs from Ghana, where gold, bauxite, logs and cocoa provide an income of nearly $200 a head, to Niger, in whose desert lands, on the fringes of the Sahara, so many of the 3 million inhabitants live outside the market economy that no calculation of per capita income is possible at all." Incidentally, the need to distinguish between ex-British Nigeria and ex-French Niger points to another difficulty: In some cases the frontiers traced by the former colonial powers cut across natural geographical (in this case riparian) boundaries.

[34] *Ibid.*

lic) decided to set up a common market of their own, adopted a flag for their "Afro-Malagasy Union," and pressed for annual meetings with President de Gaulle on the model of the British Commonwealth. In addition, the two outsiders, Guinea and Mali, have been drifting back to France—the official reason being provided by French recognition of Algerian independence—and French-speaking Africa has once more come to look like a bloc. Since Franco-African ties plainly cut across pan-African barriers, there have been cries of protest from Ghana and—less logically —from Cairo, which fancies itself the headquarters of the anti-Western camp. Elsewhere, the new union has had a mixed reception. In general, the formerly British-controlled territories tend to be suspicious of Eurafrica and the EEC (this is true even of Nigeria, which otherwise ranks with the "conservative" or "Monrovia" group of states, as against the "radical" Casablanca bloc), so that there is a danger of political divisions hardening along the old colonial frontiers.

Part of the cure may lie in nonpreferential aid on an Atlantic basis, i.e., by stabilizing world prices for tropical products and in general supplementing the French effort, which is now quite out of proportion to what is being done by the other Atlantic countries and has tended to place the ex-French territories in a privileged position. In principle, there is no reason why this cannot be done. The "Casablanca group" (Egypt, Morocco, Ghana, Guinea, and Mali) includes in Mali a country that is both a member of the franc zone and an associate of the Common Market. The group's politics—which in the case of Egypt at any rate are purely destructive and totally irrelevant to Africa's real problems—need not interfere with economic regionalism, even if Nigeria as well as Ghana decide to stay out of the Common Market. It is quite wrong to discuss this topic in terms of "radicalism" versus "conservatism." By Western standards—certainly by American standards—all these new countries are "radical": the Senegal of Léopold Senghor no less than the Guinea of Sékou Touré. All are addicted to various forms of centralized planning, state control over the economy, and national-socialist ideologies to match.[35] But only Ghana and Guinea have adopted a fellow-traveling attitude towards the Soviet bloc, and even they have fallen considerably short of Cuba's record in this respect. It can of course be held that the relative sophistication displayed by the British and French governments when faced with such tendencies has had something to do with moderating their enthusiasm for the Soviet example; but a simpler explanation probably is that no African country is really a suitable field for Communist forms of control. Sékou Touré has been at pains to stress that there is no class struggle in his country because there are no classes, a most un-Leninist observation. When these regimes describe themselves as socialist, they are quite simply saying that they favor central planning as against the kind of free-for-all that businessmen and economists in the West have come to regard as the only natural and proper form of development.[36]

And just as it is wrong to treat the Monrovia-Casablanca split as a difference over "socialism," so it is a mistake to suppose that formerly British-controlled territories such as Nigeria in the West, or Tanganyika in the East, are likely to follow Britain into the European Common Market. In fact, both have given warning that they may leave the Commonwealth if the United King-

[35] For an indication of how the French-educated elite in West Africa views the matter, see M. Senghor's address to a Chatham House audience and the subsequent discussion, in *International Affairs*, April, 1962; the President of Senegal represents the pro-Western wing of African nationalism, as reflected in the policies of the Brazzaville group of ex-French territories, but this does not make him less of a socialist. For the Communist impact, see Kolarz, *ibid.*; also M. Roberts, "African Trade Unionism in Transition," *The World Today*, October, 1961.

[36] Mr. Kolarz (*loc. cit.*) observes quite rightly: "Sékou Touré and Modibo Keita, who much admire the Russian and Chinese models, are probably no greater enthusiasts for economic planning than the Senegalese Premier, Mamadou Dia, who derives his inspiration from Emanuel Mounier's personalist philosophy." The same writer adds: "Nkrumah himself, and also Modibo Keita and Sékou Touré, would have to go, to make the three national-democratic parties of West Africa ripe for a Communist take-over." A European may perhaps be pardoned for feeling that the United States could have saved itself some trouble if its opinion-makers had taken an equally detached view of Castro instead of treating him either as a romantic hero or as a card-carrying threat to the American way of life.

dom becomes a signatory to the Treaty of Rome. If these threats are carried into effect, the political division between French-speaking and English-speaking Africa would run parallel to an economic line-up associating some African countries closely with Europe, while leaving others in the cold; though one may suppose that the United States would come to their aid. In that case, pan-Africanism would run up against economic and political barriers stretching from Europe across the Mediterranean into Central Africa; and doubtless the Sino-Soviet bloc would do its best to aggravate the resulting tensions and hostilities. If one looks ahead beyond 1967, when the new round of preferential agreements now being negotiated between the EEC and its African associates expires, it is possible to envisage a situation where the European taxpayer—especially the French taxpayer—will grow tired of the burden, while African leaders will feel strong enough to do without preferential treatment. Britain's future absorption into Europe may make it easier in the long run (though more difficult in the short term) to amalgamate the English-speaking and French-speaking blocs; but the ex-French territories derive such formidable advantages from their continued association with France (and through France with the EEC) that one does not quite see why they should renounce it even for the sake of pan-Africanism—in any case a much hazier concept than enthusiasts for a "United States of Africa" seem at present willing to concede.

Nothing that has been said so far relates—except in the most indirect fashion—to the problems of Algeria and the two other Arab States in what was formerly French North Africa: Morocco and Tunisia. Morocco is a member—as its name implies—of the Casablanca group, which holds two Arab and three African countries together in an uneasy alliance. But its traditional links are with Tunisia and Algeria, the latter probably destined to become the strongest of all North African countries. Ultimately it is a matter of political choice whether these regions will align themselves with the rest of the Continent in a pan-African assembly or prefer an Arab-Islamic orientation that would link them with the Middle East on the one hand, and with Mediterranean countries such as France, Italy, and Spain on the other. There is no convincing economic reason why they should do either, though Algeria's dependence on Saharan oil and French capital investment supplies a possible pointer. The three formerly French-controlled North African territories, with their French-speaking elites and their economic ties with France, are in any case designed by nature and history to form a confederation. If all goes well, this could become the northern counterpart of Eurafrica. Needless to say, all may not go well. Communism and Nasserism —the "national-socialist" form of Pan-Arabism—can be relied upon to join forces against such a development, which would rob Cairo of much of its importance and undercut the Sino-Soviet bloc's efforts. If they fail, it will not be because the three North African countries are likely to opt in favor of what is comically known as "free enterprise," but because their political elites may come to see greater advantages in being associated with Western Europe in general, and France in particular, than in relying on Sino-Soviet support, although they will certainly not refuse help from any quarter. If Europe can digest an Arab Socialist Republic in Algeria—ultimately in the whole Maghreb (Arab Northwest Africa), for the Islamic monarchy in neighboring Morocco is not likely to last more than a few years alongside a radical Algerian republic with a bigger army and mounting oil royalties—it need not fear Soviet competition or Nasserist maneuvers. There are some signs that the French-trained elites of Algeria, with their barely concealed preference for Paris over Cairo, are not really anti-Western, though their social radicalism is quite genuine—a good deal more genuine than that of the Nasser regime, which by comparison begins to look more and more like a caricature of fascism at its shoddiest.

In passing it may be observed that it looks as if the French are more fortunate with their former Arab and African protégés than a reader of the Anglo-American press might have supposed from the information he obtained from that source in recent years. It is certainly remarkable that after more than seven years of savage warfare, Franco-Algerian relations are not a great deal worse; and it has recently appeared that General de Gaulle's shock tactics in expelling Guinea from the French Union in September, 1958, did no permanent damage, whereas Britain got small thanks for the far more understanding treatment she gave Dr. Nkrumah in neighboring Ghana. Perhaps the moral is that as long as African leaders get what they want, the ceremonial does not matter a great deal to them. Possibly, too, the French policy of cultural assimilation pays off in the long run. It has certainly resulted in the creation of an educated elite that continues to look to Paris rather than Cairo, Moscow, or Peking.

Can one draw up a provisional balance sheet either of Eurafrica or of the emerging Arab confederation of the Maghreb (Algeria-Tunisia-Morocco), let alone the Pan-African union projected in Cairo and Accra? It will be evident from what has been said that the rift between the French- and British-oriented states in Africa is partly a legacy from the colonial era and in part a reflection of the division of Europe into the competing Six and Seven. If the European split can be healed, it will at least become possible for the ex-French and ex-British territories in Black Africa south of the Sahara to submerge their differences. If the split is perpetuated, economic frontiers will harden along the old political and language boundaries, and a rational solution—which would involve joint planning of resources—will become almost impossible. From the "European" viewpoint, Britain's entry into the European Economic Community should make it easier to construct a free-trade area embracing the enlarged EEC and most of the African countries formerly controlled by London and Paris, plus the ex-Belgian Congo. A system of preferences extended by the whole of Western Europe to the whole (or almost the whole) of Africa is, however, scarcely the ideal solution from the U.S. viewpoint, since it would inevitably work against Latin American exports. One sees in this example how difficult it is to reconcile European and Atlantic interests. Yet Eurafrica is too promising a concept to be sacrificed on the altar of free trade, and what is more, neither the EEC nor many of the politically conscious Africans are willing to sacrifice it. It is easy enough to argue that Pan-Africanism holds greater attraction in the long run, as perhaps it does.[37] But meanwhile it does nothing to help the Africans solve their most pressing economic problems, any more than pan-Americanism has been notably successful in aiding the Latin American countries to industrialize. Indeed, the two doctrines seem to have much in common. Both appeal to a sense of unity based on history and geography, though in the case of Africa it is difficult to see what the Arab States along the Mediterranean have in common with the rest of the Continent, except for being located in an area for which the geographers have conventionally employed the same traditional term. Perhaps the notion that Morocco has closer ties with Ghana than with neighboring Tunisia is due to be exploded sooner than the Cold War strategists in Cairo and Accra are ready to believe. In economic terms, the division of Africa into the rival "Casablanca" and "Monrovia" blocs is irrational and corresponds to nothing save the fleeting ambitions of a few political figures. It has no basis in geography, culture, or language and has arisen solely through divisions among the political elites. The lesson of the recent past in any case is the unity of the Arab Maghreb and the corresponding integration of Black Africa into an economic whole sustained by an enlarged EEC (including Britain). Whether these arrangements should be styled "Eurafrica" or not is a relatively minor point. It is not even important whether one or more of the states in question continues to hanker after "positive neutralism" as the external counterpart of "African socialism." Unless one believes as a matter of faith that any association between Europe and Africa must be harmful to the emergent peoples in what has long been called the Black Continent, there seems no reason why this particular legacy of the colonial era cannot be liquidated quite painlessly and in such a way as to promote both the independence and the industrialization of the new African countries.

The problem, such as it is, arises not so much from the legacy of colonialism as from the enduring unbalance between the in-

[37] Jackson, *loc. cit.*

dustrialized core of the Western world and its agrarian hinterland. In this respect Latin America, which freed itself from foreign domination a century and a half ago, is not significantly better off than Africa and Asia. Recent international studies[38] have laid stress on the permanence of a pattern with which the world has slowly become familiar: growing surpluses of food in the wealthy countries of North America and Western Europe, plus Australia–New Zealand, while shortages and malnutrition persist in much of the remainder, the so-called undeveloped or "underdeveloped."[39] There seems every reason to believe that by 1970 the food surpluses of the industrial countries will have grown even larger. On the other hand, there also impend surpluses of tropical products, such as sugar and cocoa, which could ideally help the backward countries to obtain the food, fertilizers, and machinery they need but will not get if prices are depressed; hence the desire for stable world prices or guaranteed export markets. This need presses far more hardly upon the poor countries than upon the rich, which are now applying modern production techniques to farming with such good effect that their dwindling agricultural populations pour out a growing cornucopia of unsalable surpluses. In North America it is now accepted that the urban population cannot consume all the food that is grown, despite deliberate acreage shrinking; Western—though not Eastern—Europe is likely to reach the same stage by 1970. At the same time, the market in these countries for tropical

[38] See in particular the report issued by the Food and Agriculture Organization of the United Nations in May, 1962, on probable world food supplies in 1970.

[39] Considering the number of people employed in eking out a living from every acre of soil in Egypt, India, or China, these terms have a curious ring, especially when one contrasts their swarming populations with the empty spaces of North America, Argentina, and Australia. "Development" is clearly a value term. It would perhaps be more accurate to say that the poor countries have for centuries had the wrong kind of development. Yet during the transition period to a more diversified form of economic life, their monocultures represent the best chance of accumulating investment capital. Sugar produced competitively under tropical conditions is a case in point. One need only think of its importance to Cuba! It is in this area that the advanced countries can ease the transition for the backward ones.

products (including quasi-luxuries like cocoa and coffee) does not grow fast enough to absorb the surpluses of the Latin American regions and the former colonial territories in Africa and Asia. Their own subsistence crops being inadequate, while their exports encounter inelastic markets, these countries face mounting difficulties at the very moment when their political elites have decided to break out of the circle by investing heavily in ambitious industrialization schemes.[40] Even if investments are switched from industry to farming, most of the countries in question are unlikely by 1970 to have emerged beyond the poverty line, i.e., beyond the point where they manage to grow just enough food in terms of energy (calories) to keep their populations from starving.

The orthodox liberal solution to this problem is familiar. "The way to feed Hong Kong or India is to buy their textiles. The way to feed Nigeria or Tanganyika is for Europeans to consume more coffee and chocolate. This can be done—by pulling down American and Common Market protective tariffs or excise taxes—by opening the doors, at whatever temporary cost to American mill-workers, European peasants, vested interests on either side of the Atlantic."[41] Unfortunately this leaves unanswered the question what is to happen if American workers and European peasants prove obdurate. One of the aims of the Common Market is to reduce Europe's dependence on outside imports, though this has been balanced by granting special privileges to Europe's former African colonies. But such privileges go against the universalism of the liberal school. It is also uncertain how that school would react, were it suggested that Europeans and Americans could probably consume more sugar, coffee, cocoa, and

[40] " 'Drink your own coffee' is no answer to a famine of rice or grain." (*The Times*, May 3, 1962, editorial.) The argument of course applies to China and Cuba as well as to India or Nigeria. Indeed the Sino-Soviet relationship is not in this respect so far removed from the traditional nexus between industrial and backward countries as Communist propaganda would like to make people believe. China remains dependent on the U.S.S.R. in much the same way that India depends on the West. Of course such obvious truths are seldom admitted in public.

[41] *The Times, ibid.*

other tropical foodstuffs, if their citizens in the mass really possessed that degree of "affluence" with which they are credited by liberal economists in their more expansive moments.[42] The fact seems to be that Western "affluence" is not great enough to make a significant difference when it comes to purchasing the export crops of the poorer countries—except where political considerations have tipped the balance, as in the case of Eurafrica. In the end it seems likely that the United States will have to do for Latin America what Western Europe is currently doing for its African hinterland: Pour in the necessary investment funds in the form of grants rather than loans, and at the same time supply a guaranteed market for export crops. Even so it is going to be a close-run thing. For Western Europe—already saddled with the necessity of having to drag Spain, Portugal, Greece, Turkey, and Northwest Africa into the modern world—the additional need to look after the interests of Black Africa south of the Sahara imposes a burden democratic electorates find hard to bear, but which nonetheless cannot be shirked. This may help to account for the fact that the national legislatures of the various European countries increasingly devote their time to strictly domestic matters.

BEYOND IMPERIALISM

It seems appropriate to conclude the discussion of this subject with some brief reflections on the well-worn theme of imperialism. Has the colonial chapter really been closed, or is there some truth in the assertion that Western relations with the backward, tropical, and subtropical countries have been no more than superficially revamped and are currently about to enter what is described as a "neocolonialist" stage of economic exploitation veiled

[42] Cf. Gass, *loc. cit.*; also by the same author "The New Frontier Fulfilled," *Commentary* (New York), December, 1961, especially his remarks on the school of thought represented by Professor John K. Galbraith and Mr. Arthur Schlesinger, Jr. It is one of the many oddities of the present intellectual situation that the absurd term "affluent society," and the implications that go with it, have been uncritically swallowed even by writers like Mr. Richard Crossman. We are all affluent now—but we can't afford to buy the food the poorer countries try to sell.

by the formal trappings of independence? The charge, when directed against Britain and France, is the more plausible since it can be argued that something of the kind has indeed marked the relations between the United States and most Latin American countries over the past century. It can also be held that, quite irrespective of power relationships, the "normal" exchange of goods and services between developed and undeveloped areas inevitably works out to the detriment of the latter, unless a conscious effort is made to correct the imbalance.[43]

The point at issue, however, is not whether Western capital investment in the past—with or without overt political control, i.e., "imperialism" in the strict sense of the term—has damaged and distorted the economies of backward areas, but whether this phase has now given way to a different kind of relationship. Socialists have traditionally denounced the capitalist-imperialist nexus, without denying that it was responsible for *some* degree of progress. The current controversy turns upon the question whether "planned" development—as instanced among others by the relations between the EEC and the African states—represents something radically new or a continuation of the old "unequal relationship" at a higher level. European socialists—who have taken a prominent part in helping to liquidate the old colonial system—could in principle subscribe to all, or most, of the charges hurled against it by Leninists and/or radical nationalists and still maintain that it is absurd to talk of neocolonialism when considering the relationship of Asia or Africa to Europe under present conditions. They might also argue that it is perverse to saddle them with the sins of U.S. "private enterprise" in Latin America. The analogy would hold only if Afro-European relations were typified by what has been going on in the formerly Belgian Congo since 1960. But, in fact, the extraordinary doings

43 For a more or less documented statement of the Leninist viewpoint, see Paul A. Baran, *The Political Economy of Growth* (New York, 1960). For a more balanced discussion, see Bert F. Hoselitz (ed.), *The Progress of Underdeveloped Areas* (Chicago, 1952). The conventional liberal wisdom is set out with great rhetorical effect by W. W. Rostow in *The Stages of Economic Growth* (London and New York, 1960).

of the Union Minière in Katanga represent a type of "monopoly-capitalist" activity that is rapidly going out of fashion. The notion that this kind of primitive skulduggery typifies the present order of things is really not worth controverting. Nor is it apparent that these antics form part of a global pattern that could with any plausibility be interpreted in Leninist terms, i.e., as an attempt on the part of "the monopolists and their governments" to secure physical possession of strategic raw materials.

This point leads to what is really the decisive consideration, namely the growing irrelevance of theoretical arguments derived from the pre-1914, or even the pre-1939, era. Every year that passes makes it plainer that shortage of colonial raw materials, and the need by hook or crook to seize control of them, simply does not describe the reality of present-day industrial capitalism, whether planned or unplanned. The exact opposite is the case: Many of these raw materials are being superseded by industrial techniques making use of products available in the industrially developed countries themselves. The real danger facing the backward countries is that their exports will be squeezed out by the development of synthetics. Statistics relating to the consumption of raw materials in industrial countries since the early 1950's indicate that the use of crude materials (cotton, wool, rubber, jute, copper, etc.) has lagged far behind the consumption of synthetics and other processed materials (synthetic rubber, aluminum, plastic materials and fibers, etc.). In consequence of these developments, the flow of capital tends to be diverted from extractive industries (mining, plantations) towards manufacturing. On balance, this is clearly an advantage to the developing countries, though of course it does nothing to solve their surplus-labor problem. The new forms of foreign investment are directly linked to new techniques, and they also demand workers with modern skills, though fewer in number than did the old mining and plantation economy, which reached its peak on the eve of the 1914–18 war. Even if it be argued that this inflow of foreign capital results in a political partnership with the local bourgeoisie, the latter is at any rate becoming a genuine entrepreneurial class (i.e., in Communist parlance a "national" bourgeoisie) rather than a reactionary "comprador" class living off the crumbs of foreign exploitation. In fact, this is precisely what is happening; that it should be happening because Western industrial society has itself been revolutionized by new techniques is quite in accordance with Marxist principles—though Soviet propagandists, for obvious reasons, have no interest in proclaiming the fact.[44]

The Leninist model of a stagnant Western capitalism clutching at the life-line of colonial superprofits extrapolated certain features of an era that came to an end with the 1914–18 war, though even then the bulk of foreign investment did not go to the colonies but to developed countries in Europe or the Americas. Since then, the economic importance of the colonial hinterland has dwindled to such an extent that it has become a major political preoccupation of the rival blocs (East and West) to raise public funds for development purposes, largely in the hope (which may be frustrated) of securing political sympathies and averting a desperate outbreak on the part of chronically underfed and overpopulated countries. Such private investment as can be prevailed upon—not without difficulty—to venture forth into the hinterland typically yields a lower rate of profit than capital invested in Europe or North America. The few notable exceptions to this rule—principally oil—do not seriously alter the general picture. Oil investments indeed belong to the earlier phase, which is why they are always quoted by writers anxious to prove that the Leninist model is still operative. In terms of the real problems encountered by countries such as India or Brazil, they are of course quite marginal, and where—as in the Middle East and North Africa—they have genuine importance, the post-independence pattern makes it certain that they are going to be

44 For a Marxist critique of the traditional (and now quite sterile) Leninist viewpoint, see *International Socialism* (London), Summer, 1962. It may be observed that even at the time when Lenin wrote (1916), his portrayal of an "overripe" capitalism seeking outlets in backward colonial countries while shunning the developed areas was seriously out of focus. Today it hardly requires emphasis that capital does not flow overwhelmingly from industrial to undeveloped areas—quite the contrary: Investments are increasingly based on an interchange between industrially developed countries.

used for the purpose of financing industrialization—as is right and proper. By contrast, the fantastic games still played in Arabia and along the Persian Gulf by newly oil-rich sheikhs and princelings make good copy for journalists and propagandists, but their political significance is minute.

In our age, when the emergent countries are clamoring for capital investments which the developed industrial centers are reluctant to make available, it may seem odd that nationalists should go on quoting Lenin's theses on colonial exploitation as a feature of the "highest" stage of a supposedly overripe and moribund capitalism; but such intellectual lags are not unusual. Moreover, it can be held that the emergent countries are entitled to demand planned public investment in basic services and/or modern manufacturing industries rather than a continuation of the old wasteful system, which developed a few sectors of the economy while distorting or neglecting the remainder. This is a legitimate argument between the Western countries and the ruling elites of their former dependencies. It has nothing to do with the weird notion that Africa is a stamping-ground for "monopolists" in search of profits denied to them at home. The real problem arises from the enormous claims levied upon the European countries by their less-developed partners, now understandably in a hurry to industrialize, and simultaneously faced with a population explosion.

In the case of Algeria, to take one notable example, it has been calculated that merely to hold living standards at their present level—in the face of a population growth curve that has doubled its numbers from 5 to 10 million since 1920 and promises to raise it to 15 million by 1980—the former metropolis would have to invest between $5 billion and $6 billion in Algerian industry—exclusive of oil production and pipeline construction —over the next twenty years. A plan to raise living standards by 2 per cent annually would require the investment of $10 billion; raising standards by 4 per cent a year would call for some $20 billion by 1980. Clearly such efforts are more likely to be made (if at all) by a semi-authoritarian regime in France than by a parliamentary democracy dependent on the voters. This may be among the reasons why all factions of Algerian nationalism greatly prefer the Gaullist regime to its predecessor.

If the Leninist formula of equating capital exports with colonialism is outmoded, the nationalist argument that without massive injection of public capital the vicious circle of poverty, overpopulation, and inadequate investment cannot be broken is well-founded. So is the insistence that such investments must in the main be guided to the key sectors of the economy, not left to short-range considerations of profitability. It is within these terms—familiar to European socialists, and increasingly to intelligent conservatives and liberals as well—that the argument now tends to work itself out. It gains nothing from being presented in terms of stale controversies between Leninists and *laissez-fairists*. Now that the leading European countries have been shorn of their colonial possessions (without suffering the threatened disaster), while their former dependencies are experimenting with "mixed" public and private economies, it becomes possible to transcend the dispute over "imperialism as the highest stage of capitalism." Clearly, the colonial chapter is closed, while the maturation of Europe's industrial economy involves both an exceedingly fast rate of growth and a conscious departure from the state of affairs summed up in the phrase "anarchy of production." Whatever else imperialism may have been, it was plainly not the last stage in the development of the society that is now about to give itself a supranational political organization.

V

THE NEW SOCIAL ORDER

POLITICS IN THE PLAN ERA

> We shall not try to turn our free society into a kind of fascist or communist state. We shall not ask for powers to fix all wages and salaries throughout the land. We shall not try to control all prices. . . . We shall promote [our incomes policy] in the only legitimate way a free and democratic system admits, by trying to persuade people that it is right and that it is in their own interests . . .

Thus spoke the Prime Minister of Great Britain, addressing a Conservative women's conference in May, 1962. The fact that Mr. Macmillan was thereupon rebuked for indulging in *laissez-fairism* by no less an Establishment organ than the London *Times* spoke volumes for the evolution of political thinking in Europe since 1945; it likewise served to illuminate the gulf dividing European from American politics in the 1960's. On the face of it, nothing could seem more reasonable, even commonplace, than the Prime Minister's utterance. Yet the traditional organ of Conservatism would have none of it:

> there are various powers and measures far short of complete wage and price control which a government could take in pursuance of a policy of a socially just, economically efficient, and non-inflationary wages structure . . . persuading people that something is right and in their own interests is not, in fact, the farthest a government may legitimately go in a free and democratic system: there is also the little matter of enforcement. Taxes are not gathered in this country, or any other, simply by persuading people that it is right and in their own interest for them to pay up. . . . [To argue that bargaining over

wages] is so important a freedom that its abridgment . . . would threaten the basis of a free society . . . is a bold assertion in an age which accepts with equanimity, and indeed demands, a high degree of state regulation of the economy.[1]

Dr. Johnson observed that if a man knows he is to be hanged in a fortnight it concentrates his mind wonderfully. The British economy in 1962 was not in quite such desperate straits, but it was facing the very real problem of promoting rapid growth without wage and price inflation. In the circumstances it was perhaps not surprising that the country's leading newspaper should have lent its weight to the cause of planning, i.e., central control, for this was now coming to be regarded as *the* great issue in the national life. State regulation of wages and prices is only an extreme—and perhaps impracticable—example of a trend that in recent years has made it necessary to rethink the principles on which democratic politics should be based. These principles could not, in the Britain of 1962 (and *a fortiori* on the European Continent), be formulated in classical liberal terms:

> when freedom is invoked it makes some difference whether the emphasis is on the traditional liberal or the traditional socialist understanding of that versatile concept. According to the liberal view any fresh proposal for state intervention threatens to inhibit private freedom of action. . . . The socialist view, crudely stated, holds that money buys freedom, that freedom of action is largely illusory for those who lack the means to take advantage of it. On this view a policy of state intervention which has the object of promoting a general and diffused prosperity should enlarge rather than diminish the sum of freedom.[2]

The editorial had no doubt that the vocabulary of liberalism was frequently employed to defend a particular notion of how the economy should operate: "One may hear it said that wage determinations must be free, otherwise the market mechanism is hobbled. . . . This use of 'free' should be recognized for what

[1] *The Times*, June 4, 1962, editorial.
[2] *Ibid.*

it is, part of the description of a particular theory of economic activity . . ."

A century ago, this "particular theory" had the status of dogma, at any rate for the mid-Victorian public that read *The Times*. A little later it came to be described as "Manchester liberalism," or *laissez-fairism*, and Conservatives as well as Socialists acquired the habit of dissociating themselves from its more unwelcome consequences, though few people seriously questioned its doctrinal foundations. The great depression of the 1930's introduced governments and central banks to the Keynesian notion that the level of employment might be regulated by adjusting the budgetary mechanism, while leaving the determination of wages and prices to the free push and pull of market forces (which were also class forces, though this was not generally stressed in public). By the 1960's, unemployment had ceased to be a problem, but the inflationary consequences of full employment had meantime raised a different specter: Was economic growth compatible with monetary stability if employers and unions were left free to fight it out in the market? Was there a choice between inflation and stagnation? Or if not, was the true solution—rapid growth with stable prices—possible under liberal democracy? Might it not be necessary to impose a wages-and-prices policy upon employers and unions alike, and who was to do the imposing? There was, to be sure, the example of Holland and Sweden, where such policies had been voluntarily adopted, and more or less consistently adhered to. But in Sweden this had been done under a Social-Democratic regime now (in 1962) already thirty years old, and in Holland it rested upon a Catholic-Socialist compromise, which also operated in Belgium and Austria and was tending to become the dominant political reality all over Continental Western Europe.[3] With Scandinavia governed by Socialists—for Denmark and Norway were solidly Social-Democratic,

3 In West Germany this was masked by the continuance of the Adenauer regime, but few observers doubted that by 1965 at the latest the Federal Republic would be governed by a "black-red" Catholic-Socialist coalition on the Austrian model. As for France, its semiplanned economy appeared to be successful in the measure in which it diverged from the traditional liberal model, and the Gaullist regime itself was committed to *dirigisme*.

and Finland in general approximated to this pattern—and the bulk of Europe, including Italy, gravitating towards coalition regimes with Socialist participation, the vestigial differences between the EEC group and the original Seven appeared to be irrelevant to what was now coming to be the main issue: How was a balance to be struck between liberalism and socialism, market forces and central control, private enterprise and planning?

The fact that in 1962 the question could be posed in these terms—not as an abstraction, but as something for governments, including the British Government, to make up their minds about —indicated how far removed European politics were by now both from the prewar ambience and from the transatlantic debate. For although the latter touched upon the same issues—at any rate since the advent of an Administration unwilling to sacrifice economic growth to financial orthodoxy—the terms in which it was conducted corresponded to the pre-1914 atmosphere in Edwardian Britain rather than to the European climate of the 1960's. For Americans, the question appeared to be whether liberalism could be made to square with conscious and purposeful direction of society. For Europeans, the liberal philosophy was only one element in a situation that had plainly outgrown the traditional framework of free enterprise and reliance upon the market. The question was how much freedom could be salvaged for the individual—the industrial worker or salaried employee as well as the private entrepreneur—within a planned economy in which the basic decisions were made at the center. To that extent, the "socialization" of economic life—to which even the Catholic Church had begun to lend cautious support, with a Papal Encyclical in 1961 seeking to legitimize the new departure —was publicly recognized as an irreversible trend to which doctrine had to accommodate itself. Governments and political parties were left with the task of creating a mental climate in which the great organized interests could be persuaded to surrender their "freedom" to wreck the economy by pushing sectional bargaining beyond the safety limit. The issue was the same in free-enterprise Belgium and in Socialist Sweden (which had managed to operate economic planning without nationalizing its

principal industries). In the degree to which it cut across previous alignments, it embarrassed all the main democratic parties,
since none could afford to proclaim in public that its venerable
doctrines must in practice be accommodated to a liberal-socialist
compromise.

The Communists, needless to say, were outside this discussion,
since their ossified dogma committed them to the notion that no
basic evolution of Western society was possible without violent
political upheaval and the "dictatorship of the working class,"
i.e., of their own party. Where, as in Italy, this stubborn faith
was beginning to crumble at the edges, the consequent spread of
"revisionist" heresies seemed to presage a general crisis of doubt.[4]
Elsewhere, e.g., in France, the retention of Leninist-Stalinist
orthodoxy was purchased at the price of a doctrinal rigidity so
great that it alarmed the more intelligent and flexible members
of the Party, without as yet affecting the leadership's obstinate
adherence to a policy of opposing both democracy and economic
modernization. In both countries, doctrinal disputes between
orthodox and revisionists clearly corresponded to a political rift
between Stalinist diehards and liberalizers, with the former committed not merely to theoretical "catastrophism," but also to a
deliberate policy of hindering economic growth. If this strategy
obtained the support of the workers, the modernization of Western Europe would be retarded and its resistance to the Soviet bloc
weakened. Hence the difficulty caused for the Italian Communist
Party by the decision, early in 1962, of the Socialists to lend their
support to a Christian-Democrat government that tried to institute something like a functioning planned economy. And
hence, too, the three-cornered struggle between the Gaullist
regime, the democratic opposition parties, and the Communists
in France: the first two committed to economic growth and planning, the latter instinctively determined to hinder the process
in order to prevent the emergence of a genuinely modern industrial society in which the Communist Party would "wither

4 See Leopold Labedz (ed.), *Revisionism: Essays in the History of Marxist
Ideas* (London and New York, 1962), especially Part IV.

away," unless it managed to transform itself into something quite new and not yet seen—a Communist movement genuinely reconciled to democracy. In this struggle, the interest of the French and Italian workers plainly required democratic participation in society's effort to renovate itself, while the strategic concern of world Communism dictated the opposite line. Hence the emerging rift within these parties, and the long-range chances of an internal transformation that would replace the old Stalinist leadership with a "revisionist" one no longer fettered by utopian and destructive ideas of total revolution.

Stalinism, however, is not, in the 1960's, a major issue in West European politics. Its association with the U.S.S.R. and the satellites renders it unattractive to all but the most backward regions west of the geopolitical frontier. Powerful in Greece and Italy, and a potential menace in Spain and Portugal, the Communist Party has in most of Western Europe been thrown upon the defensive. Though in France it still conserves a massive electoral following, its paper strength is disproportionate to its effective hold over the bulk of the industrial workers. Where it grows in size, it seems at the same time to lose its punch. This is not simply a corollary of boom conditions and rising income levels: It points to a deep-seated change of attitude that, in time, is bound to sap the faith of the Party cadres in the effectiveness of the traditional strategy. As the working class becomes more firmly integrated into the new society now growing up on the ruins of the old Europe, the Communist Party cannot indefinitely maintain an attitude that made sense in the apocalyptic climate of the 1940's. Failing a major catastrophe, it must come to terms with the reality of an increasingly modern and prosperous society in which the industrial workers are no longer outsiders, but rather the mass basis of a new social and political hierarchy. It must, in short, become "reformist" or face the danger of losing a large part of its clientele. Where it is not a mere sect, as in Britain and Scandinavia, but a mass movement, this choice is the more urgent because the workers expect "their" party to promote structural changes vaguely associated with "socialism." If the Communist Party fails as an instrument of such change, as it has already failed as an instrument of revolution, of what use is it to its followers?

It must not be thought that the dilemma is uniquely attributable to the industrial boom, or that it affects only the Communist Party. Insofar as Western Europe is beginning to resemble the United States—in respect to income levels, social fluidity, and the breakdown of inherited class and caste structures—its society tends to reproduce some of the patterns of a modern industrial democracy with which Americans are familiar. Concurrently, there arises the problem of reshuffling the traditional division into agrarian-conservative, bourgeois-liberal, and labor-socialist (or communist) parties. These divisions stem from the "first industrial revolution," and are now in part outmoded, at any rate in the more advanced regions of Western Europe. The traditional class structure—landed proprietors, bourgeois owners of industry and commerce, industrial proletariat—which underlies the familiar Marxist three-class model, has begun to dissolve under the impact of technological change and social unheaval. At the same time, the role of the state has changed: from an "executive committee of the bourgeoisie" (in Marx's familiar phrase—originally coined in 1848, when Louis Philippe was on the throne of France's "bourgeois monarchy") it has turned into the arbiter of a society in which capital and labor confront each other as equals, while the growing technocratic and managerial stratum aspires to the coordinating role. Hence the problem of formulating a political doctrine that responds to the altered situation without renouncing traditional attachments.

The issue is not altogether novel. In a sense it has been troubling political theorists since the early years of the century, which was also the time when the European Socialist movement first made the acquaintance of "revisionist" doctrines. But it was only after World War II that thinking really began to catch up with the facts. Even now we still lack an adequate theory of how industrial democracy operates, or can be made to operate, in the age of world-wide economic planning; but we are at least beginning to acquire the rudiments of one. It is, for example, becoming evident that the state can no longer be thought of either as a policeman "holding the ring" while competing private interests slug it out in the market place, or as the instrument of the possessing class in control of the means of production. Such notions—more or less adequate in the nineteenth century, when the first industrial revolution made its impact on Europe—simply will not do in present-day circumstances. A fully developed industrial democracy, with mass organizations barely controllable by an elite of elected leaders, cannot be adequately described in terms derived from classical liberal philosophy. But neither is the traditional socialist doctrine altogether operative in an environment which in many respects resembles that foreseen by Saint-Simonians and Marxians. It is just because so many of their predictions have come true—not, as is sometimes argued, because things have worked out differently—that socialist doctrines have begun to wear a somewhat antiquated look. As a theory of how the industrial revolution would progressively destroy the inherited class structure, socialism—like positivism, which was conceived at the same time, in the 1830's and 1840's—has fully justified itself. Where in recent years it has begun to falter is in its ability to render a coherent account of what is now beginning to be called "the second industrial revolution."[5]

INDUSTRIAL SOCIETY

The concept of industrial society is indeterminate as between the rival economic systems of capitalism and socialism, and for this reason tends to be looked upon with some suspicion by economists and politicians alike. Considering the frequent misuse of an allegedly neutral and "value-free" sociology to underpin conclusions agreeable to the defenders of the *status quo*, this mistrust cannot be described as unjustified. Nonetheless, there is a sense in which an industrial society can be said to have a struc-

[5] For this and the following chapter, see among others: Jean Fourastié, *La grande métamorphose du XXe siècle* (Paris, 1961); Raymond Aron, *La société industrielle et la guerre* (Paris, 1958); Ralf Dahrendorf, *Class and Class Conflict in Industrial Society* (London, 1959); by the same author, *Gesellschaft und Freiheit* (Munich, 1961); G. D. H. Cole, *Studies in Class Structure* (London, 1955).

ture peculiar to it. There is no need to inquire whether societies should be regarded as "organic wholes," or indeed whether the economic "base" can be clearly differentiated from the "social superstructure." There are alternative ways of looking at such matters, but as long as all concerned are agreed that the concepts of "growth" and "evolution" are applicable to the totality of the system, it does not matter much in what language we express the intuition that the "whole" has a specific mode of functioning. The difficulty lies rather in determining the particular historical stage which has been reached at a given moment as a result of some major political upheaval coinciding with a basic change in the underlying social texture. The impact of the two world wars on European society appears to mark a genuine "historical change," inasmuch as it hastened the collapse of the old pre-1914 social order, which, broadly speaking, rested upon a symbiosis of bourgeois and prebourgeois elements, with the latter generally in control of the state. The significance of this fact is open to various interpretations, depending on whether one accepts the notion that bourgeois society is not a completely self-sustaining organism but requires political rule by a nonbourgeois stratum for the most part drawn from the ancient territorial nobility or the bureaucracy and its hangers-on.[6]

This problem is not peculiar to Europe. It has its counterpart in Latin America (though not in the United States). But for historical reasons it is of primary importance to West Europeans, because Western Europe is the only part of the world to have evolved a fully developed bourgeois-capitalist society on the ruins of a feudal past. For the same reason, it is the only Continent where authentic conservative, liberal, and socialist (or communist) parties genuinely confront one another. Elsewhere, one or the other of these elements is commonly missing. Thus the United States has not so far evolved a socialist labor movement

[6] Cf. Joseph A. Schumpeter, *Capitalism, Socialism and Democracy* (London and New York, 1950), pp. 134 ff; for a recent critique of Schumpeter's position, see Allen M. Sievers, *Revolution, Evolution, and the Economic Order* (Englewood Cliffs, N.J., 1962).

(though Australia has done so, and Canada seems about to follow suit), while in some preindustrial countries, parties or movements bearing the socialist label are plainly no more than organizations of the political elite, quite unconcerned with the interests of the working class (which may not even be in existence). The extreme case—but one which by now is not at all uncommon—is that of a "socialist" movement in fact spearheading a capitalist form of economic development. One may hazard the guess that in a good many, if not all, backward countries, this particular form of delusion or self-delusion ("ideology" in the strict Marxist sense) is likely to have a fairly lengthy run. To the despairing question "How can we sell capitalism to the masses?" the obvious answer would appear to be, "By calling it socialism." Such stratagems need not be conscious; they are indeed more likely to be successful if the exponents of the official creed are in good faith. But for obvious reasons they can work only in backward countries and with fairly unsophisticated electorates (if indeed there is any intention of consulting the voters at all). Where democracy and literacy have already had a trial run, most people are likely to see through such conscious or unconscious maneuvers whereby the political elites seek to mobilize support for industrialization policies that must initially demand heavy sacrifices, notably from the peasantry. A relatively backward country that introduces the apparatus of parliamentary democracy *before* industrialization is complete may actually find that while the ruling elite of army officers, politicians, and intellectuals is on the side of forced-draft modernization, the peasant voters will have none of it. In a situation of this kind, the elite then faces the awkward choice of scrapping either democracy or modernization. Turkey is a case in point. In such cases, if the ruling minority decides to press on with modernization against the will of the backward majority, it may find it necessary to seek a legitimation in "socialism." Its political doctrine will then be undemocratic and may come to bear some resemblance to either Fascism or Stalinism—as the case may be—though in point of fact it simply serves to speed industrialization, quite possibly laying the foundation of a subsequent development along fairly ordinary capitalist lines.[7]

This particular problem clearly belongs to the typology of backwardness. In non-Soviet Europe it is of importance only in Turkey, Yugoslavia, Greece, and the Iberian peninsula. Western Europe proper—including Italy, which suffered its last relapse under Fascism—has moved out of the range of forced-draft modernization, and into an era of rapid self-sustained progress under conditions where industrialization begins to pay dividends. In a situation of this kind, the only real threat to political stability comes from mass unemployment (which hits the workers) and/or inflation (which affects primarily the salaried middle class). Political alignments consequently tend to shape themselves around the twin issues of full employment and monetary stability. In a fully industrialized society, "conservatism" signifies not defense of precapitalist interests (e.g., in agriculture), but rather the maintenance of middle-class values and standards such as home ownership, educational privileges, and various amenities associated with possession of individual property. "Liberalism" may come to stand for economic planning—a far cry from Cobdenite or Gladstonian orthodoxy. "Socialism" signifies concern for the status of lower-paid wage earners, while the historic goal of superseding "private ownership of the means of production" is tacitly abandoned, at any rate so long as the economy maintains full employment. The classical case is Scandinavia under Social-Democratic management, but Britain and the remainder of Western Europe show signs of following suit. Under circumstances of this sort, with growing wealth making for political quiescence, socialism loses its revolutionary edge, so that it is finally left to a minority of syndicalists and other enthusiasts to keep the pure flame of faith burning. It is, however, misleading to attribute this change in the political climate to *embourgeoisement* on the part of the workers or their leaders. The fact is that

---

[7] See Rostow, *op. cit.*, where, however, the mechanics of the process are discussed in abstraction from social realities such as class conflict. Rostow regards nationalism as the prime instrument of modernization and does not give sufficient attention to the role of pseudosocialist movements.

a society of this kind, though it may still be capitalist, cannot any longer be described as bourgeois.

The common ground occupied by social classes and political parties in contemporary Western Europe is the welfare state. This term is to be understood as signifying something beyond the enactment of legislation on public housing, unemployment compensation, progressive taxation, and other measures designed to equalize incomes and guarantee a minimum of social stability. Basically, it relates to the maintenance of full employment in a "mixed economy," which is still capitalist in the sense that the majority of investment decisions are made by private firms. Compared with the 1930's, when the unregulated market economy collapsed all over the Western world, the change is twofold: In the first place, the authorities now acknowledge their responsibility for maintaining something like full employment; secondly, the expansion of the public sector, plus governmental control over the central banks, enables them to adopt countercyclical measures, even if "business" (i.e., the private sector) lacks the necessary confidence to invest. A structure of this type is still basically a market economy, in that most decisions are decentralized and made by private individuals; but government intervention restricts the free play of the market in the interest of social stability and an adequate rate of growth. Income redistribution, through taxation and expansion of the social services, has the twofold object of ensuring economic growth and limiting inequalities. The rationale of this policy stems from the recognition that the traditional large disparities in income are no longer needed to provide the savings necessary for capital investment. This role is now increasingly shouldered by the state and by institutional saving of a kind not dependent on private wealth. The welfare state thus rests upon a mixed economy in which the public sector is large enough to set the pace for the kind of growth rate which society considers desirable.

The European boom of the 1950's and 1960's has been in part at least attributable to the adoption of this degree of conscious control over the economy; so, on the other hand, has the inflationary pressure which has now become the chief obstacle to balanced growth. The mixed economy sets targets which are difficult to reconcile: full employment, high investment, equitable income distribution, democratic decision-making, and price stability. The tug between public and private interests, and at a remove between rival political parties, turns upon the issue of achieving a proper balance. In principle, there is nothing in this picture that does not apply to the United States as well as to Western Europe. America led the world in the great depression of the 1930's and in the subsequent introduction of full employment and welfare measures (though it took the war to lift the economy out of its stagnation). Since 1946, the United States has been officially committed to the goal of maintaining a condition of more or less full employment. Yet for reasons having to do with the sociopolitical texture—notably the greater prestige of the business community as compared with Europe—the changeover to Keynesian, or welfare-state, economics has been half-hearted, while the West European governments have consciously adopted the mixed economy as the guideline of public policy. (Even West Germany has done so in fact, though not in form). The Keynesian doctrine that an unregulated market economy will tend to equilibrate at a level below the maximum—or even the optimum—employment of capital and labor is not seriously challenged in Europe, and since mass unemployment is no longer politically tolerable, the governments concerned have more or less consistently adopted the necessary measures to ensure a rate of investment adequate to a state of (almost) full employment. Such measures do not necessarily entail regular budget deficits, but they do make for a level of public spending that precludes a return to low taxation; they also demand a constant effort at income redistribution so as to maintain purchasing power. The record shows that when not upset by wars leading to sudden price fluctuations, the system can cope with inflation while maintaining a rapid rate of growth. The secret of success is public control, not the automatism of the market, which by itself tends towards cyclical depressions and a rate of growth significantly below the optimum level.

Intellectually, the mixed economy is validated by the Keynesian orthodoxy in economics; politically, it corresponds to the pressures generated by a democracy with a strong organized labor movement. And since it is indeterminate as between capitalism and socialism, it can be operated by conservatives, liberals, and socialists alike. Stability is guaranteed as long as the parties respect the principle of balance between the public and private sectors of the economy, with the authorities reserving the right to lay down the general guidelines demanded by public opinion (or, what comes to the same, enforced by the mechanism of majority rule in a democracy). If labor is in power, the system acquires a "laboristic" bent which, however, does not alter its character sufficiently to make it possible for socialists to feel quite at home with it. Laborism is not socialism, though it tends in that direction. In itself it represents a compromise solution whereby society consents to leave the principal means of production—though not essential public utilities such as railways and power stations—in private hands, on the tacit understanding that the regulated market economy will conduce to a state of full, or almost full, employment. Governmental imposition of a growth rate adequate to this purpose follows from the discovery—now scarcely denied any longer by reputable economists—that the market economy by itself tends to stabilize below the full-employment level. The resulting system will naturally be judged by its ability to promote a faster rate of growth, and a correspondingly more rapid rise in living standard, than the market economy of liberalism. Success in this regard being granted, the awkward conclusion from the standpoint of traditional socialism arises from the need to subordinate—temporarily at least—social equality to economic efficiency. There are strong theoretical and practical reasons for doubting whether a genuinely socialist community—i.e., one aiming consciously at the elimination of economic conflict, and ultimately at virtual equality among all citizens—can guarantee a fast rate of growth; it may even have to pay for social equality with economic stability. If this prospect were placed before the electorates of industrial countries, they would probably reject it in favor of a less egalitarian system —either entrepreneurial and liberal or centrally planned—which promised satisfaction of consumer demands. Under democratic conditions, this is perhaps the main obstacle to full socialization, and the principal threat to traditional socialist aims.

It hardly needs emphasis that all this relates only to highly industrialized, and fully democratic, societies. Under preindustrial conditions, state intervention has an altogether different function, though the difference is veiled by the current habit of describing as "socialist" both the welfare state in advanced and the authoritarian state in backward countries. In the latter, state control of the economy aims at speeding the process of industrialization, whereas in a fully developed welfare democracy of the Western type, the need for central control of the market economy arises from the maturity of an industrial society which has outgrown the liberal stage. There is indeed a common factor linking the two types, inasmuch as in both cases it is the failure of the market to sustain a high rate of growth that compels the intervention of the public authorities. In this rather general sense, the imposition of central planning in backward countries can be described as "socialist," though in the long run it may lead to the emergence of a "normal" capitalist market economy. But for theoretical purposes, the two cases must be rigorously distinguished, if only because antidemocratic movements feed on the confusion engendered by describing as "socialist" any and every form of state control, no matter what its political content. If Western democratic socialism is in question, it should be plain that industrial maturity is among its preconditions, just as it should be evident that "socialist" dictatorships are a concomitant of backwardness. The kind of socialism appropriate to industrial society is democratic, and conversely the mixed economy that responds to democratic pressures under conditions of industrial maturity has a socialist, or socializing, bent: not—as conservative writers, following Schumpeter and Hayek, tend to assert—because the intellectual climate is hostile to private enterprise, but rather because the private sector is seen to play a subordinate part in mobilizing society's economic resources and ensuring a sufficiency of aggregate demand. The fact that this particular problem arises under conditions of full industrial maturity—i.e., after the phase of "primitive accumulation of capital" has been left behind—naturally alters the character of the debate between defenders and critics of the market economy. Controversy between liberals and socialists occurs not before but *after* liberal democracy has stabilized itself, and it concerns the problem of safeguarding individual and group freedoms within an increasingly planned and centralized economy. Terminology apart, this debate has little in common with the argument over dictatorial rule in backward countries, where "surplus value" has to be squeezed out of a reluctant peasantry for the purpose of financing industrial construction. "Socialization in a state of maturity," to employ Schumpeter's phrase, is a problem peculiar to cultures that have passed beyond this primitive stage. This is the ultimate reason why arguments between Eastern Communists and Western Socialists tend to be fruitless. Even where both sides employ Marxian language, they are not talking about the same thing.[8]

To stay for a moment longer with the mixed economy and the welfare state: For all the latter's socializing tendencies, it differs radically from a genuinely socialist system, in that the public authorities do not themselves engage in production, but rather act to provide markets for commodities produced by privately owned industry and farming. To the extent that this distinction obtains, even Yugoslavia under a self-styled Communist regime is not completely socialist. It is, however, unnecessary for a socialist system to dispense with pricing and the market. The fact that this has been done in the U.S.S.R. proves nothing except the mental rigidity of the planners. Likewise, there is no need for socialist authorities to do away with private farming. In principle it would be possible for the Soviet Government to restore private property in agriculture (and in small-scale manufacturing and

8 See Schumpeter, *op. cit.,* pp. 219 ff.; Sievers, *op. cit.,* pp. 37 ff.; Karl Polanyi, *The Great Transformation* (Boston, 1957), 223 ff. Polanyi has shown once and for all that the collapse of the unregulated market economy in the 1930's was not accidental but represented the close of a chapter in economic history and the opening of a new one. His conclusions are naturally colored by his socialist presuppositions, but they do not differ significantly from those of the antisocialist Schumpeter.

trade) without compromising the socialist character of the system. That this is not being done has no relevant cause except doctrinal fanaticism, and its sole result is to promote inefficiency and irrationality. A socialist system is compatible with a market economy, provided the basic decisions are made by the planners and provided the public sector is dominant, which in practice means that it must embrace large-scale industry and banking. Conversely, the mixed economy in Western Europe is not socialist as long as governments merely act to ensure a high level of aggregate demand, thus providing the fuel for private investment.[9] As long as capital accumulation proceeds primarily under private control, one cannot speak of socialism. The proper designation of political parties operating a democratic welfare state of this kind is "laborist" rather than "socialist," and the British Labour Party has shown wisdom in retaining its traditional appellation, though it could equally well style itself "Social-Democratic" without misleading anyone: After all, the German and Scandinavian Social-Democrats have long made it plain that the operation of a mixed economy through democratic controls defines the kind of society they want to maintain. This attitude clearly reflects more than the political caution of leadership strata. It is in tune with the limited goals of a mass electorate that, for the present, aims primarily at the satisfaction of consumer demands and the attainment of middle-class living standards. The mixed economy is adequate for these purposes, and as long as it yields economic dividends, the bulk of the working class will be indifferent to the argument that it is not socialism (understood as the elimination of private property in the means

---

[9] Sievers, *op. cit.*, p. 100: "To the extent that the welfare state provides consumers with additional income on a countercyclical basis, it also contributes to the stabilizing of the market system." See also Henry Smith, *The Economics of Socialism Reconsidered* (London and New York, 1962). This is not the place to ventilate the question whether countercyclical policies can be effective unless the "mixed" economy has a large public sector. There is a well-known joke to the effect that Keynesian theories are admirably adapted to a socialist economy but cannot be made to work properly under capitalism because of the instinctive hostility of the business community to anything that looks like central planning.

of production, and "workers' control in industry"). A democracy may vote itself a fully socialist system, but so far this has not happened. Possibly it will not happen until society has become wealthy enough to dispense with the urge for economic growth. The residual surplus could then at last be devoted to noneconomic (and nonmilitary) purposes; plainly for most countries this is a rather distant goal.

The tensions that emerge at this stage of social evolution are common to all mixed societies, whether governed by conservative, liberal, or laborist parties. Basically, they arise from the unsolved problem of establishing a social mechanism whereby conflicting sectional claims can be harmonized without damage to the public interest. By itself, the market economy cannot organize more than the material forces of society. Since these forces are not harmonious, they have to be arbitrated, and once the welfare state is in being, the role of arbiter falls to the government. The great economic interests are so many "solidarity blocs" pressing their sectional claims upon the authorities. Under nineteenth-century liberalism this problem solved itself automatically in favor of the business class, which was virtually in control of the market economy and could inflict crises of "confidence" and mass unemployment upon society whenever its claims were disregarded. Under welfare-state democracy, with capital and labor confronting each other as equals or near-equals, their sectional bargaining tends to promote constant inflationary pressures unless the government steps in. Inflation benefits the strongest sectors—monopolistic industry and the most powerful labor unions—at the expense of the weaker and more numerous members of society. Wage and price increases emerging from the inflationary spiral may even make consumer goods too expensive for the mass of buyers and thus precipitate the familiar cyclical depression due to insufficient demand. If the traditional disciplines of competition and unemployment are no longer adequate to restrain sectional conflicts in a fully democratized society, the public authorities have to step in and impose price and wage controls. Hence the extreme sensitiveness of labor movements to the issue of a wages policy, without which the system cannot be operated.

In the long run it may indeed be to the advantage of trade unions and labor parties to take the initiative in formulating such a policy, which is anyhow in tune with the central tenets of social-ism. But it is precisely at this point that socialist doctrine and laborist interest fail to harmonize. Nothing sounds more reason-able than to say that society must, in the last resort, decide how it wants to remunerate miners, nurses, policemen, etc.; but in practice, "society" boils down to the government of the day and/or the central planning authorities, however democratically controlled. By what criterion—other than that of the market, which may no longer be effective—does one decide how much more a schoolteacher should be paid than a street cleaner? "Where should it all begin? The direct advance will be tentative and slow, and even if ideas of relative value were widely accepted by the public, their application in a free society would not be auto-matic."[10] It is indeed precisely because Western industrial society is free and democratic that the operation of a planned economy raises problems quite unheard-of in lands where freedom is merely a name.

The inability to perceive these facts is among the marks of Soviet theorizing, which still operates with the concept of bour-geois-proletarian class conflict, as though nothing had happened since 1914. The obverse of this mistake is made by those inter-preters of the "conventional wisdom"—with American academ-ics well to the fore—who discuss the welfare state as though it merely signified (in the words of a recent survey already cited) "government responsibility for assuring to all citizens a standard of living at a 'health and decency level' and basic security against life's economic hazards."[11] Although these aims have consistently figured in the literature of Fabianism and "collectivist liberalism" since before 1914, it does not follow that they adequately de-scribe the present state of affairs in Western Europe. (They may designate the current aims and limitations of American liberal-ism, but that is a different matter.) In reality, social-welfare legis-

[10] John Cole, "Approaches to an income policy," *The Guardian*, June 8, 1962.

[11] Dewhurst, *et al.*, *op. cit.*, p. 863.

lation and income redistribution are aspects of a socialization process that circumscribes the operation of the market economy. The other half of this process is constituted by the expansion of public ownership, and by the deliberate establishment of a balance between the public and private sectors. What underlies the whole movement is the persistent tension between social and market values, with the former gradually getting the upper hand. It is misleading to describe this by saying that "the proletariat at the base of the income pyramid and the idle rich at the peak have both disappeared, and people everywhere are acquiring middle-class habits and attitudes along with middle-class incomes."[12] This is the language of political propaganda. The "idle rich" never mattered to anyone but sensational journalists, and the disappearance of the proletariat does not turn the working class into a middle class. (If it is in the "middle," who is at the bottom?) Least of all does it follow that industrial society retains a "bourgeois" complexion. There cannot be a bourgeoisie without a proletariat, and if the one is fading out, so is the other, and for the same reason: Modern industrial society does not require either for its operation. It is useless to pretend that one can have bourgeois society without classes, or a differently stratified society in which everyone belongs (a) to the middle class, (b) to no class at all. Yet American sociology seems largely devoted to the hopeless task of affirming both these contradictory propositions at once. It thus threatens to become the inverted mirror image of the Soviet theorizing it is trying to combat.

The reality is that contemporary industrial society is increasingly "postbourgeois," the nineteenth-century class structure tending to dissolve along with the institution of private entrepreneurship on which it pivoted. Hence the uncertainty that afflicts so much of current political thinking. The "crisis of socialism" is also a "crisis of liberalism," not to mention the conservative defenders of preindustrial traditions, which indeed are now virtually identified with backward countries. In Western Europe proper, "conservatism"—whether on the British Tory

12 *Ibid.*

model or the corresponding Christian-Democratic formations in Continental Europe—is in principle classless rather than aristocratic, and in practice a defensive organization of the old and new middle classes. Like other political movements it is torn between the conflicting claims of social and market values, though the dominant role of the business community within the middle class tends to weight the scales persistently in one direction. Conversely, the evolution of the traditional socialist movement since 1945 has proceded along the lines of transforming it into an alliance of organized labor and a section of the professional middle class, with the technical intelligentsia as its core. It is this transformation that distinguishes modern socialism from the pre-1945 variety and that causes political figures like Mr. Gaitskell or M. Mendès-France to present so strange an appearance against the background of cloth-capped class consciousness typical of the traditional labor movement.[13]

If the foregoing remarks deal primarily with the conflicting claims of liberal and socialist theorizing, the reason is that one cannot seriously speak of a conservative sociology (setting aside the traditional Catholic doctrine, whose practical application appears for the moment to have run aground amid the sandbanks and shallows of the "corporate state"). Western European Christian-Democracy is a "solidarity bloc" of middle-class and peasant interests, held together by the desire to slow down the tempo of social change so as to make it tolerable to those concerned, plus a left wing of Catholic labor unions with quasisocialist tendencies. Its doctrine is necessarily eclectic, though on the whole democratic. Elsewhere, conservatism presents itself as an amalgam of traditional preindustrial, and modern big-business, atti-

[13] The defeat of the British Labour Party in the 1959 general election gave rise to a lively controversy on this subject, which at one stage threatened to disrupt the Party, until the "modernizers" got the upper hand. It also produced some interesting literary by-products; see in particular Mark Abrams and Richard Rose, *Must Labour Lose?* (London and Baltimore, 1960), and S. M. Lipset, "Must the Tories Always Win?" in *The New Leader*, November 7, 1960. Possibly the discussion would have benefited if the participants had been less obsessed with the notion that opinion polls are a safe guide to the class structure.

tudes. The "thinking" it inspires is of the kind associated with privileged classes all over the world: Mountains labor and bring forth the *status quo*. It would be unprofitable to inquire into the rationale of British Toryism since the end of Empire deprived it of its traditional *raison d'être*, and in any case it does not possess a distinctive theory of modern society. The same may be said of other conservatives parties committed to the defense of traditional hierarchies and established values. Gaullism makes a partial exception: Its intellectual spokesmen appear to be moving towards a doctrine in which technocratic echoes mingle with authoritarian notions of planning and state control. They seem at least to have grasped the fact—apparently still concealed from their liberal critics—that parliamentary government of the classical kind is no longer feasible. At this point they encounter their left-wing opponents, who are likewise committed to central planning, though with more emphasis upon popular participation. On the whole, conservative parties and schools of thought appear uncertainly suspended between preliberal and postliberal attitudes and modes of thought. At the extremes, Fascist slogans of elite rule, and Communist harping on the class struggle, set up a minor cacophony of discordant noises. For all their verbal ruthlessness, these totalitarian movements are beginning to look somewhat dated when set against the backdrop of contemporary Western society, though they are still capable of impressing and confusing the intellectual elites of backward countries. Of the two, Fascism derives some short-term advantage from its traditional association with nationalism, but fails all the more decisively in the long run. Its intellectual equipment is anyhow too meager to warrant serious consideration. The rival totalitarian movement is in temporary disarray, Stalinism having been discredited, at any rate in Western Europe, which leaves the Communist Party with the problem of bringing its petrified doctrine up to date. We are thus left with the difference between liberal and socialist theories of what has been happening to Europe's traditional structure, and with the political philosophies respectively derived from classical liberalism and nineteenth-century

socialism—the latter of course primarily Marxian, though not exclusively so.

It would be tempting at this point to engage in a critical review of what has been happening to socialist theory since its formulation by Saint-Simon, Proudhon, and Marx in the past century. The temptation has to be resisted. The subject is endless
and calls for separate treatment. But since a good deal has been
said, in the course of this analysis of European developments
since 1945, about the transformation of the market economy into
something resembling a synthesis of liberal capitalism and socialism, a word of caution may be in place: It is beginning to
look as though the mixed economy may become the forerunner
of something resembling a genuinely planned one, but it does
not necessarily follow that democratic socialists will be any hap-
pier than liberals with some of the political consequences of this
evolution. Leaving aside the Soviet orbit, which is perhaps too
immature politically and economically to count for our purpose
—many of its problems of growth seem due to lack of capital and
similar marks of underdevelopment—it is still possible to say
that, despite the growth of central planning, democratic forms
of public life have been preserved and even strengthened. It cannot be denied, however, that there has in recent years been a
remarkable outcrop of technocratic tendencies—notably in such
unlikely places as France. By technocracy is meant a tendency for
authoritarian regulation of economic life, of a kind that is not,
properly speaking, either liberal or socialist, and whose pivotal
elements are neither employers nor industrial workers, but the
planners themselves and their hangers-on, plus the managerial
stratum as a whole. If this tendency should continue unchecked,
state control may come to mean—temporarily anyhow—the rule
of a new privileged stratum (not a "class," and certainly not a
"new class," but rather a political elite with technical functions
and a near-monopoly of specialized knowledge). This would be a
curious gloss on some of the utopias we have been promised. The
awkward thing is that such a state of affairs might even have to
be regarded as "historically progressive" (whatever that may
mean) while it lasts. So far, this is no more than a rather large

cloud on the horizon. It will probably depend on the political maturity of democratic electorates whether the threat materializes.

FREEDOM AND EQUALITY

Forty-five years after the French Revolution, most of Europe had absorbed the consequences of that upheaval, and liberalism had become respectable, though democracy had not. It is pertinent to inquire whether four and a half decades after the cataclysm of 1917, the Russian Revolution has likewise ceased to appear either very promising or very alarming. No doubt the point where the comparison breaks down is marked by the actual political relationship between the U.S.S.R. and the West. In the 1830's, Jacobinism had run out of steam, and France had ceased to terrify her neighbors. In the 1960's, Bolshevism looks distinctly old-fashioned, but the Soviet Union is far from a reassuring presence. Hence the persistent habit of viewing all contemporary social transformations in terms of whether or not they correspond to the forecasts made by Marxism-Leninism. Yet it is becoming increasingly obvious that this is the wrong way to approach the subject. Classical Marxism has been quietly absorbed into democratic socialism and—partly—into academic philosophy and sociology; as for Leninism, it is simply an irrelevance. No one, whatever his political predilections, can even begin to make sense of the European scene today by applying Leninist categories. The only rational approach is to disregard altogether what Soviet writers may have to say about matters outside their own country and to treat Western Europe as a society that has outgrown the particular phase of class conflict associated with earlier stages of the industrial revolution. To say this is not to fall in with the current academic fashion of pretending that there never was such an era; it is simply to recognize that it is now closed.

Once this is admitted, one can begin to ask meaningful questions. One can, for example, ask in what sense Western Europe may be said to have undergone a social transformation during the past half century. Sociologists in Britain and elsewhere have in recent years debated this question and come up with answers which, for all the inevitable disagreements due to conflicting viewpoints and predispositions, have enough in common to suggest some degree of unanimity over fundamentals.[14] Thus it is possible to differ over the extent to which welfare legislation has really transformed the conditions of life of the majority, and yet to agree that something like a social revolution has occurred by comparison with the pre-1914 age, when mass unemployment and pauperization were the rule. The same half century saw a radical improvement in health conditions, and here again it may be questioned how much of this was due to technological change, how much to growing wealth, and how much to social legislation.[15] Whatever the precise answers to these and similar questions, few people would deny that West Europeans live today in an environment that differs significantly from the pre-1914 one (if only because the automobile has transformed daily life). To take an example: The number of children born to each family in Britain during the late nineteenth century was well over four, while at present it does not reach two and a half, and this change signifies not only a greater life expectancy for the majority, but also a radical alteration in the status of women, especially working-class women, about half of whom around 1900 gave birth to between seven and fifteen children. Anyone is free to dispute that this has been primarily the consequence of welfare legislation, but no one can deny that it amounts to a transformation in living conditions, social habits, and mental patterns. The same may be said of the spread of home ownership and the acquisition of "consumer durables" by a growing stratum of

[14] See Cole, *op. cit., passim;* Aron, *op. cit.;* Dahrendorf, *Gesellschaft und Freiheit,* pp. 133 ff.; also Peter Laslett, "The Social Revolution of our Time," *The Listener,* January 11, 1962; Richard Wollheim, "Socialism and Culture," Fabian Tract 331, May, 1961; V. L. Allen, "White Collar Revolt," *The Listener,* November 30, 1961.

[15] Laslett notes that whereas in 1898 no fewer than 13,000 people in England and Wales died of the measles, by 1948 this number had dropped to about 300, while diphtheria deaths fell from 7,500 to 150. He suggests that such changes "can only be counted as marking a deliberate transformation consciously contrived," though the term "revolution" is not necessarily appropriate to them.

semiskilled workers, white-collar employees, and technicians no longer subject to frequent unemployment. That this is not the tiny "labor aristocracy" of Leninist imagination is evidenced by the fact that in their daily practice the Communist parties themselves have quietly adapted themselves to the existence of this stratum, and even drawn support from it. Here, too, one may question whether this is more than an acceleration of trends visible before 1914, but the salient fact is that the acceleration has coincided with the sociopolitical changes already mentioned. To the extent that full employment tends to even out income differentials and living standards between skilled and unskilled workers, or between workers and clerical staffs, the social changes thereby set in motion amount to an alteration of the class structure, which in turn is politically relevant. Social leveling makes for political leveling, and thus ultimately renders it easier to operate a democratic system based on some degree of consent and mutual comprehension. In the measure that this happens, democracy ceases to be "bourgeois democracy," without thereby becoming socialist. This is only one instance of the semantic problem encountered by sociologists who take these terms seriously. There is nothing wrong with the terms; some of them happen to be in need of adaptation because the situation has changed.[16]

When it comes to assessing the political relevance of changed patterns of income or employment, we encounter the familiar problem of disentangling factual from value statements, but even at the factual level it is not always easy to distinguish what is happening from its presumptive consequences. To take another instance, the statistician notes that whereas in 1900 personal domestic service was the principal occupation of all employed women in England—there being 1.5 million servants among the 4 million women at work—by 1960 the female domestic servant

[16] For some of the implications of this splitting up of the modern industrial labor force, see Cole, *op. cit.*, pp. 26 ff. The most recent trend towards the numerical contraction of the actual work force, and the parallel expansion of clerical and administrative occupations, has led to a further differentiation within the industrial pyramid, with technologists and research workers forming themselves into a new elite based on special training. None of this precisely fits the inherited categories, liberal or socialist.

had almost disappeared, while simultaneously the number of women clerks employed in offices reached the number of domestic servants sixty years earlier. So far, so good. It is, however, much more difficult to establish whether the high proportion of women workers in clerical jobs is connected with the fact that "almost two-thirds of the unorganized employees in Britain are in white-collar employment."[17] There is an obvious presumption to that effect, but it may also be that antiunion tendencies affect male and female clerical employees equally. Meanwhile, in recent years, full employment, social leveling, inflation, and office mechanization have quietly combined to erode the status differences between blue-collar and white-collar workers, and to that extent facilitated the task of union organizers and induced hitherto resistant strata to practice collective bargaining, and even go on strike. These conflicting tendencies are simultaneously at work, and—depending on their orientation—rival schools of sociology and political philosophy will interpret their relevance differently. The most one can say, without overtly taking sides, is that conservatives will emphasize status differences and try to promote a graded hierarchy, while liberals will stress the importance of skill and the "career open to the talents," and socialists will, as before, put the emphasis on equality and the greatest satisfaction of the greatest number. And each party will claim, with evident sincerity, to be concerned with "social justice"—the definition of "justice" being a value problem and thus ultimately a philosophical issue. Yet all concerned are dependent on the same set of facts and must somehow shape their policies to take account of social trends that are only in part open to conscious direction.

It is of course precisely this margin of freedom—freedom to shape the conditions under which people live and work—that constitutes the real field of political conflict. Socialist egalitarianism, liberal insistence on free competition, conservative preference for traditional status differences are relevant insofar as there exists an area of actual choice. One assumes that there is a certain range of possibilities—midway between "material reality"

[17] Allen, *loc. cit.*

and "ideological differences"—where people can actually decide how they want to live or what sacrifices they are prepared to make. The assumption is true for some individuals under most circumstances, but it is only in a rapidly evolving and socially fluid environment that the majority of people are conscious of it as a real possibility. This is perhaps the nearest one can come to a description of what "democracy" actually means to the electorate of a fully industrialized society. It clearly means something qualitatively different from the organization of class and sectional interests, although these are never lost sight of. When there is a modicum of security, with the basic material needs more or less satisfied or guaranteed in principle, democracy assumes the form of debate and conflict over alternative ways of organizing social life. Housing and education may then become more important than the level of incomes. It would be foolish to pretend that Western Europe as a whole has already passed into this stage, but some parts of it have, and the trend is plainly in this direction. Against such a background, the residual conflicts between "Christian Democrats" and "Social Democrats," "Conservatives" and "Liberals," reduce themselves to a search for alternative ways of organizing the collective life of a community with a certain fundamental consensus of values tacitly shared by "middle" and "working" classes alike.

From the sociologist's standpoint, the validity of this picture will largely depend on one's notion of how important the inherited class structure still is, or indeed whether we are not perhaps moving into a situation where classes in the traditional sense will cease to have much meaning. Liberals of course have always disclaimed any major concern with class, while socialists and—for different reasons—traditionalists have made the most of it. In liberal-individualist doctrine, class differentiations are regrettable and transitory residues of the fixed status groups ("estates") of preindustrial society, whereas socialists have tended to affirm that, on the contrary, classes come into being as a consequence of the process of industrialization, which counterposes entrepreneurs ("owners of means of production") and propertyless salaried workers. Nowadays, liberals and orthodox Marxists tend to suffer from the same fixation upon what happened between 1830 and 1930, when the industrial revolution transformed European society, to the accompaniment of acute conflict between bourgeoisie and proletariat. The result is that both schools go on arguing over an issue that is rapidly becoming marginal: namely, whether modern postbourgeois industrial society is split into classes. It would be more sensible to inquire what sort of stratification is likely to take place once the technological revolution has been absorbed; but social theory is always a few steps behind the facts. In a country like Britain, where the old preindustrial aristocracy has retained its social privileges and some political influence, one can even find people arguing in all seriousness whether titles of nobility should continue to be bestowed upon businessmen and union leaders. All this belongs to the serio-comic side of social life and has little, if any, political relevance. "Class" as the embodiment of social control by a privileged minority, and "class" as the more or less illusory possession of conventional marks of social distinction, are different matters. The first is a serious theoretical and practical issue; the second is best left to journalists and popular novelists.[18]

If one abstracts from trivialities such as "status consciousness" or "Establishment culture," which have really to do with caste rather than class, one is left with the problem of characterizing a society that is still largely capitalist but no longer bourgeois. In such a society, stratification tends to correspond partly to ownership of capital, partly to rank within the industrial hierarchy, with organizers, scientists, and technologists usurping some of the prerogatives of the old entrepreneurial stratum. Although

[18] To avoid misunderstanding, it should be emphasized that these remarks refer to Western Europe. In the United States—so far as an outsider can judge—the official credo prescribes belief in the proposition that (a) in a democracy there are no classes, (b) everyone belongs, or ought to belong, to the middle class, (c) it depends entirely upon an individual's evaluation of his own personal social status to which class he belongs. The last-named notion, for obvious reasons, is popular among authors of fiction. Of late, it has also acquired some currency among European political writers who have mistaken the jargon of market research for sociology, but it does not have the force of dogma it appears to possess in the United States.

there are good reasons for rejecting the well-known concept of a "managerial revolution"—if only because "the managers" have hitherto been remarkably reluctant to think and act as a group.[19] —this emergence of a hierarchy partly based on technical skill does constitute something new. It also poses a problem for adherents of all the major political schools. Conservatives tend instinctively to welcome the idea of status hierarchies, but their sympathies have hitherto been engaged on the side of preindustrial cultures and landed aristocracies: It is difficult to make Burke's or Hegel's philosophy rhyme with the reality of modern society. Liberals are all for industrial progress and scientific management, but most of them still fight shy of technocracy and central planning. Socialists favor planning and public ownership, but are reluctant to legitimize major status and income differentials. Fascism—perhaps the only consistent elitist doctrine in existence—has been discredited by the criminal lunacy of its adherents. Stalinism as a doctrine accords fairly well with the reality of untrammeled rule by a political elite drawn in large part from the new directing stratum, but most Communists, for political reasons, are now compelled to proclaim that they are opposed to it; and in any case even the more intelligent and critical among them have not yet grasped the *social* significance of Stalinist rule. This is another instance of political theory lagging behind the facts. We live in an environment that has been transformed by technological change, two world wars, and a social upheaval, but politicians and writers go on debating the issues in terms drawn from past controversies. A degree of conservatism in such matters is useful, because there are after all some factors that do not change; but in important respects social theory is now seriously out of step. Just as many Europeans of the older generation have not yet digested the fact that the sovereign nation-state has become a piece of useless lumber, so there is a marked reluctance to acknowledge that the issue of freedom and equality cannot be posed any longer in the traditional nineteenth-century manner. Democracy in Western Europe is now firmly

19 See Cole, *op. cit.*, pp. 98 ff.

established, but its theoretical clarification leaves much to be desired. This is not solely due to the Marxists, though in recent years they have added to the confusion by closing their eyes to some quite evident social changes and ignoring Marx's own hints on the subject; it is the fault of all parties. They are reluctant to admit that the reality confronting them is no longer quite that to which their doctrines were once attuned.

A good instance of this lag is provided by recent attempts to revise socialist doctrine so as to make it relevant to current practice. In West Germany, this has taken the form of a wholesale abandonment not only of the remnants of Marxist terminology, but even of the traditional socialist commitment to public ownership (though not of public control over the market economy). In France, on the other hand, we have in recent years witnessed the curious spectacle of M. Mendès-France—a Keynesian liberal if ever there was one—blossoming out as the leader of the more left-wing of two Socialist parties. Apparently this has been due— aside from personal factors—to a growing belief among progressive economists and planners that the French economy requires more energetic central direction than it is likely to obtain under the somewhat conservative Gaullist regime, for all the latter's evident technocratic leanings. In Italy, the Socialists appear to be moving towards partnership with the ruling Christian-Democrats, thereby reinforcing a general West European trend. The British case is the best known of all, though not necessarily the best understood. It is usually interpreted as a struggle over the Labour Party's traditional commitment to public ownership of industry (quaintly described as "Marxist" in some quarters, though in fact the platform was drafted by the patriarch of Fabianism, Sidney Webb).[20] There is reason to believe, however,

20 The relevant clause of the 1918 document, which for the first time committed the Labour Party to a socialist doctrine, refers briefly to "the common ownership of the means of production and the best obtainable system of popular administration and control of each industry or service." (See Henry Pelling, *A Short History of the Labour Party* [London and New York, 1961], p. 44). This elastic formula makes a vague concession to syndicalism, which in practice has not borne fruit.

that the attempt to modernize the party's image would have led to a violent dispute even if the leadership had not chosen (rather foolishly, in the opinion of some uncommitted observers) to make an issue of this particular clause in the program. The conflict really turns upon the question whether "socialism" means more than central control and the administration of a "planned" economy that is also a "mixed" one. Of course it does, but modern "revisionist" Socialists are loth to admit in public that, for the time being, the only practical goal is how to make the mixed economy work. It goes against the grain to have to acknowledge that this halfway house is the most that can be hoped for, just as Conservatives and Liberals are reluctant to concede that it is also becoming their own habitat. Let it be remarked once more that even a "socialist" planned economy, i.e., one in which the public sector dominates the field and embraces all or most of large-scale industry, may—and probably will—fall short of the socialist ideal of income and status equality. Indeed, it may conflict with it, inasmuch as economic efficiency will make for large differentials in income (though not in privately owned wealth) and authority. We are really dealing with three different problems: the mixed economy; socialist planning; and the (possibly unrealizable) goal of a society from which economic conflict has disappeared. It is only the last-mentioned that corresponds to socialism as an ethical ideal, as distinct from an economic blueprint.

For evident reasons, these issues are intimately linked with social dominance and political power. In a fully open society, class consciousness would either disappear or depend on each individual's temporary occupation or achievement. But no such society exists—least of all in Britain, where the social order is weighed down by irrelevant status differences on top of the inherited class structure. By any criterion, Britain is less democratic than most European countries, not to mention the United States. It is, on the other hand, so fully industrialized as to give very great potential political weight to the organized working class. Precisely for this reason, the built-in weaknesses and limitations of this class and its political party are apparent to the naked eye. One can almost risk saying that the brief experiment of Labour rule in postwar Britain has been instructive chiefly for its effect in making plain the political immaturity of the working class. On the other hand, there is no doubt that the thinking minority within the labor movement tends instinctively to press for goals that ultimately transcend the welfare state and issue in something that can perhaps be designated as socialism. Whether this is feasible in the present generation (and in a country so dependent on world trade as Britain) is another matter. If it should turn out to be a utopian expectation, one can confidently forecast a further growth of romantic rebelliousness among the minority of active Socialists committed to something radically different from the present order. Romanticism and utopia go together. What is unattainable appears the more desirable, and conversely, desires fasten upon the future because the present is both unattractive and unalterable. It may be that European Socialism faces a "crisis of conscience" as it becomes more evident that the current social compromise is the best that can be obtained for the time being. At any rate, these are among the real issues, as distinct from the spurious ones so often ventilated in newspapers and election tracts.[21]

If Socialists are in a quandary over "laborism" and the permanence of the welfare state, so are their opponents. To be consistent they have to assert that centralized management of the economy, and public provision of social services, are undesirable expedients, temporarily adopted for the sake of necessity but not to be retained a moment longer than required. This litany is indeed the persistent theme of the more old-fashioned kind of

---

[21] The 1956 Labour Party platform, *Towards Equality,* which inaugurated the retreat from complete socialization, was described by an unfriendly critic as an unsuccessful attempt to replace Marx by Freud. Behind this kind of irony lurks the uncomfortable awareness of some Conservatives that the Britain they are trying to preserve is a remarkably undemocratic country. It is true that the Labour Party has in recent years seemed to worry more about equality of status than about public ownership; it is also true that social equality is what many Tories dislike most.

Conservative and Liberal rhetoric, not only in Britain. It can be summed up in the statement that "the true object of the Welfare State, for the Liberal, is to teach people to do without it."[22] How far the surviving exponents of self-help—now linked with the antiplanners in a rearguard outflanked on all sides by the steady drift of events—genuinely believe in the practicality of such slogans is another matter. It is easy enough to assert that the individual should be master of his fate; that he should be free to spend his income as he sees fit; and that his personal liberty is best guaranteed by ownership of property. When it comes to making these prescriptions work, individualism commonly turns out to have meaning chiefly for those who already possess some property. For the others, it translates itself into the suggestion that they would do better to entrust their savings to private (i.e., corporate) welfare and insurance bodies instead of relying on the community. Why this should make them more independent is not explained, just as one is never told why private schools are preferable to state schools (except for the obvious reason that they may be able to provide superior education for a wealthy minority). The fact is that European liberalism for the most part remains obstinately middle-class in its outlook; its assumptions do not fit the reality of a society in which the great majority are salary earners, for whom the only choice is between publicly provided services or none at all. These services may in many instances be second-rate compared with the best that private enterprise can provide; but they are better than nothing, and nothing is precisely what most people would be getting if they were dismantled. In this instance, the conflict between freedom and equality translates itself so clearly into an argument between a privileged minority and the great majority that it is not sur-

22 Professor Alan Peacock, quoted by Mr. P. Towsend, in the *New Statesman,* April 14, 1961; for the fullest and most consistent exposition of the pure *laissez-faire* doctrine, see F. A. Hayek's major work, *The Constitution of Liberty* (London and Chicago, 1960). It is only fair to add that this testament of nineteenth-century liberalism proved too much even for *The Economist,* whose reviewer described it as a theoretical "Tower of Pisa, skewed at its foundations and pointing a long way out of true."

prising to find democratic electorates steadily turning their backs upon parties committed to classical liberalism.[23]

In intellectual terms—though not politically—the case for modern Conservatism is more easily stated. Genuine Conservatives are in the happy position of not believing in either freedom or equality, except for a minority, so that for them this particular problem does not exist. If they possessed the courage of their convictions, they would restrict voting rights to owners of property, plus the upper ranks of the managerial hierarchy; since this is not feasible, they rely on rearguard actions and the strengthening of corporate positions and privilege. Ultimately, a long spell of Conservative rule would presumably issue in the piecemeal demolition of liberal democracy and the institution of a "corporate state," with the controllers of the great corporations firmly in charge of the government as well as the economy (which might be more or less "planned" in the interest of preserving the *status quo*). Such a state of affairs has many attractions for stagnant classes and traditional-minded people, and might even tempt a few businessmen. The only trouble is that it would promote economic stagnation of a kind that no modern industrial country can afford, on pain of being taken over by more energetic rivals. Conservatism in practice thus inevitably disappoints its ideologists, who pine for a stable hierarchial order, with fixed status positions and a minimum of public debate. When in office, and under pressure to secure public support, Conservatives in a democracy unfailingly acquire the label "progressive," and a progressive Conservative is really not very different from a Liberal. Corporate rule has never been seriously attempted except under Fascism; and it was a failure even then. The fact is that modern electorates cannot be made to believe in such obvious shams, and a modicum of consent being required, the experiment can get under way only in the most stagnant and backward countries.

Does all this mean that there are no genuine problems left,

---

[23] Except where (as lately in England) they have revamped their platform to take account of the existence of salary earners. But in such cases it becomes questionable whether they should still describe their doctrine as "liberal."

and that Western European society has now acquired the kind of political stability that eluded it in the interval between the two world wars?

Not quite. Pluralist democracy has indeed come to stay, and even looks like becoming so deeply entrenched that most people may soon be unable to conceive of any other way of managing public affairs. Stability, however, continues to elude us. This is in part due to the international tensions that inevitably refract themselves on the European level; in part it arises from the dynamic of industrial society and from the unsolved problem of "marrying" its scientific techniques to political and social institutions capable of giving expression to the popular will; and in part it may be surmised that it stems from the awkward circumstance that the popular will itself is still unformed.

To begin with the last-mentioned consideration, it is by no means certain yet that popular feeling—as distinct from official "public opinion"—has come to terms with the erosion of national sovereignty, the diminished role of Europe on the world scene, and the new relationship between the old imperial powers and their former subjects. The violent convulsions produced in France by the Algerian war are symptomatic of a disorder that exists elsewhere in a milder form: It can be witnessed in contemporary Britain whenever racialism is given a chance to raise its head. The "end of empire" has had a traumatic impact upon important strata of society, and it is still an open question to what extent the new European consciousness can effectively fill the emotional void left by the dissolution of traditional attachments. Unfortunately, it is an illusion—to which liberal and socialist intellectuals are particularly prone—to suppose that in these matters the popular mind can be relied upon to come spontaneously to the rescue of advanced thinkers and progressive minorities. In the long run it is doubtless true that democracy favors enlightenment and the abatement of tensions, but it does so only if a lead is given by those in control and backed up by the intelligentsia; the latter's attitude being probably the key factor. In a way this is a reassuring thought, since it implies that rational discussion will in the end have an effect in molding popular attitudes; but it also underlines the danger of trusting to luck. Controlling minorities of the wrong sort can do enormous damage without encountering any significant resistance. The experience of Germany during the Third Reich is proof of it. Contrary to the sentimental populist myth, the "common man" is not necessarily on the side of enlightenment. Sociologists know that working-class attitudes are basically more conservative than middle-class ones, and that the values they conserve are not wholly admirable. Democracy supplies a mechanism whereby these attitudes can in time be changed, but only a mechanism. The machinery has to be powered by people who feel sufficiently strongly about their beliefs to brave temporary unpopularity. It is probably safe to risk the generalization that within each social class the main resistance to progress comes from the bottom rather than the top. Majority attitudes are always ambivalent on the subject of change. Even the "revolutionary proletariat" (where it still exists, i.e., in backward countries now going through the first phase of the industrial revolution) is made up of individuals who in their private lives are obstinately attached to traditional values—and often all the more rebellious politically because their habitual way of life has been disturbed. But even under Western conditions, working-class conservatism is probably a bigger handicap to liberal or socialist movements than all the real or imagined machinations of entrenched reactionaries. The latter indeed would be unable to operate with any degree of success if they could not evoke deeply rooted popular sentiments. Especially in relation to foreigners and, *a fortiori,* members of other "races," such sentiments tend to be instinctively hostile—whatever sentimentalists may assert to the contrary.

Now it may be questioned whether such problems of adaptation to change are easier to cope with under circumstances where there is no firm commitment to principles or values tacitly accepted by the whole society. Modern democracy is pluralist, not only in that it allows people to divide their loyalties among a multitude of free associations, but also in its tendency to make do without a framework of universally shared beliefs and convictions. The obverse of liberalism is cultural relativism, and while this makes for tolerance it also makes for uncertainty over first principles. There is perhaps no inherent reason why contemporary Western society should not eventually develop a new consensus to take the place of the vanishing religious integration; but it has to be recognized that at present we are in a rather uncomfortable in-between stage, with the traditional loyalties losing ground and nothing very definite taking their place for most people. In Western Europe this process has been going on for some two centuries, but here, too, the recent acceleration has led to a qualitative change in feeling. Where formerly skepticism over fundamentals was confined to small intellectual elites, it has now been democratized and generalized, to the point where one can hardly open a newspaper, or turn on the radio, without coming upon a discussion (usually rather unsatisfactory) on the "loss of faith," or the "spiritual uprootedness," experienced by what is vaguely known as "the modern age." This situation seems to be peculiar to highly civilized countries and is therefore likely to become more acute. Conservatives will of course blame progressives for aggravating this state of affairs by undermining traditional beliefs, and they may even be tempted to clamp an artificial consensus upon societies whose evolution points away from religious attachments. Such anxieties are at least justified in the sense that rapid technological and social change does threaten the stability of institutions whose permanence has long been taken for granted. It is, for example, by no means certain that the family can survive the collapse of the bourgeois mode of life. What this is likely to mean in terms of cultural strains and psychological changes can at present barely be surmised.

Lastly, if one wants to speculate over the probable future of Western Europe as a distinctive civilization, there is the impact of mass education—or half-education—upon a culture that has long been stratified into an elite and the rest. This is once more a general problem, but it is one that Europeans are peculiarly conscious of, because the growth of equalitarianism does impose special strains upon a society whose patterns were formed under quite different conditions. Even today, with all the spread of mass education, this society has not really begun to close the gap between the privileged elite and the masses; in some areas it may even be widening. Here, too, political choices suggest themselves at the same time that democracy becomes a reality for the majority—a majority that is only now beginning to enter into the heritage of former ruling classes. Inevitably there are tensions, and some tendencies towards extremism, whether democratic or authoritarian. Not all conservatives are as candid as Clive Bell, who years ago calmly laid it down that "civilization requires the existence of a leisured class, and a leisured class requires the existence of slaves. . . . On inequality all civilizations have stood. The Athenians had their slaves: the class that gave Florence her culture was maintained by a voteless proletariat: only the Esquimaux and their like enjoy the blessings of social justice."[24] Taken seriously and pushed to their conclusion, such sentiments issue in fascism or some other form of elitism. The danger for democrats lies in supposing that these notions can be effectively countered by preaching the gospel of complete equality; whereas, in fact, with the present level of mass culture, radical egalitarianism could only produce a general retreat to something distinctly inferior to what we have. Even if educational standards were drastically improved, it would still remain true that creativeness is, and always must be, the prerogative of a minority (though not necessarily a socially privileged one). The relationship between a society and its culture—or if one likes, its intellectual elite—is inevitably a "dialectical" one: There has to be tension as well as consent. The failure to recognize this is among the reasons why Soviet literature is so unutterably boring, but "socialist realism" in the U.S.S.R. is not the only instance of officially sponsored conformism and mediocrity. There is a problem here that becomes more acute as modern society becomes more democratic, while at the same time the channels of communication are controlled either by governments with an ax to grind, or by commercial hucksters with no aim beyond the maximization of profit. Again, there is nothing specifically European about this conjunc-

[24] *Civilization* (London, 1947), pp. 127, 130; cf. C. A. R. Crosland, *The Future of Socialism* (London and New York, 1956), pp. 238 ff.; Wollheim, *op. cit., passim.*

tion, but it so happens that public opinion in Western Europe is only now becoming conscious of it.

To sum up, Western Europe is belatedly "Americanizing" itself and in the process acquiring some of the characteristic strains, as well as the familiar material appurtenances, of a fully industrialized society. "Mass culture," democratic pluralism, the impact of piecemeal socialization, and the retreat from overseas empire and unrestricted national sovereignty are all making their impact more or less simultaneously. This is among the reasons why European political alignments have remained more sharply defined and "ideological" than the corresponding American patterns. When a traditional society goes into the melting pot, it inevitably reacts more violently than does a civilization that is still moving ahead under its own steam and along fairly familiar routes. American public life has commonly struck the European as relatively free from grave conflict, and for the same reason as somewhat uninteresting. This state of affairs may change as Americans increasingly come to divide over genuine issues of foreign policy, racial equality, and social organization, as distinct from the rather spurious disagreements that have hitherto seemed to monopolize their attention. Even so, it seems probable that Europe will continue to set the pace in formulating sharply defined issues in political philosophy. The range of deeply contrasting national and cultural patterns—one need only consider the historic differences separating, e.g., Sweden from Spain—is such that European life, however standardized technologically, can never approach the relative uniformity of the United States. Nor is there any good reason why it should. In a world of continental agglomerations, Europe's intricate pattern of national and regional differences is not the least of its charms.

There is, too, the uneven impact of world-political tensions upon the various members of the European-Atlantic world. Although West European "neutralism" is a chimera, it is not unreasonable to hold that both the major world powers have an interest in not wrecking the highly industrialized, and correspondingly fragile, civilization of Western Europe. By thermonuclear standards, the European nation-state is anyhow an anachronism.

While this realization may promote pan-European schemes at the military level, it cannot fail to make each of the countries concerned more conscious of the need for peace and international organization. These countries are thus likely to become pace-makers in movements for lessening world tensions and giving greater authority to supranational bodies such as the United Nations. One sees the tendency at work in small, peaceful countries such as Holland or Ireland, and it is hardly possible to doubt that in time this pattern will become characteristic of Western Europe as a whole—always supposing there is no catastrophe. Democracy and pacifism have a tendency to reinforce one another, notably in countries which no longer play a major role on the world scene. The alternative—a cohesive industrial and military bloc strong enough to rival the superpowers—seems improbable for geographic and strategic reasons. A certain degree of fragmentation is likely to persist, and with it—alongside the drawbacks that go with relative military inferiority—the ability to experiment with a variety of social forms, political patterns, and intellectual creeds. Such pioneering efforts may in the long run benefit the rival superpowers, now frozen into rigid attitudes by the pressures and dangers of planetary conflict. Paradoxically, in this age of thermonuclear stalemate, medium-sized and smaller countries are relatively freer to try out bold new ideas than are the giants. At any rate, it is in such terms that thinking Europeans tend to view the future. The alternative is one that most of them do not wish to contemplate, and it may be that in refusing to believe that the end of the nation-state is also the end of European history, they are wiser than the pessimists.

CONCLUSION

Eighteen years after the close of World War II, some of the strains produced by the upheaval have disappeared, their place being taken by others. Chief among these is the thermonuclear stalemate, which has increasingly tended to "freeze" both national frontiers and international alignments. In a Europe cut in two by the advance of the Soviet empire to the heart of Germany, this freezing process has been superimposed upon the armed confrontation of the two great international camps along a line running roughly through the center of the Continent. Although "Europe" remains in some sense a reality underneath the artificial divisions imposed upon it by the Cold War, it has become evident that, for an entire historical period, Eastern and Western Europe are due to follow divergent paths. The tacit recognition of this fact underlies the current discussion over Western Europe's place within the Atlantic world, for it would clearly be senseless to debate this topic on the assumption that the Iron Curtain is likely to be raised in the near future. A Europe in which ideas, no less than individuals, could travel freely from the Pyrenees to the Urals—the Europe that existed before the great divide of 1914–18—would not be in need of American protection against the standing menace of Soviet expansion. It is this threat that imposes upon the nations of Western Europe—including some former great powers now reduced to secondary status by the technological revolution of the nuclear age—the need to group themselves in the Atlantic Alliance. Talk of "European neutralism" in these circumstances is doubly senseless. Not only does it ignore the quite patent threat implicit in Soviet policies and attitudes; it also abstracts from the existence of the East European countries now attached to the U.S.S.R. To be at all meaningful, "neutralism" would have to embrace them too, which is tantamount to saying that the U.S.S.R. would have to be induced to withdraw and let the political system imposed upon its satellites be replaced by something akin to democracy. It requires an inordinate amount of optimism to believe that this is likely to happen, at any rate within the coming decade; and until it does happen, all talk of "disengagement" and "neutralization" belongs to the realm of fantasy.

The Atlantic Alliance is thus imposed upon Western Europe by factors outside its control. This circumstance is the major obstacle to harmonious relations between the United States and the principal European nations, who until lately were masters of their destiny and free to contract whatever alliances they considered suitable. In the measure that these nations—or their political and intellectual elites through which they express their collective feelings and ambitions—retain memories of this recent past, they are bound to view the United States as a temporary overlord, whose sudden elevation to the rank of *primus inter pares* corresponds neither to innate virtues nor to the long-range interests of the Western world as a whole. When all is said and done, this feeling is the prime source of anti-American sentiment in quarters where the Atlantic Alliance is reluctantly accepted as a political necessity. If the U.S.S.R. ceased to appear as a constant threat to the independent existence of all European countries and their democratic freedoms, it is fairly certain that this underlying impatience would soon translate itself into a determination to have done with America's physical presence in Europe. Conversely, the certainty that Soviet pressure is likely to endure, probably for a generation, helps to cement the Alliance, but also tends to make Europeans more conscious of the need to attain a greater measure of political unity among themselves. For, irrespective of whether or not the protective American umbrella is viewed as a permanent part of the political landscape, it is no longer possible to doubt that the European nation-state

by itself is simply not built *à l'échelle nucléaire.* This conviction
is shared—whatever they may say in public—by those European
governments (with the British and French well in the lead) who
stress the need for an "independent national deterrent." Indeed,
it is precisely because all concerned are aware that Europe is
moving towards integration, that a race is in progress among
traditional rivals such as Britain and France to reach the supranational goalpost with the maximum of modern technological
equipment. The political orientation of the coming Western
European grouping of formerly sovereign states and nations must
to some extent depend upon the specific weight of its major constituents. The question, e.g., whether Britain's nuclear forces
are to remain intertwined with America's Strategic Air Command, or to become part of a unified European command, has its
bearing upon the political complexion of a future European government and parliament—supposing such a construction emerges
by 1970 or thereabouts, when Western Europe's economic unification will have been completed and the serious business of creating a federated political structure will presumably be under way.

It is in these terms, and against this background, that the rather
longwinded discussion of Western Europe's economic prospects
in Chapters II–IV of this study may justify itself. Its purpose was
to describe the infrastructure of the integrated Western Europe
of tomorrow. This implies some political assumptions about
what is possible and probable, and also—why deny it?—a certain
choice as to what is desirable. It so happens that in this instance
the more probable outcome—a European confederation including
Britain—also appears to the author to be the more desirable one;
but the argument outlined in the preceding chapters would stand
even in the somewhat improbable event of the British deciding
to be merely economic associates of their Continental neighbors.
A political structure centered, for the time being, on the ancient
core of Western Europe would be a second-best; but in principle
it would represent just as drastic a break with the tradition of
sovereign nationalism as a looser confederation embracing Britain
and Scandinavia. Moreover, it is difficult to believe that in the
long run it would not spread to the political boundaries of West-

ern Europe. Britain can in any event hardly afford to be left out. The advantages of joining may not be very obvious, but the dangers of remaining on the sidelines are likely to become increasingly evident.

It is quite a different matter to suggest that such a degree of political unification, coming on top of the economic integration now in progress, must necessarily improve relations between a federal, or confederal, Western Europe and the United States. There is no precedent for a freely arranged union of formerly sovereign states, and it is still uncertain how far the ancient nationalist content can be replaced by a new consciousness that is both European and democratic. Whatever the precise circumstances, some expectations are likely to be disappointed: A genuinely democratic Western Europe may be at once too socialist and too pacifist to suit American tastes; a Europe in which the old conservative and aristocratic elites retain major importance is unlikely to be a comfortable ally; a streamlined, technocratic Europe, with a rapid rate of economic growth and rising standards of consumption, may come to resemble the United States, to the point of depriving Americans of their favorite excuse for spending their vacations abroad. Perhaps the only certainty one can offer with a clear conscience is the prediction that Western Europe will continue to be an irritant to its transatlantic friends, and an insoluble puzzle to Soviet and Far Eastern sages. Its complexities do not lend themselves to any simple formula, such as capitalism vs. socialism, and its further evolution is likely to baffle the orderly minds of propagandists and political theorists in the new centers of world power. The dialectic of East-West conflict can be relied upon to keep the Atlantic Alliance in tolerably good political health; beyond this near-certainty any prediction risks the fate of being disproved almost before it has been committed to the permanence of printer's ink.

SHORT READING LIST

(The titles listed are those cited in the text, except for pamphlets and periodicals, plus some additional works of general interest)

CHAPTER I

BARRACLOUGH, GEOFFREY. *History in a Changing World.* London and New York: Oxford University Press, 1955.

BELOFF, MAX. *The Great Powers.* London: Allen and Unwin; New York: The Macmillan Company, 1959.

————. (ed.). *Europe and the Europeans: A Report prepared at the request of the Council of Europe.* London: Chatto and Windus; New York: Humanities Press, 1957.

BOYD, ANDREW AND FRANCIS. *Western Union. UNA's Guide to Western Recovery.* London: Hutchinson & Co., 1949; Washington, D.C.: Public Affairs Press, 1949.

DALTON, HUGH. *High Tide and After.* London: Frederick Muller, 1962.

DEHIO, LUDWIG. *Germany and World Politics in the Twentieth Century.* New York: Alfred A. Knopf, 1959.

EDEN, ANTHONY. *Full Circle.* London: Cassell & Co., 1960; Boston: Houghton Mifflin Company, 1960.

DE GAULLE, CHARLES. *War Memoirs,* vol. II. London: Weidenfeld and Nicolson; New York: Simon and Schuster, 1959.

GOTTMANN, JEAN. *A Geography of Europe.* New York: Henry Holt and Company, 1954.

HALECKI, OSCAR. *The Limits and Divisions of European History.* London: Sheed and Ward, 1950; New York: The Ronald Press, 1952.

HARROD, ROY F. *The Life of John Maynard Keynes.* London: Macmillan & Co., 1952.

HUGHES, H. STUART. *Contemporary Europe.* Cambridge, Mass.: Harvard University Press, 1961.

Mosse, George L. *The Culture of Western Europe.* Chicago: Rand McNally & Company, 1961; London: John Murray, 1962.

Namier, Lewis B. *Europe in Decay.* London: Macmillan & Co., 1950.

Robertson, A. H. *The Council of Europe: Its Structure, Functions and Achievements.* London: Stevens & Sons; New York: Frederick A. Praeger, 1961.

Royal Institute of International Affairs. *Atlantic Alliance: NATO's Role in the Free World.* London and New York: Oxford University Press, 1952.

Shackleton, Margaret Reid. *Europe: A Regional Geography.* London–New York–Toronto: Longmans Green & Co., 1950.

Weber, Alfred. *Farewell to European History.* London: Kegan Paul, 1947.

Woodward, Lewellyn. *British Foreign Policy in the Second World War.* London: Her Majesty's Stationery Office, 1962.

Chapter II

Benoit, Emile. *Europe at Sixes and Sevens.* New York: Columbia University Press, 1961.

Deniau, Jean François. *The Common Market.* New York: Frederick A. Praeger, 1960; London: Barrie and Rockliff, 1961.

Kitzinger, U. W. *The Challenge of the Common Market.* Oxford: Basil Blackwell, 1961.

Mackay, R. W. G. *Towards a United States of Europe.* London: Hutchinson & Co., 1961.

Marjolin, Robert. *Le Marché Commun et l'Unification de l'Europe.* Brussels: Société Royale d'Economie Politique, 1961.

Meade, James E. *UK, Commonwealth and Common Market.* London: Institute of Economic Affairs, 1962.

Pinder, John. *Britain and the Common Market.* London: The Cresset Press, 1961.

Perroux, François. *L'Europe Sans Rivages.* Paris: Presses Universitaires de France, 1954.

Pryce, Roy. *The Political Future of the European Community.* London: Stevens & Sons, 1962.

Robertson, A. H. *European Institutions.* London: Stevens & Sons; New York: Frederick A. Praeger, 1959.

Strang, William. *Home and Abroad.* London: André Deutsch, 1956.

Streeten, Paul. *Economic Integration: Aspects and Problems.* Leyden: A. W. Sythoff, 1961.

CHAPTER III

DEWHURST, J. FREDERICK *et. al. Europe's Needs and Resources: Trends and Prospects in Eighteen Countries.* New York: The Twentieth Century Fund, 1961.

DUPUIGRENET-DESROUSSILES, GUY. *Niveaux de vie et coopération économique dans l'Europe de l'Ouest.* Paris: Presses Universitaires de France, 1962.

FOURASTIÉ, JEAN. *La grande métamorphose du XX-ième siècle.* Paris: Presses Universitaires de France, 1962.

V.D. HEYDTE, F. A., AND SACHERL, K. *Soziologie der deutschen Parteien.* Munich: Isar Verlag, 1955.

MCKENZIE, R. T. *British Political Parties.* London: William Heinemann; New York: St Martin's Press, 1955.

MEADE, J. E. *The Theory of Customs Unions.* Amsterdam: North Holland Publishing Company, 1955.

————. *et al. Case Studies in European Economic Union.* London: Oxford University Press, 1962.

MENDÈS-FRANCE, PIERRE, AND ARDANT, GABRIEL. *Economics and Action.* London: William Heinemann; Paris: UNESCO, 1955.

NOVE, ALEC. *The Soviet Economy.* London: Allen & Unwin; New York: Frederick A. Praeger, 1961.

PICKLES, DOROTHY. *The Fifth French Republic.* London: Methuen & Co.; New York: Frederick A. Praeger, 1960.

RÖPKE, WILHELM. *Jenseits von Angebot und Nachfrage.* Zurich: Eugen Rentsch Verlag, 1958.

SHANKS, MICHAEL. *The Stagnant Society: A Warning.* London: Penguin Books; Gloucester, Mass.: Peter Smith, 1961.

SHONFIELD, ANDREW. *British Economic Policy Since the War.* London: Penguin Books, 1959.

THOMSON, DAVID. *Democracy in France.* London and New York: Oxford University Press, 1952.

CHAPTER IV

ACHESON, DEAN GOODERHAM. *Power and Diplomacy.* Cambridge, Mass.: Harvard University Press, 1958.

ALLEN, HARRY C. *Great Britain and the United States: History of Anglo-American Relations.* London: Odhams Press, 1954; New York: St Martin's Press, 1955.

ARNDT, H. W. *The Economic Lessons of the Nineteen-Thirties.* London–New York–Toronto: Oxford University Press, 1944.

BARAN, PAUL. *The Political Economy of Growth.* New York: Monthly Review Press, 1957.

FRIEDMANN, WOLFGANG G. *An Introduction to World Politics.* London: Macmillan & Co.; New York: St Martin's Press, 1960.

HOSELITZ, BERT F. (ed.). *The Progress of Underdeveloped Areas.* Chicago: The Free Press of Glencoe, 1952.

KENNAN, GEORGE F. *American Diplomacy 1900–1950.* Chicago: University of Chicago Press, 1951.

———. *Realities of American Foreign Policy.* Princeton, N.J.: Princeton University Press, 1954.

MANDELBAUM, KURT. *The Industrialization of Backward Areas.* London: Oxford University Press, 1945.

ROSTOW, W. W. *The Stages of Economic Growth.* London and New York: Cambridge University Press, 1960.

SETON-WATSON, HUGH. *The Pattern of Communist Revolution.* London: Methuen & Co., 1953.

STRACHEY, JOHN. *On the Prevention of War.* London: Macmillan & Co., 1962.

CHAPTER V

ABRAMS, MARK, AND ROSE, RICHARD. *Must Labour Lose?* London and Baltimore: Penguin Books, 1960.

ARON, RAYMOND. *La société industrielle et la guerre.* Paris: Librairie Plon, 1959.

———. *Paix et guerre entre les nations.* Paris: Calman-Lévy, 1962.

BELL, CLIVE. *Civilization.* London: Pelican Books, 1947.

COLE, G. D. H. *Studies in Class Structure.* London: Routledge & Kegan Paul; New York: Humanities Press, 1955.

CROSLAND, C. A. R. *The Future of Socialism.* London: Jonathan Cape; New York: The Macmillan Company, 1956.

DAHRENDORF, RALF. *Class and Class Conflict in Industrial Society.* London: Routledge & Kegan Paul; Stanford, Calif.: Stanford University Press, 1959.

———. *Gesellschaft und Freiheit.* Munich: Piper Verlag, 1961.

HAYEK, FRIEDRICH AUGUST VON. *The Constitution of Liberty.* London: Routledge & Kegan Paul; Chicago: University of Chicago Press, 1960.

LABEDZ, LEOPOLD (ed.). *Revisionism: Essays in the History of Marxist Ideas.* London: Allen & Unwin; New York: Frederick A. Praeger, 1962.

MENDÈS-FRANCE, PIERRE. *La République Moderne.* Paris: Gallimard, 1962.

PELLING, HENRY M. *A Short History of the Labour Party*. London: Macmillan & Co.; New York, St Martin's Press, 1961.

POLANYI, KARL. *The Great Transformation*. Boston: Beacon Press, 1957.

SCHUMPETER, JOSEPH A. *Capitalism, Socialism and Democracy*. New York: Harper & Brothers; London: Allen & Unwin, 1950.

SIEVERS, ALLEN M. *Revolution, Evolution, and the Economic Order*. Englewood Cliffs, N.J.: Prentice-Hall, 1962.

SMITH, HENRY. *The Economics of Socialism Reconsidered*. London and New York: Oxford University Press, 1962.

TOPITSCH, ERNST. *Sozialphilosophie zwischen Ideologie und Wissenschaft*. Neuwied: Hermann Luchterhand Verlag, 1961.

INDEX

INDEX

Abrams, Mark, 195n
Adenauer, Konrad, 45, 49, 53, 55, 177
Algeria, 79, 158 f., 163 f., 173
Allen, V. L., 199n
Aron, Raymond, 29n, 182n
Atlantic Community, V, 24 f., 32 f., 35, 40, 84, 134 ff., 144 ff., 151; as free-trade union, 144 ff., 151 ff.; in relation to Africa, 161 f.
Attlee, Clement, 15, 17

Baran, Paul A., 170n
Barraclough, Geoffrey, 8n
Barrat-Brown, Michael, 73n
Bauer, P. T., 68n
Beaton, Leonard, 36n
Beloff, Max, 5n, 6n, 7n, 8n, 13n, 24n, 26n
Bell, Clive, 213n
Benoit, Emile, 58n, 66n, 72n, 154n
Bevin, Ernest, 17, 52n
Bidault, Georges, 18
Blum, Leon, 18n
Bolshevism, 198; see also Lenin, Leninism
Boyd, A. and F., 17n
Brazzaville group, 160
Brunner, John, 103n

Cairo, 161, 166
Casablanca group, 161 f.
Castro, Fidel, 162n
Catlin, George, 26n

Chamberlain, Austen, xii
Christian-Democrats, 45 ff., 179 ff., 195 ff.
Churchill, Winston, 14, 15, 16n, 17, 18n, 25, 26
Class structure, 181, 182 ff.; see also socialism
Clayton, Will, 145n
Cole, G. D. H., 182n, 199n, 200n
Cole, John, 193n
Colonialism, 170 ff.
Commissariat du Plan, 102, 115 f.; see also planning
Common Market: see European Economic Community, and passim; postwar growth rates, 93 ff.; comparison with Britain, 98 ff., 135 ff.; contrast with COMECON, 85n, 110
Commonwealth, British, XI, 20, 21, 37 f.; as trading area, 53, 56, 137 ff.; food exports, 142 f.
Congo, 155 ff., 165, 170
Conservative Party, British, 12, 20, 36, 100, 104, 141n; Conservative doctrine, 175 ff., 209 ff.
Corporatism, 83, 209
Council of Europe, 17 ff., 41 ff.
Crosland, C. A. R., 213n
Crossman, Richard, 169n
Cuba, 167n
Cyprus, 6n, 119n, 129 f.

Dahrendorf, R., 182n

229